T0207397

Communications in Computer and Information Science 817

Commenced Publication in 2007
Founding and Former Series Editors:
Alfredo Cuzzocrea, Xiaoyong Du, Orhun Kara, Ting Liu, Dominik Ślęzak,
and Xiaokang Yang

More information about this series at http://www.springer.com/series/7899

Sander Münster · Kristina Friedrichs
Florian Niebling · Agnieszka Seidel-Grzesińska (Eds.)

Digital Research and Education in Architectural Heritage

5th Conference, DECH 2017, and First Workshop, UHDL 2017
Dresden, Germany, March 30–31, 2017
Revised Selected Papers

 Springer

Editors
Sander Münster (iD)
Media and Information Technology
Technical University of Dresden
Dresden, Sachsen
Germany

Kristina Friedrichs
University of Würzburg
Würzburg
Germany

Florian Niebling
University of Würzburg
Würzburg
Germany

Agnieszka Seidel-Grzesińska
University of Wrocław
Wrocław
Poland

ISSN 1865-0929   ISSN 1865-0937 (electronic)
Communications in Computer and Information Science
ISBN 978-3-319-76991-2   ISBN 978-3-319-76992-9 (eBook)
https://doi.org/10.1007/978-3-319-76992-9

Library of Congress Control Number: 2018936910

Printed on acid-free paper

This Springer imprint is published by the registered company Springer International Publishing AG part of Springer Nature
The registered company address is: Gewerbestrasse 11, 6330 Cham, Switzerland

Preface

Urban history, drawing on architectural heritage and cultural history, is one of the key areas in digital humanities. Regarding the research interest, digital libraries play an important role, especially for visual media such as photographs, paintings, or drawings, but also for physical and virtual models. Owing to the wide field of possible research, different approaches, methods, and technologies have emerged – and are still emerging.

For a long time, funding priorities for digital cultural heritage in general—and digital supported research on urban history in the EU and in Germany in particular—focused primarily on technological aspects. These included cost minimization, the ease of use of software tools for creating digital 3D reconstructions, and specific cases of application. One focus has been on digital research environments for the digital humanities. While DARIAH[1] and CLARIN[2] develop and operate virtual research environments for humanities scholars, especially for text-related research approaches, projects like DC-NET[3] focus on e-infrastructures for preserving cultural heritage. ARIADNE[4] and associated projects are dedicated to supporting archaeological information management on a European level. Complementing these, the EUROPEANA[5] virtual library and its sub-projects are dedicated digital repositories for digital cultural heritage assets in Europe, which collect and aggregate resources from museums, libraries, and archives.

Regarding the role of digital libraries and repositories as main facilitators, previous funding programs have not sufficiently considered the fact that digitally supported urban history research is conducted and applied in complex socio-technical arrangements. Against this background, a paradigm shift has taken place in funding politics since 2010. Besides the further development of technical infrastructures like research environments and digital repositories, human resources, transnational knowledge exchange and cooperation, social and economic impacts, valorization and dissemination are increasingly important objects of funding. An evaluation of the FP5-7 research funding programs stated that: "Foster[ing] the dissemination, transfer and take-up of program results" has been seen—in these programs—as an underrepresented issue. By contrast, the Horizon 2020 work program aims for "an understanding of Europe's intellectual basis," the use of "new technologies [...] as they enable new and richer interpretations of our common European culture while contributing to sustainable economic growth," and the development of innovative research infrastructures to foster research, education, and publication of "knowledge-based resources such as collections

---

[1] https://dariah.eu. Accessed 2.12.2017.
[2] https://www.clarin.eu/. Accessed 2.12.2017.
[3] http://www.dc-net.org/. Accessed 2.12.2017.
[4] http://www.ariadne-infrastructure.eu/. Accessed 2.12.2017.
[5] https://www.europeana.eu/. Accessed 2.12.2017.

[or] archives [...]"[6] to a European audience. In this changing context, the question arises as to how research and education of urban history can be supported by digital libraries.

The primary objective of the conference "Digital Encounters in Cultural Heritage" (DECH) and the workshop "Urban History in the Age of Digital Libraries" (UHDL), held in March 2017 in Dresden as a joint event, was to concentrate on the area of tension between the fields of culture, technologies, and education. This book presents major findings and aims to highlight crucial challenges for further research and to encourage debate between the sciences. We showcase contributions on theoretical and methodological issues, application scenarios and projects, as well as novel approaches and tools. The 33 submissions to the joint event were reviewed by a joint Program Committee. The reviewers selected which paper was to be accepted for the conference and which for the workshop. After the conference, 13 papers were invited for the revised and selected papers volume: 11 from the DECH conference and two from the UHDL workshop track. These include the following five areas:

1. Research on Architectural and Urban Cultural Heritage

Do computing methods lead to new and ground-breaking research questions, approaches, or insights into architectural and urban cultural heritage research? This general question has been primarily addressed in terms of research contexts, research objects, or phases in the research process. In most cases, the use of computing simply extends nondigital possibilities, without much change to the pre-digital approaches and research questions. Nevertheless, digitalization has dramatically altered research qualities, quantities, and workflows. This section will present three chapters about insights and research approaches in the field of cultural heritage fertilized by the employment of digital technologies.

2. Technical Access

During the past few years, various new technological opportunities have arisen from big data, Semantic Web technologies, and the exponential growth in data accessible via digital libraries such as EUROPEANA. The immense effort invested in digitization and rapid changes in technologies and formats have greatly increased the importance of sustainability in recent years. Long-term data storage, availability of models, and the interoperability of data formats are major challenges to existing digital infrastructures. Moreover, novel approaches such as the photogrammetric reconstruction of historical buildings from image databases allow for contextualization and intuitive access to data. This section includes two articles focusing on technical workflows and tools to support research and education in the field of urban history.

---

[6] European Commission (2015) HORIZON 2020 Work Programme 2014–2015. European research infrastructures (including e-Infrastructures), p. 4.

3. Systematization

Both research on urban history from the perspective of humanities and the development of supporting digital technologies are attracting attention from art history, digital cultural heritage studies, and information sciences. These multidisciplinary settings present various challenges due to the specific requirements of interdisciplinary work, such as common grounds, project strategies, or critically reflected methods. The widespread impact of digital humanities has created a high demand for research to be put to practical use. The applicable techniques, valid strategies, classifications, and quality standards need to be determined. Against this background, this section includes five articles about methodologies, practices, and standards for utilizing digital technologies for cultural heritage research.

4. Education in Urban History

Education and support through digital libraries plays only a minor role in scholarly discourses on cultural heritage and in particular urban history. There is still no broad consensus on specific education paradigms, or a canon of didactic settings in digitally supported teaching on urban history, and as yet no larger studies have been conducted in this area. In this section, two articles highlight perspectives to employ digital technology and to educate a broad audience about urban and landscape history.

5. Organizational Perspectives

Concerning application of digital methods, numerous associations were funded and a lively scholarly community has arisen during the last decades. One of the most renowned associations worldwide is the CIPA Heritage Documentation, an International Scientific Committee (ISC) of ICOMOS, and ISPRS (International Society for Photogrammetry and Remote Sensing). This last chapter is dedicated to gain an insight in CIPA's activities as well as to highlight challenges and perspectives of cultural heritage on a global level.

We would like to acknowledge the important work done by the chapter reviewers. We also thank the sponsors, Program Committee members, supporting organizations, and volunteers for making the joint event held in Dresden in March 2017 a success. Without their efforts, the event would not have been possible.

February 2018
Sander Münster
Kristina Friedrichs
Florian Niebling
Agnieszka Seidel-Grzesińska

Organization

Reviewers

Fabrizio I. Apollonio	University of Bologna, Italy
Stefan Bürger	Julius-Maximilians-Universität Würzburg, Germany
Emanuel Demetrescu	Istituto per le Tecnologie Applicate ai Beni Culturali, Italy
Andreas Georgopoulos	National Technical University of Athens, Greece
Robert Hecht	IÖR Dresden, Germany
Frank Henze	BTU Cottbus, Germany
Isto Huvila	Uppsala University, Sweden
Christina Kamposiori	University of London, UK
Thomas Koehler	Technische Universität Dresden, Germany
Piotr Kuroczynski	Hochschule Mainz, Germany
Marc Erich Latoschik	Julius-Maximilians-Universität Würzburg, Germany
Ivan Lee	University of South Australia, Australia
Davide Mezzino	Carlton University, Canada
Mieke Pfarr-Harfst	TU Darmstadt, Germany
Nikolas Prechtel	Technische Universität Dresden, Germany
Fulvio Rinaudo	Politecnico di Torino, Italy
Antonio Rodríguez	Anahuac Mayab, Mexico
Mario Santana Quintero	Carlton University, Canada
Danilo Schneider	Technische Universität Dresden, Germany
Jin Shang	Tsinghua University, China
Alex Ya-Ning Yen	China University of Technology, Taiwan

Contents

Education in Urban History

Organizational Perspectives

Research on Architectural and Urban Cultural Heritage

A Tentative Map of Influences Between Urban Centres of Genre Painting in the Dutch Golden Age - An Exercise in "Slow" Digital Art History

Daniel Isemann[1](✉), Tuan Anh Tran[1], and Adriaan Waiboer[2]

[1] University of Regensburg, Regensburg, Germany
daniel.isemann@ur.de
[2] National Gallery of Ireland, Dublin, Ireland

Abstract. In this work we explore the creative influences between Dutch cities in terms of the uptake of genre painting motifs developed or elaborated upon in one city by painters from other cities. Concentrating on the seventeen leading genre painters of the period 1650–1675, we use data about their whereabouts and judgments about pairwise directed influences between these painters' individual works which have been collected as part of the international exhibition project *Vermeer and the Masters of Genre Painting: Inspiration and Rivalry* (2017–2018) organised by the National Gallery of Ireland in collaboration with the Musée du Louvre, Paris, and the National Gallery of Art, Washington. We use three different ways to quantitatively aggregate art historians individual judgements on paintings to estimate the role Dutch towns played as centres of genre painting. Finally, we compare this with the corresponding 'gut feeling' of one of the art historians involved.

Keywords: Digital art history · Urban history
Quantifying creative influence · Dutch genre painters
Data aggregation · Network analysis

1 Introduction

The present study is set within an examination of creative and artistic influence between genre painters of the Dutch Golden Age or rather between the individual works of certain genre painters. Due to political and socio-economic factors after the Reformation, the Low Countries saw the development of a vibrant art market and the rise of new types of paintings including so-called genre paintings, that is scenes of everyday life painted for the free market [5]. The authors of the exhibition catalogue *Vermeer and the Masters of Genre Painting: Inspiration and Rivalry* argue that the leading painters of this genre in the third quarter of the seventeenth century were strongly influenced by each other's works [10]. Their many cross-currents were strengthened by the fact that the northern

© Springer International Publishing AG, part of Springer Nature 2018
S. Münster et al. (Eds.): UHDL 2017/DECH 2017, CCIS 817, pp. 3–21, 2018.
https://doi.org/10.1007/978-3-319-76992-9_1

Netherlands had a network of canal barges that was unrivalled in Europe and afforded relatively easy travel between urban centres [1, Chap. 1].

In this paper we introduce a data set which was created as part of this exhibition project with a view to investigating such inspiration-taking and influences in detail. We also present a weighting and aggregation scheme, which was devised to aggregate and quantify the influence one artist may have exerted over another. This must of course not be interpreted as an attempt at measuring an objectively observable quantity, but rather as an approximation of relative influence and influentialness which may perhaps trigger further investigation, debate or rebuttal. We then apply this weighting and aggregation scheme to aggregate the data set from a geographical perspective (by city or metropolitan area). Cities and towns, much more than just an agglomeration of people and housing, have significance as economic hubs and form cultural centres and breeding grounds for ideas which emanate a certain intellectual influence. In recent years a city's aptitude for fostering creativity has even been argued, albeit controversially, to be an important factor in urban development and planning [4, 7]. In the context of this paper we use a detailed data set originally created for a different purpose, to investigate the question which Netherlandish towns in the third quarter of the seventeenth century produced the most influential group of high end genre paintings (in terms of the quantity and quality of the influence they exerted on other similar paintings) and how these centres of genre painting inspired each other. In addition, we present preliminary attempts for evaluating such a "data driven"[1] approach, by looking at internal correlations in the data and comparing our aggregate results to a summary judgement by a domain expert.

The paper is organised as follows: after presenting related work in the following section, we outline the nature and purpose of our data set and the weighting and aggregation scheme developed together with art historians. Afterwards we present the results of our data analysis and of first, tentative evaluations of the aggregation method. The paper concludes with a discussion of the results and the method and an outlook on future work.

2   Related Work

Against the backdrop of recent developments in digital art history [6] art historians have employed systematic data collection and analysis, including network analysis of relevant historical actors (artists, dealers etc.). Recent work on history painting in Amsterdam [9] drew on the *ECARTICO* database [8],[2] an extensive collection of information on over 25.000 people involved in the cultural industries of the early modern Low Countries. The database includes information on family relations and collaborations next to other more conventional attributes (date of birth, death, professional roles).

---

[1] Some authors would likely argue that our approach should be called "capta driven" as our atomic units of information are not objective measurements, but individual expert observations (cf. [3]).

[2] Cf. also http://www.vondel.humanities.uva.nl/ecartico/ (last accessed 1/3/2018).

Similarly, the *Cornelia* database developed in the context of the MapTap project [2] gathers information on over 4000 historic actors related to manufacturing tapestries in early modern Antwerp, Brussels and Oudenarde. Koenrad Brosens and colleagues have used network analysis on this data collection to gain new insights into the role women have played in the capital-intensive and complex tapestry business (ibid.). The authors refer to their methodological approach as 'Slow Digital Art History', because it depends on careful, complex and manual data gathering (hence 'slow') before any 'digital' methods can be applied to the data set.

In contrast to the projects mentioned above the present study is based on network data not between actors, but between artifacts, namely paintings. The data can be described as influence networks between paintings which record whether or not a painting has possibly served as a source of inspiration for another painting.

3   Method

In order to shed more light on the nature, quality and quantity of creative inspiration between various masters of Dutch genre painting, art historians working at the Netherlands Institute for Art History (RKD), The Hague, and the National Gallery of Ireland, Dublin, have compiled over 950 assessments between individual pairs of genre paintings from seventeen different artists, which express that one painting has likely served as a source of inspiration for another. The nature of inspiration taking can vary in strength from including indistinct elements, that vaguely reflect another work, to copying a secondary object (say in the background of the scene), to emulating a central figure constellation of a work, to creating a downright copy or pastiche of an entire work, to name just a few examples. The multitude of possible borrowings and the various qualities of inspiration taking have been discretized by the art historians involved in the exhibition project into five categories of increasing 'connection strength', ranging from 1 (weakly/vaguely inspired) to 5 (copy or pastiche). Figure 1 gives an overview of the five connection strength categories, illustrated by a prototypic example each. Some of the individual judgments regarding influence links between paintings were taken from the literature, while others were created specifically for the exhibition project *Vermeer and the Masters of Genre Painting: Inspiration and Rivalry*.

As judgments of this kind in art history are typically beset with uncertainties and often disputed among experts each individual assessment was additionally tagged with a 'probability level' which can take one of five discrete values: *certainly*, *most likely*, *probably*, *possibly* and *perhaps*. These terms are common qualifiers of statements in art historic literature and a deliberate decision has been made to use these discrete levels instead of real numbered representations of probabilities as too fine grained distinctions appear hard to justify in a setting where expert judgment is the sole source of the probabilities.

The seventeen artists featured in the data set are (in alphabetical order): Cornelis Pietersz Bega, Gerard ter Borch, Quiringh Gerritsz van Brekelenkam,

(a) Category 1: assigned to works that contain indistinct elements that can be traced back to a model or that only vaguely reflect a model.

(b) Category 2: assigned to works that contain one or two basic elements borrowed from a model, but where the artist has used these elements in a different context and has therefore created a distinctly autonomous work of art.

(c) Category 3: assigned to works that contain three to four elements borrowed from a model, including at least one significant element, which the artist has used in a somewhat similar context;

Fig. 1. Examples illustrating the connection strength categories. Classification of paintings into the categories refers to defined *basic* (e.g. thematic motif, coloring etc.) and *significant* (e.g. primary subject, overall composition etc.) image elements.

(d) Category 4: assigned to works that contain several borrowings from a model, including more than one significant element, but that are still autonomous enough that they cannot be labelled as copies, partial copies or pastiches.

(e) Category 5: assigned to copies, partial copies, pastiches (be they mirrored or not).

Fig. 1. (*continued*)

Gerard Dou, Pieter de Hooch, Ludolf de Jongh, Nicolaes Maes, Cornelis de Man, Gabriel Metsu, Frans van Mieris, Michiel van Musscher, Eglon van der Neer, Caspar Netscher, Jacob Ochtervelt, Godfried Schalcken, Jan Steen and Johannes Vermeer. At least ten of these can be considered the preeminent masters of genre painting of the period in question, with the remainder still belonging to an elite circle of artists.[3]

The idea behind assigning discrete categories for likelihood and connection strength was to allow for room to capture variation while at the same time constraining expert judgement on such a complex issue enough to warrant some degree of intersubjective agreement. Moreover, these categorisations were collected with a view to aggregate influence or inspiration taking from the individual

---

[3] Cf. [10, p. 254], where Dou, ter Borch, Steen, Metsu, de Hooch, Vermeer, Maes, van Mieris, van der Neer and Netscher are singled out as "the ten most significant genre painters active in the third quarter of the seventeenth century" (ibid).

instance observations (between pairs of paintings) to the level of artists. In order to do so the categories for both likelihood and connection strength were assigned numerical weights. These weights were negotiated in a discussion process between art historians and knowledge engineers (Table 1). The probability weights were chosen to approximate the likelihood with which experts would expect the corresponding statements to hold. The intuition behind the connection weights was that a direct copy should be seen as roughly ten times as important as the weakest forms of artistic borrowings and that weights should not be linear but rather exponential putting more emphasis on the stronger forms of influence.[4]

Table 1. Weights for probability level and connection strength

(a) Probability weights		(b) Connection weights	
Probability level	Weight	Connection strength	Weight
Certainly	1	5	10
Most likely	0.85	4	5.61
Probably	0.7	3	3.16
Possibly	0.5	2	1.78
Perhaps	0.25	1	1

The aggregation scheme based on these weights, which was likewise negotiated with art historians, consists of a formula in which corresponding weights are multiplied and then added up. Thus for two sets of paintings A and B the weight of the influence between them would be calculated as follows:

$$weighted\ influence(A, B) = \sum_{i \in I(A,B)} p(i) \cdot c(i) \qquad (1)$$

Here $I(A, B)$ is the set of all individual influences paintings from A had on paintings from B according to our data and $p(i)$ and $c(i)$ are the probability weight and connection weight, respectively, assigned to connection i.

It is worth pointing out that the semantics of the two weights (probability $p(i)$ and connection strength $c(i)$) suggest that their values are not entirely uncorrelated. A vague connection between two paintings (in terms of connection strength) by its very nature appears to be less certain (on average) than more explicit forms of connections. The strongest form of connection, between a work and a copy or pastiche thereof, is so clearly observable, that one would expect domain experts to regularly assign the highest probability level to these links. As it turns out this is indeed the case for the 965 observations that were recorded for the project: the 12 cases of connection strength 5 (copy or pastiche) where all assigned the probability level *certainly* (cf. Fig. 2, top right). In general, however,

---

[4] The values between the extremes of 1 and 10 were thus calculated according to the following formula: $f(x) = (10^{\frac{1}{4}})^{(x-1)}$.

the Pearson correlation between the two discretized values ($r = 0.325$, $p < 0.001$) points to a weak, albeit statistically significant correlation. We may therefore assume that the two weights assigned to each data point express correlated, but appreciably different aspects of the influence instances.

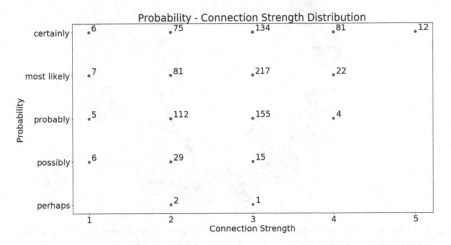

Fig. 2. Plot showing probability levels and connection strengths and the frequencies of their combined occurrence in our data set; Pearson correlation: $r = 0.325$, $p < 0.001$.

The most important type of aggregation envisaged at the outset of the project was aggregation to the level of artists. In this case the set of paintings A in Eq. 1 above represents all the works in our data set by one artist (the 'influencer') and the set of paintings B represents all the works in our data set by another artist (the 'influenced'). Aggregating all the observations on pairs of paintings in this way we arrive at a value intended to represent how much one artist influenced another. Swapping the two artists results in a value intended to represent the flow of influence or inspiration in the opposite direction. Doing this for all 17 artists in the data set we arrive at values intended to express the mutual influences. Given the nature of the data set, these 'measures of influence' can of course only pertain to the domain of genre paintings in the third quarter of the 17th century. Figure 3 shows a visualisation of these values as directed edges between artists, where the heaviest edge has been normalised to the value of one and all other edges have been linearly scaled down accordingly.

The figure illustrates, for instance, strong influences by van Mieris on Ochtervelt and by ter Borch on Metsu and Netscher and considerable influences by Dou on Schalcken, by van Mieris on van der Neer and by ter Borch on van Mieris. The more minor influences, however, are too numerous to be clearly distinguishable let alone interpretable in a visualisation such as this. A framework for visualising and analysing the influence links on the painting and artist levels has been presented elsewhere. Such analysis and visualisations have also influenced the exhibition project and its presentation to the public.

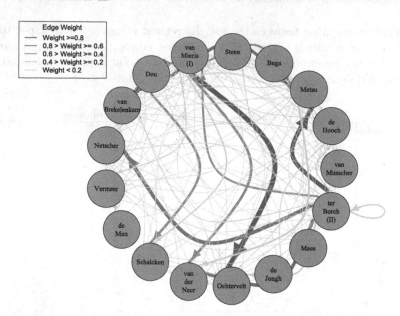

Fig. 3. Influence network between artists with frequency count weighted by probability and connection strength weights (multiplied) as edge weights.

In the present study, however, we use the data to examine not individual instances of inspiration taking or the question of the overall influence an artist's oeuvre had on his contemporaries, but to evaluate the relative importance of urban centres of high-end genre painting in terms of how often motifs first developed or elaborated upon in a given city influenced the works by painters from other cities. In addition, our aim is to investigate the robustness of our approach by comparing our aggregated results to expert judgement and by examining correlations in our data.

In order to aggregate the connection data not by artist, but by geographic location, we needed to cross-reference the painting connections with information on where paintings were most likely created. This information may in part be derived from the whereabouts of the artists at particular points in time. Vermeer, arguably the most well-known of the seventeen painters, spent his entire life living in Delft, but some of his peers lived and worked in different places at different times. Information on their known or presumed whereabouts has been published in various articles and monographs. As part of the exhibition project, information on the artists' whereabouts was gathered and collected from such sources in a tabular format which documents notable stays or residencies of the artists. Each artist has several entries, representing an event or period that has a geographical location assigned to it. Included are entries such as birth and death, visits, longer stays, residencies and travels.

Based on these records we first identified the main places of residence for each artist together with the rough time spans the artist lived there (see Table 2). In this process we took into consideration:

- the length of an artist's stay
- where an artist painted his more important works
- where an artist painted his genre scenes

Concerning the last point note, for instance, that Nicolaes Maes worked longer in Amsterdam than in Dordrecht, but he never painted any genre scenes in the former. Places in the vicinity of metropolitan centres were counted towards these. Thus Ludolf de Jongh's stay in Hillegersberg from approximately 1666 to

Table 2. Artists' whereabouts: listed are places of residence or longer stays together with approximate time spans. Only places relevant to the artists' oevre of genre paintings were considered.

Artists	Whereabouts (with rough timespans)
Cornelis Pietersz Bega	Haarlem: ca. 1631–ca. 1664
Gerard ter Borch	Deventer: ca. 1652–ca. 1673, ca. 1675–1681
Quiringh Gerritsz van Brekelenkam	Leiden: ca. 1648–ca. 1669
Gerard Dou	Leiden: 1613–1675
Pieter de Hooch	Rotterdam: ca. 1629–ca. 1652
	Delft: ca. 1653–ca. 1661
	Amsterdam: ca. 1662–after 1684
Ludolf de Jongh	Rotterdam: ca. 1628–ca. 1632, ca. 1640–1679
Nicolaes Maes	Dordrecht: 1634–ca. 1649, ca. 1654–ca. 1674
Cornelis de Man	Delft: 1621–ca. 1643, ca. 1652–1706
Gabriel Metsu	Amsterdam: ca. 1654–1667
Frans van Mieris	Leiden: 1635–1681
Michiel van Musscher	Rotterdam: 1645–ca. 1661
	Amsterdam: ca. 1662–1705
Eglon van der Neer	Amsterdam: ca. 1635–ca. 1650, ca. 1658–ca. 1664
	Rotterdam: ca. 1665–ca. 1681
Caspar Netscher	Deventer: ca. 1654–ca. 1658
	The Hague: ca. 1659–ca. 1660, ca. 1662–1684
Jacob Ochtervelt	Rotterdam: 1634–ca. 1674
Godfried Schalcken	Dordrecht: ca. 1654–ca. 1692
Jan Steen	Delft: ca. 1654–ca. 1656
	Leiden: ca. 1657–ca. 1660
	Haarlem: ca. 1661–ca. 1671
Johannes Vermeer	Delft: 1632–1675

1679 was counted towards Rotterdam and Jan Steen's residence in Warmond, similarly, towards Leiden. This resulted in eight cities and towns which were included in our analysis: Amsterdam, Delft, Deventer, Dordrecht, Haarlem, The Hague, Leiden, Rotterdam.

In the next step we filtered the influence network of paintings for such works, that belonged to artists and time spans that allowed us to associate them with one of the cities mentioned above. Starting out with 965 individual assessments of inspirational influence between paintings and filtering for the time spans in which the artist whereabouts were relevant and reasonably certain (cf. Table 2) we arrived at 601 entries which we could use for our analysis covering a total of 583 paintings from our seventeen artists. To aggregate the resulting data to city level we compared three aggregation schemes of increasing complexity against each other: first we did a raw count of inspiration links between cities, then we weighted the count by the assigned 'probability level' (cf. Table 1a) and finally we used both the assigned 'probability level' and the assigned 'connection strength' as described by Table 1 and Eq. 1 above.[5] In the following section we present a discussion and visualisations of the resulting aggregations.

4 Results

The resulting aggregated weights for each city pair according to each of the three aggregation schemes outlined above are presented in the an appendix (cf. Tables 4, 5 and 6). They can be visualised as directed graphs with weighted edges (Figs. 4, 5 and 6). As the raw weights have a big spread and the numbers are not comparable across the three aggregation schemes, we scaled the weights relative to the heaviest weight and assigned a value of one to the heaviest edge (as indicated before in relation to Fig. 3).

Generally speaking all three figures show similar networks of influence. In all three cases the aggregated influence from Deventer to Rotterdam forms the heaviest edge (with weight 1 by convention). A noticeable difference is that the combined weights lead to a stronger reflexive edge on Deventer (probably due to the more detailed borrowings that Caspar Netscher made from his teacher ter Borch). The influence of Deventer on The Hague is more pronounced in the graph weighted by probability only. Overall we can see that influence across cities is at the least as important as influence within cities. In each of the three aggregation schemes the top two edges are inter-city edges. On the other hand, in each of the three schemes two of the five heaviest edges are reflexive.

As we have pointed out for the case of artists before (cf. Fig. 3) the scope of such visualisations can of course only extend to the domain of genre painting and the time span 1650 to 1675 as well as the selected artists, as these restrictions governed the gathering of the data. Having emphasized that, we were interested in how well the aggregation of art historians individual judgements (individual connections between paintings, probability and strength assignments, weight

---

[5] Note, that the second aggregation scheme ('probability only') results from setting all the $c(i)$ to 1 in Eq. 1.

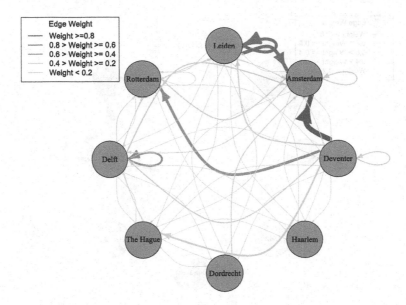

Fig. 4. Influence network between cities with raw frequency count as edge weights.

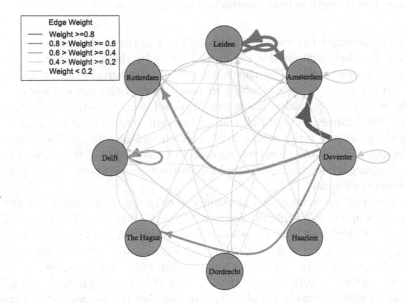

Fig. 5. Influence network between cities with probability weighted frequency count as edge weights.

assignments) to city level under these constraints corresponds to the same art historians intuitive summary judgments. For a first, rough approximation of this we added one more aggregation step by summing up the weights of all outgoing edges per city thus arriving at a value arguably representative of the city's overall

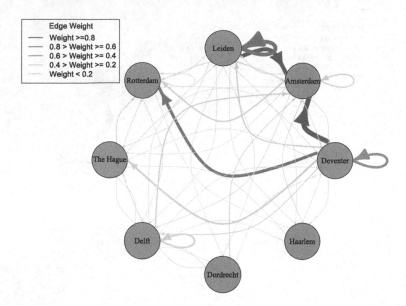

Fig. 6. Influence network between cities with frequency count weighted by probability and connection strength weights (multiplied) as edge weights.

capacity to influence the cream of genre painters in the Netherlands (from 1650 to 1675). We then compared a ranking of cities by these values in decreasing order to a similar ranking by the last author based on his expert intuitions. As an art historian he was involved in every step of the process such as setting the weights, negotiating the aggregation scheme, collecting and recording the individual influences and delineating relevant centres of genre painting as well as the stays and residences of artists which had significance for their genre painting oeuvres. He was, however, unaware of the results of the various mathematical aggregations, basing his ranking instead on his knowledge, experience and informed intuition.

Aggregating the weights and ranking the cities by their influence results in the rankings in Table 3, with the column "Expert" denoting the opinion of the last author. Calculating rank correlation with Spearman's ρ between the expert ranking and the rankings derived from our aggregation schemes, the aggregations by frequency count and using only probability weights showed a positive correlation, with $r_s = 0.738$ and p $= 0.046$. Note that the rankings resulting from these aggregation methods are identical. In contrast to this result, aggregation by combined weights did not show a statistically significant correlation with the expert ranking ($r_s = 0.452$, p $= 0.267$). The discrepancy between the aggregation by combined weights and the other two aggregation schemes with respect to the expert ranking may in part be due to the fact, that with eight items the size of the ranking is on the short side of what is normally considered a good range for Spearman's test (typically 10–30). Comparing the three rankings derived from the different aggregation schemes directly against each other we see a different

Table 3. City rankings by 'genre painting influentialness' in decreasing order. The first column is based on the intuitions and experience of the last author, the others on the aggregate values according to each of our three aggregation schemes.

Expert	Raw frequency	Probability only	Combined weights
Leiden	Deventer	Deventer	Deventer
Deventer	Leiden	Leiden	Leiden
Amsterdam	Delft	Delft	Delft
Delft	Amsterdam	Amsterdam	Amsterdam
Dordrecht	Dordrecht	Dordrecht	Rotterdam
The Hague	Rotterdam	Rotterdam	Dordrecht
Rotterdam	The Hague	The Hague	The Hague
Haarlem	Haarlem	Haarlem	Haarlem

picture. Here the two identical rankings based on aggregation by frequency count and probability weights showed a positive correlation with the ranking based on aggregation by both weights, with $r_s = 0.786$ and $p = 0.027$. We conclude the paper with a discussion of the observed results and a reflection on the method.

5   Discussion

We have presented a limited experiment in "Slow Digital Art History" (as introduced in [2]). Using a carefully collected and expertly curated data set on painting to painting influences (qualified by values for *connection strength* and *probability*) we attempted to draw conclusions on the aggregated influentialness urban centres had on others with regard to the chosen domain and time frame. Our results corroborate the hypothesis that inter city influence played a big part (compared to intra city influence) and we could produce aggregated city rankings which are positively and significantly correlated with an expert ranking of overall city influence. However, we could not reproduce the expert ranking directly and it is worth pointing out that the aggregation method which was expressly sanctioned by domain experts (i.e. the one using both, probability and connection strength values) did not produce a ranking significantly correlated to the expert opinion.

Naturally, these results have to be taken with a pinch of salt. As we have pointed out the rankings are slightly on the short side of what is typically considered a good range for robust rank correlations and our expert ranking for comparison is based on the opinion of just one expert. Still they give rise to a number of interesting questions: Is the aggregation scheme based on both weights overshooting the mark? Perhaps because the positive correlation between probability and connection strength leads to an undue emphasis on the clearer and less disputed connections? Or does the aggregation of atomic expert observations indeed reveal aspects which though absent from the summary expert judgment, warrant consideration? Why do the mathematical aggregations point to Deventer as most influential city and expert intuition to Leiden? Is this because of the fact that Leiden was home to no less then four masters of genre painting compared to Deventer's two (apparently very influential) masters? Is the influence of ter Borch and Netscher, the two Deventer masters unduly exaggerated in the data?

It is these and similar questions which we see as a rewarding and promising effect of the outlined approach, which will hopefully trigger fruitful debates and perhaps lead to deeper insights into the domain at hand or comparable domains treated similarly.

A further observation, which may by of interest, is that the different aggregation schemes did not produce very different results (all three mathematically aggregated rankings were highly correlated, two even identical). The scheme with the combined weights was developed in discussions between computer scientists and art historians with a view to an aggregation based on fine-grained expert judgments. For the chosen purpose, however, it was no more effective than simple counting. While our results are preliminary and the individual weight judgments carefully created by art historians form an incredibly valuable resource in its own right, we have not been able to disprove that for data aggregation a less sophisticated – in other words: slightly faster – approach to digital art history may be good enough.

We have been careful throughout the paper to point out the limitations of our approach. Any results or conclusions derived from the aggregations are subject to the individual judgements that went into generating the data, the chosen weights and the aggregation scheme and only pertain to the selected set of works. Even with these caveats in place we are aware that not everyone will subscribe to an analysis which centrally revolves around an influence relation between works of art, perhaps fearing that such an approach makes too strong assumptions about the way artists interacted with each other. In this context we can only emphasise that we do not imbue the influence relation with strong ontological assumptions. Influence between two works does not necessarily entail that the artists in question have met nor that one artist has seen the other work in the original. Influence in that sense may be indirectly mediated through copies, prints or other mechanisms. We also would not like to advocate that our type of analysis should replace or supersede subject- or motif-based classification systems. Rather it offers an additional and alternative way of looking at influence and fashions in genre painting which has the strength that conjectures and hypotheses can be derived from a number of easily retrievable basic observations. These observations in turn may of course be called into question, either individually or en bloc, based on differing assumptions. Either way our approach hopes to engender a discussion which is more strongly grounded in recorded observations.

Acknowledgements. The authors would like to thank everyone involved in the exhibition project *Vermeer and the Masters of Genre Painting: Inspiration and Rivalry* who supported and enriched this research and made it possible in the first place, as well as three anonymous reviewers for valuable feedback and suggestions.

Appendix

Table 4. The table shows the influence Town A had on Town B, based on the aggregation of the raw frequency count, presented as the absolute weight (Weight) and normalized to the highest absolute weight (Normalized Weight)

Town A	Town B	Weight	Normalized weight
Deventer	Amsterdam	74.5	1.0000
Leiden	Amsterdam	52	0.6980
Leiden	Leiden	47	0.6309
Deventer	Rotterdam	42	0.5638
Delft	Delft	31	0.4161
Deventer	The Hague	28	0.3758
Delft	Amsterdam	20.5	0.2752
Deventer	Leiden	20	0.2685
Deventer	Delft	18.5	0.2483
Amsterdam	Amsterdam	17	0.2282
Amsterdam	Rotterdam	17	0.2282
Deventer	Deventer	17	0.2282
Dordrecht	Amsterdam	14	0.1879
Amsterdam	Delft	13	0.1745
Rotterdam	Amsterdam	13	0.1745
Delft	Rotterdam	10.5	0.1409
The Hague	Rotterdam	10	0.1342
Delft	Leiden	10	0.1342
Leiden	Rotterdam	9.5	0.1275
Leiden	Delft	8.5	0.1141
Amsterdam	Leiden	8	0.1074
Rotterdam	Rotterdam	7	0.0940
Deventer	Haarlem	7	0.0940
Leiden	The Hague	7	0.0940
Haarlem	Amsterdam	6.5	0.0872
Dordrecht	Delft	6.5	0.0872
Delft	Dordrecht	6	0.0805
Leiden	Dordrecht	6	0.0805
Leiden	Haarlem	6	0.0805
Delft	Deventer	5.5	0.0738
Amsterdam	The Hague	5	0.0671

(continued)

Table 4. (*continued*)

Town A	Town B	Weight	Normalized weight
Dordrecht	Leiden	4	0.0537
Amsterdam	Deventer	4	0.0537
Amsterdam	Haarlem	4	0.0537
Dordrecht	The Hague	4	0.0537
Haarlem	Rotterdam	3	0.0403
Leiden	Deventer	3	0.0403
Rotterdam	Delft	3	0.0403
Delft	Haarlem	2.5	0.0336
Rotterdam	Deventer	2.5	0.0336
The Hague	Amsterdam	2	0.0268
Dordrecht	Deventer	2	0.0268
The Hague	Delft	2	0.0268
The Hague	Deventer	1.5	0.0201
Haarlem	Leiden	1	0.0134
Delft	The Hague	1	0.0134
The Hague	Haarlem	1	0.0134

Table 5. The table shows the influence Town A had on Town B, based on the aggregation of the probabilities of connections, presented as the absolute weight (Weight) and normalized to the highest absolute weight (Normalized Weight)

Town A	Town B	Weight	Normalized weight
Deventer	Amsterdam	62.63	1.0000
Leiden	Amsterdam	43.85	0.7002
Leiden	Leiden	40.8	0.6515
Deventer	Rotterdam	34.75	0.5549
Delft	Delft	27.8	0.4439
Deventer	The Hague	26.95	0.4303
Delft	Amsterdam	17.2	0.2747
Deventer	Deventer	16.85	0.2691
Deventer	Leiden	16.2	0.2587
Amsterdam	Rotterdam	14.63	0.2335
Amsterdam	Amsterdam	13.7	0.2188
Deventer	Delft	12.65	0.2020
Dordrecht	Amsterdam	10.95	0.1749

(*continued*)

Table 5. (*continued*)

Town A	Town B	Weight	Normalized weight
Rotterdam	Amsterdam	10.55	0.1685
Amsterdam	Delft	9.05	0.1445
The Hague	Rotterdam	8.05	0.1285
Delft	Rotterdam	7.83	0.1250
Delft	Leiden	7.2	0.1150
Leiden	Rotterdam	6.95	0.1110
Amsterdam	Leiden	6.63	0.1058
Rotterdam	Rotterdam	6.4	0.1022
Deventer	Haarlem	6.25	0.0998
Haarlem	Amsterdam	5.9	0.0942
Leiden	The Hague	5.3	0.0846
Leiden	Delft	4.95	0.0790
Delft	Dordrecht	4.6	0.0735
Leiden	Haarlem	4.4	0.0703
Delft	Deventer	4.23	0.0675
Dordrecht	Delft	4.05	0.0647
Amsterdam	The Hague	3.78	0.0603
Leiden	Dordrecht	3.75	0.0599
Amsterdam	Haarlem	3.1	0.0495
Amsterdam	Deventer	2.8	0.0447
Dordrecht	The Hague	2.8	0.0447
Rotterdam	Delft	2.7	0.0431
Dordrecht	Leiden	2.68	0.0427
Haarlem	Rotterdam	2.4	0.0383
Rotterdam	Deventer	2.2	0.0351
The Hague	Deventer	2	0.0319
Leiden	Deventer	1.7	0.0271
Delft	Haarlem	1.55	0.0248
The Hague	Delft	1.55	0.0248
The Hague	Amsterdam	1.4	0.0224
Dordrecht	Deventer	1.4	0.0224
Delft	The Hague	1	0.0160
Haarlem	Leiden	0.43	0.0068
The Hague	Haarlem	0.35	0.0056

Table 6. The table shows the influence Town A had on Town B, based on the aggregation of the combined weights, i.e. both probability weights and connection weights, presented as the absolute weight (Weight) and normalized to the highest absolute weight (Normalized Weight)

Town A	Town B	Weight	Normalized weight
Deventer	Amsterdam	179.47	1.0000
Leiden	Amsterdam	147.93	0.8243
Leiden	Leiden	141.76	0.7899
Deventer	Rotterdam	115.6	0.6441
Deventer	Deventer	98.26	0.5475
Deventer	The Hague	71.11	0.3963
Delft	Delft	65.71	0.3661
Amsterdam	Rotterdam	54.08	0.3014
Amsterdam	Amsterdam	50.8	0.2831
Delft	Amsterdam	50.27	0.2801
Deventer	Leiden	49.69	0.2769
Deventer	Delft	34.02	0.1896
The Hague	Rotterdam	29.97	0.1670
Rotterdam	Amsterdam	29.58	0.1648
Dordrecht	Amsterdam	27.5	0.1532
Leiden	Rotterdam	25.16	0.1402
Amsterdam	Delft	22.73	0.1267
Haarlem	Amsterdam	22.58	0.1258
Delft	Rotterdam	21.83	0.1216
Rotterdam	Rotterdam	21.81	0.1215
Amsterdam	Leiden	21.25	0.1184
Delft	Leiden	19.92	0.1110
Leiden	The Hague	19.2	0.1070
Leiden	Haarlem	17.75	0.0989
Deventer	Haarlem	16.44	0.0916
Leiden	Delft	12.95	0.0722
Amsterdam	The Hague	12.08	0.0673
Delft	Deventer	11.8	0.0657
Amsterdam	Haarlem	10.91	0.0608
Leiden	Dordrecht	10.47	0.0583
Dordrecht	Delft	8.87	0.0494
Dordrecht	The Hague	8.85	0.0493
Amsterdam	Deventer	8.37	0.0466
Delft	Dordrecht	8.19	0.0456

(*continued*)

Table 6. (*continued*)

Town A	Town B	Weight	Normalized weight
Rotterdam	Delft	7.36	0.0410
The Hague	Delft	6.98	0.0389
Haarlem	Rotterdam	6.62	0.0369
Dordrecht	Leiden	6.52	0.0363
Rotterdam	Deventer	4.61	0.0257
The Hague	Amsterdam	4.42	0.0247
The Hague	Deventer	4.16	0.0232
Leiden	Deventer	3.99	0.0222
Dordrecht	Deventer	3.46	0.0193
Delft	Haarlem	2.76	0.0154
Delft	The Hague	1.78	0.0099
Haarlem	Leiden	1.34	0.0075
The Hague	Haarlem	1.11	0.0062

References

1. Blanning, T.C.: The Pursuit of Glory: Europe, 1648–1815, vol. 6. Penguin (2007)
2. Brosens, K., Alen, K., Slegten, A., Truyen, F.: MapTap and cornelia. Slow digital art history and formal art historical social network research. Zeitschrift für Kunstgeschichte **79**(3), 315–330 (2016)
3. Drucker, J.: Humanities approaches to graphical display. Digit. Humanit. Q. **5**(1), 1–21 (2011)
4. Florida, R.: Cities and the Creative Class. Routledge, Abingdon (2004)
5. Gombrich, E.H.: The Story of Art, 16th edn. Phaidon Press, London (2007)
6. Klinke, H., Surkemper, L.: Editorial. Int. J. Digit. Art Hist. **1**, 6–9 (2015)
7. Landry, C.: The Creative City: A Toolkit for Urban Innovators. Earthscan, Abingdon (2012)
8. Nijboer, H., Bok, M.: Ecartico: linking cultural industries in the early modern low countries, c. 1475-c. 1725. Newsl. Consort. Eur. Res. Libr. **28**, 5 (2013).
9. Sluijter, E.J.: Rembrandt's Rivals: History Painting in Amsterdam, 1630–1650. John Benjamins Publishing Company, Amsterdam (2015)
10. Waiboer, A. (ed.): Vermeer and the Masters of Genre Painting: Inspiration and Rivalry (exh. cat. Musée du Louvre, Paris/National Gallery of Ireland, Dublin/National Gallery of Art, Washington, 2017–2018). Yale University Press (2017)

Linked Cultural Events: Digitizing Past Events and Implications for Analyzing the 'Creative City'

Harm Nijboer[1] and Claartje Rasterhoff[2(✉)]

[1] Huygens ING, Amsterdam, The Netherlands
harm.nijboer@huygens.knaw.nl
[2] University of Amsterdam, Amsterdam, The Netherlands
C.Rasterhoff@uva.nl

1 Introduction

This chapter introduces 'linked cultural events' as a novel methodological framework that allows for the systematic analysis of cultural expressions in their urban contexts. The events-based approach is inspired by datasets developed in the research program Creative Amsterdam: An E-Humanities Perspective (CREATE). This program investigates how cultural industries have shaped Amsterdam's cultural position in a European and global context (and vice versa), from the seventeenth century until the present day. By doing so, it aims to contribute to answering several major research questions (cf. [1]): Why do certain places and periods stand out in terms of cultural and creative achievements? Are their accomplishments rooted in specific urban historical contexts? What are the sources of urban creativity and – especially relevant to policy makers – how can they be unlocked?

Since a decade and a half culture and creativity have become key concepts in the rhetoric of urban planners and policy makers [2–4]. And although this focus is sometimes gratuitous there are many cities around the globe whose economies, or at least whose image, rely to a significant extent on creative and cultural industries, such as theatre, cinema, publishing, broadcasting, art, literature, music, and so on [5–7]. Amsterdam is often considered to be a highly cultural and innovative city, not in the least by its own town council, who is actively engaged in attracting, fostering, and promoting creative industries. In 2017, for instance, credit company TotallyMoney ranked the city number 1 in its list of 'The World's Most Cultural Cities', presumably due to the relatively high number of theatres, museums, galleries, concert halls, and fine-dining restaurants per capita [8]. In narratives acclaiming Amsterdam's creative potential, proponents have observed that Amsterdam has been a creative city for centuries. In the seventeenth century, the Dutch Golden Age, the city was indeed one of the most important hubs in the Western world [9]. In later centuries Amsterdam continued to function as a cradle of cultural and creative activities on both a national and international level, although it would never reach such prominence again [10, 11].

In trying to explain the long-term evolution of cities like Amsterdam as creative hubs, CREATE researchers develop research projects aimed at digitizing, collecting,

© Springer International Publishing AG, part of Springer Nature 2018
S. Münster et al. (Eds.): UHDL 2017/DECH 2017, CCIS 817, pp. 22–33, 2018.
https://doi.org/10.1007/978-3-319-76992-9_2

and enriching data on the various cultural sectors of Amsterdam, linking existing datasets and developing and applying computational search, analysis, and visualization tools. Collectively the projects form an infrastructure for combining cultural data in a network that exposes their relations and interdependencies.

In this chapter, we explore how such an approach can contribute to historiographical debates on urban creativity by means of datasets on musical and theatrical performances in Amsterdam. Scholars still have trouble addressing the dynamic relationship between cultural content and urban creative development. This can partly be understood as a consequence of different research traditions in the social sciences and humanities, but it also persists within the humanities. Cultural expressions are traditionally studied in specialized disciplines such as art history, music history, book history, and theatre history, while economic, cultural, social, and political historians study the historical context in which such expressions take shape. Through digitization, it has become possible to connect data on cultural expressions with data on the industrial or urban context. How exactly this may be done in a systematic way still remains empirically underexplored and undertheorized [12, 13]. We aim to redress this through the methodological framework of linked cultural events.

2 Theatre and Concert Programs as Linked Cultural Events

The events approach outlined here is partly data-driven, partly theory-driven. The CREATE program currently focuses on three interrelated core themes: *European Performing Arts Dataverse* (EPAD), on the history of performing arts (theatre, music, and cinema); *Amsterdam Time Machine* - a linked data hub and interface on the history of Amsterdam; *Digital History and Text Mining* - historical textual research and methodological reflections. In EPAD, data on the repertoires of various performing arts take up a particularly prominent position. Such programming data on cinema, theatre, and music generally contains information on the cultural expressions themselves, as well as on the (urban) contexts of performances. In terms of methodology, such data therefore allows us to move beyond biographical, institutional or object data, and develop a framework in which different data types and cultural activities can be studied in conjunction.

During the last two decades historians have identified programs of cinemas, theatres, and concert halls as important sources for the study of, amongst others, urban cultural life, the development of taste, and processes of canonization. William Weber's book [14] on the transformation of musical taste in the eighteenth and nineteenth centuries, for example, is based on thousands of concert programs. Indeed you will find a great many facsimiles of these programs scattered across this book, but Weber did not provide a systematic analysis of the content of these programs, nor did he structure this information in a digital resource. The focus on original documents is also present in the few projects aimed at digitizing concert programs [15–20]. All these projects function more or less as catalogs of concert programs, in the sense that they make concert programs queryable by means of meta-data but they do not provide sufficient data structure for analyzing the content of these documents.

A more advanced strategy with regard to the digitizing of programs was followed by Karel Dibbets with his Cinema Context project, which was launched online in 2006 [21]. At the time of writing Cinema Context contains 107,235 programs of Dutch cinemas from 1896 to the present. All movies (often circulating under various titles), persons, and companies in these programs have been identified and aligned to a master record. This means that Dutch titles like 'De juffrouw van de post', 'De juffrouw van de posterijen' and 'De dame van de Post en Telefonie' all link to the master record of the 1913 French movie 'Les demoiselles de PTT'. As a consequence it is possible to ask the system to list all screenings of this movie without having to know (or to state) all the alternate titles under which it is known. Where possible, Cinema Context provides a link to the well-known and well-maintained Internet Movie Database (IMDb) [21, 22].

For the CREATE datasets on musical and theatrical performances in Amsterdam we took an approach that is very similar to that of Cinema Context. The first, ONSTAGE (Online Datasystem of Theatre in Amsterdam in the Golden Age), contains information on the performances programmed in Amsterdam's public theatre during the period 1637–1772, and is currently being expanded to include the nineteenth and twentieth centuries [23–25]. The second, FELIX (Felix Meritis Programming Database), stores and links data on concerts held in the famous Amsterdam concert hall Felix Meritis between 1832 and 1888. The dataset contains over 6,500 performances of musical works from over 800 digitized concert programs [26, 27]. Currently it is being expanded to include opera programming in Dutch venues between 1880 and 1980.

In both projects we aimed at digitally structuring the content of the programs rather than building catalogues of programs. To do so, we entered verbatim transcriptions of all items (plays, compositions, composers, and musicians) mentioned in the programs in a relational database and matched different descriptions of the same subject, using various matching techniques, against a single master record. For ONSTAGE we were able to identify 96% of all plays staged in Amsterdam's public theatre between 1637 and 1772 and for FELIX we were able to identify 95% of the composers and 30% of the compositions mentioned in the concert programs (figures relate to instances, not to unique titles or names). External resources were pivotal in this identification process. We used lists of playwrights and printed editions of plays derived from the Short-Title Catalogue Netherlands (STCN) [28] to identify the entries in the theatre programs. For the concert programs we used lists of composers and compositions extracted from the International Music Score Library Project (IMSLP) [29]. Using these external resources significantly speeded up the process of identification while at the same time providing external identifiers for entities in our own data sets.

Data with links to external (web) resources, or linked data, are the building blocks of the Semantic Web, a web of data that is using more or less the same technological architecture as the better known World Wide Web, which is essentially a web of documents [30]. Basically the Semantic Web centers on two principles: (1) the use of Resource Description Framework (hereafter RDF) as a scheme to describe properties of and relationships among entities, and (2) the use of uniform resource identifiers (hereafter URIs and in practice URLs) to identify properties and entities.

RDF is a scheme, introduced in 1999, that was initially designed to describe metadata on objects (texts, images, multimedia) on the Web. The principle behind RDF is that it describes data in the form of subject–predicate–object triples. A statement like "Palamedes is written by Vondel", can be translated into the triple:

Subject: Palamedes
Predicate: is written by
Object: Vondel

If subject, predicate, and object are formally defined somewhere on the Web, we can also translate this statement in URIs:

Object: http://www.vondel.humanities.uva.nl/onstage/plays/88
Predicate: http://schema.org/creator
Subject: http://www.vondel.humanities.uva.nl/onstage/persons/5

We may then also follow this scheme to establish connections across resources, using a statement like:

Object: http://www.vondel.humanities.uva.nl/onstage/persons/5
Predicate: http://schema.org/sameAs
Subject: http://viaf.org/viaf/61555829

This states that the Vondel as described in ONSTAGE is the same as the one described in The Virtual International Authority File (VIAF).

ONSTAGE and FELIX are both accessible through a web interface that provides identifying pages for works, persons, theater shows, and concerts. These pages provide both a human readable (HTML) and machine readable (RDF), representation of the data.

By representing cultural events such as performances, screenings, and exhibitions using semantic web technology we create *linked cultural events*. This way of processing and connecting information is to a large degree homologous to the way events are linked to actors and objects in the real world. Hence linked data is to researchers of urban creativity more than a convenient way to present, retrieve, and connect data. Ideally, the very structure of the data offers the researcher a model of how cultural connections are made on both a local and a global level. However, data on the Semantic Web is seldom described in terms of events (*in flux*). More often data is described in terms of objects and their properties (*in stasis*). Inferences are needed to derive flux from stasis (and vice versa), as exemplified in Fig. 1.

State	Statement	Inference
Stasis	The author of Palamedes is Vondel	Vondel must have been writing Palamedes
Flux	Vondel wrote Palamedes in 1625	The author of Palamedes is Vondel

Fig. 1. Illustration of data description in stasis and in flux

RDF originated as a scheme for metadata, which is one of the reasons why data on the Semantic Web is likely to be described in stasis. From its inception it is geared towards the practice of cataloguing: describing objects and their properties. Besides that, data described *in flux* is much more verbose than data described *in stasis*. Nevertheless, interest in dealing with events on the Semantic Web is growing [31–33] and technologies to draw inferences from Linked Data and to transpose data from one ontology to another are advancing. Notwithstanding the limitations and complexities of Semantic Web technology, the great practical advantage of this technology is that it enables us to connect single resource data to external resources. It provides us with the contextualization that is needed to make sense of cultural events, which by their ephemeral nature are difficult to operationalize otherwise [13].

A brief treatment of the international linkages of local cultural life illustrates how operationalizing this phenomenon through linked events may assist researchers in mapping and analyzing urban culture beyond a single event or a fixed network of local actors. Figure 2 lists a basic Top 10 of composers who were programmed in music hall Felix Meritis in the nineteenth century (Fig. 2).

1. Ludwig van Beethoven (1770-1827)   424 performances
2. Wolfgang Amadeus Mozart (1756-1791)   375 performances
3. Carl Maria von Weber (1786-1826)   283 performances
4. Felix Mendelssohn (1809-1847)   264 performances
5. Gioacchino Rossini (1792-1868)   245 performances
6. Louis Spohr (1784-1859)   212 performances
7. Peter Joseph von Lindpaintner (1791-1856)   168 performances
8. Gaetano Donizetti (1797-1848)   150 performances
9. Robert Schumann (1810-1856)   137 performances
10. Johannes Bernardus van Bree (1801-1857)   102 performances

Fig. 2. Top 10 composers programmed in Felix Meritis in the nineteenth century (Source: FELIX)

Although the list contains many established names, it is also surprising in some respects. Several well-known eighteenth and nineteenth century composers are missing in this list, while lesser-known composers like Spohr, Lindpaintner and local hero Van Bree feature prominently. The music scene in nineteenth century Amsterdam was clearly internationally oriented. When we want to account for this international dimension by analyzing features of the events and the places where they took place, linking local data to external resources is the only realistic option that we have. The alternative would be to store a lot of additional data in our own system, but such a huge (think alone about the data that is worldwide available on Beethoven and Mozart) and heterogeneous dataset would be very difficult to maintain for small - and even large - research groups.

The international dimension is also present in the data on theatre performances in seventeenth and eighteenth century Amsterdam. Jautze et al. [25] have done extensive research on the ONSTAGE data to explore the impact of Spanish drama on theatre in

Amsterdam in the Dutch Golden Age. This impact was - contrary to what many would expect - considerable. Translations of plays by, amongst others, Félix Lope de Vega y Carpio (1562–1635) and Pedro Calderón de la Barca (1600–1681) turned out to be real blockbusters in the programming of Amsterdam's city theatre in the late seventeenth century. Investigating the dynamics of such phenomena requires deep internal linkage of local data. First of all, plays have to be identified as translations or even translations of translations. Moreover, by linking data on plays to external bibliographical resources like the Short-Title Catalogue Netherlands (STCN), we can get a detailed picture of their publishing history. And by linking data on plays to international resources like VIAF (Virtual International Authority File) and Wikidata, we get access to a lot of data on artefacts and actors to enrich local resources. Furthermore, external linking also serves the purpose of making our local data available in a global context.

Although primarily defined from a methodological perspective the notion of linked cultural events also reveals that the role of events is heavily undertheorized with regard to urban creativity and urban culture.

3 Linked Cultural Events and the Creative City

We argue that the systematic and relational analysis of data on cultural events contributes to a better understanding of urban creative development. Studies on urban demographics (creative class), formal and informal industrial organization (creative clusters), or structural properties of cities (creative city) have offered valuable insights in conditions and mechanisms favorable to creativity and innovation, but they tend to view the creative city as a state of being, rather than as a continuous state of becoming. The general idea in these discourses is that cultural producers and their industries are major contributors to a city's economic durability and the wellbeing of its inhabitants, as sources of distinction, creativity, and innovation. In turn, the city is thought to be crucial in the development of such industries, because urban amenities and the spatial clustering of market participants ease knowledge transfers necessary for innovation. These ideas have given way to a worldwide policy frenzy over the creative city, meanwhile criticasters have pointed to the lack of robust empirical evidence supporting these claims, as well as to the downsides of policy frameworks that reduce culture and creativity to mere assets [34].

Recent historical research emphasizes the importance of time- and place-specific characteristics and circumstances, and call for clarifications of the presumed relationships between urban contexts and innovation [35–37]. The current literature, for instance, is strongly focused on the role of economies of agglomeration, labor mobility and diversity, education, the interaction of technology and cultural industries, internationality, and public support [4, 38]. Following these insights urban creativity is often considered as the outcome of a city's infrastructure and its more or less structural properties. Little attention is being paid to what actually makes cities come to life: the cultural expressions themselves, and in particular events such as exhibitions, concerts, and theatre performances. For novelty and creativity to become innovations, cultural expressions do not only need to be produced, but also have to be presented, consumed, and valued. As we will argue, events play a key role in this.

Although cultural events feature in several ways in the social-scientific literature on contemporary urban creativity, this field does not offer us much of a structural explanation on why some places and periods are more cultural or creative than others. First of all, events are often defined in the narrow sense of the word (i.e. fairs and festivals) and studied in relation to the topics of city branding and urban revitalization [39, 40]. Secondly, in the literature on industrial organization and innovation, events such as fairs and festivals are conceptualized as temporary clusters. Their cluster-like characteristics (physical proximity and social interaction) facilitate knowledge exchange, codification, and contestation, which are in turn considered important to the dynamics of innovation and creativity [41]. In both strands of literature the focus tends to be on individual mass or niche events and their network effects for participants. However, for our research, we are not so much concerned with measuring the social, cultural, political or economic impact and spillovers of individual events in the urban community, but with 'cultural life' in the form of (webs of) events and their role in shaping urban creativity.

In contrast to the social sciences, one might expect a stronger focus on events in historical studies of urban culture. Although it would be too simplistic to define the field of history as the recollection of past events, it is how the discipline started out and it has remained at the core of historical research ever since. As a consequence, much has been written about how events should be conceptualized and about the role of events in studying and writing history. However, much of the historiographical debate on events concentrates on the question whether historians should focus on extraordinary events (e.g. wars and revolutions) or more ordinary life events (e.g. marriages and baptisms), and on the structure-event dichotomy posed and contested in the *Annales* school [32, 42]. Theoretical and conceptual thinking about history and events also expands to the field of action theory in philosophy and social theory [43]. However, in these traditions methodological reflection on the role of events remains limited.

With the increasing importance of digital resources and computational techniques in historical scholarship, a renewed methodological interest in events has emerged in recent years. Events are, for instance, seen as important devices in structuring heritage data and as building blocks for online reconstructions of historical narratives [44]. In the field of digital art history, moreover, the cultural events themselves also feature as units of analysis. The Exhibitium project, for example, aims to develop a platform for the development and analysis of available data relating to temporary art exhibitions, considering them 'complex cultural phenomena resulting in the establishment of a series of relationships between certain actors, but also in strategic factors in the promotion of social dynamics and economic movements' [45]. Most projects on events are data-driven and therefore do not explicitly aim to develop historical analytical frameworks in relation to data collection and data modeling. We emphasize that networks of events should also be considered as units of analysis that can help us identify and disentangle processes of social change.

Our approach, then, relates to a methodology more common in the social sciences: event analysis. In the study of social movements in particular, event catalogues have become standard tools to study contentious episodes, collective action, and social movements [46, 47]. By collecting data on social events in 'event catalogues', scholars aggregated counts of specific aspects of events into measures that help explain patterns of social change (e.g. variation over time, place or social category, or covariation with characteristics of settings, participants or associated events). Tilly [48] and others have argued that such catalogues and simple counts of characteristics of events fail to capture internal regularities such as recurrent sequences or causal links between events. In order to better capture the relational character of political contention, they tried to account for the interactions, conversations, and social ties within and between events by developing coding schemes defined by subject-action-object. These triplets allowed them to capture rich descriptions of individual events and of multiple episodes, mainly on the basis of unstructured textual data. Similarly, datasets of events over time have been used in the broader field of data analytics, for instance in event-based network analyses, to add temporality and dynamism to otherwise static information systems [49].

Such an approach seeks a middle ground between the depth of a single event history and quantitative measures of multiple events. Together, the structures and content of events form patterns that mark particular periods of history or changes over time, and through the emphasis on action and interaction events emerge as relational and performative phenomena that sustain and transform social structures.

To further develop these thoughts in relation to cultural events and the city, we should expand a little on the concepts of performance and performativity. When dealing with data on performances it is hard to ignore what is labelled 'the performative turn' in the social sciences. A large number of contemporary social theorists reject the notion of a cultural act or event as an expression (or representation) of a given culture. Instead culture should be understood as a collection of performative acts or events. By performativity we mean that an event calls or recalls something (a piece of art, a cultural code or trait) into being. A play, for instance, must be performed (staged, read, remembered) to be there. Beyond the performance a play is nothing but 'code'. The same goes, mutatis mutandis, for novels, music, paintings, and even concepts like masculinity and ethnicity. The importance of identifying events as the constituting elements of culture is that it allows for a non-essentialist approach of cultures and cultural communities [50].

Events, of course, as Tilly and his colleagues realized, do not occur in isolation. Each event involves the actions, narratives, and presence of a number of entities. These entities can be human agents (e.g. performers and spectators), non-human agents (organizations), material objects (places, artifacts, etc.) or immaterial objects (concepts, code). These entities are in turn likely to be involved in other events as well. Already in 1964 the ethnolinguist Dell Hymes, who was an early protagonist of the performative turn, defined 'communities' as 'systems of communicative events' [51]. Being a linguist his primary focus was of course on verbal communication, but we can easily extend this to non-verbal performative events like gesture, exhibitions et cetera.

In order to operationalize this interpretation of culture and its role in shaping patterns of urban creativity (and vice versa) for historical research, we conceptualize linked cultural events (LCEs) as the web of cultural performances that underpins the exchange of cultural artifacts, as well as the introduction of novel creations in markets (innovations). Linked cultural events, then, are performances (and, for example, also publications) that are situated in time and place, but also linked to actors across time, space, and society. On a methodological level, this means that we can operationalize the study of cultural movements through linked cultural event catalogues. Because this approach takes events as units of analysis it enables us to model cultures and cultural communities in operational frameworks that allow for advanced analysis and data handling. The centrality of events, agents, and objects and the reoccurrence of connections in webs of LCEs can, for instance, serve as an indication of the cultural impact of the entities involved.

4   Conclusion

In this chapter we have discussed the use of linked cultural events as a conceptual and methodological tool in the study of urban creativity. By offering an analytical framework for mapping and disentangling connected cultural webs, we have aimed to offer researchers a way to analyze the role of culture in relation to patterns of urban creativity. The methodological framework has two main characteristics: (1) it posits cultural events as analytical units with generic features and linkages to actors, institutions, and urban properties (linked cultural events); and (2) it is connected to a data structure that allows for querying the connections between these units of analysis (linked data). On the level of data handling the LCE approach has strong affinity with Semantic Web technology and the associated Linked Open Data paradigm, which have evolved as leading principles in the handling of historical and cultural heritage data in recent years [52]. The accompanying linked data structure has implications for both the mapping and analysis of cultural events.

Through the cases of FELIX and ONSTAGE with their linked open data structure, we have seen how we may use not only counts but also the connectivity of linked cultural events as proxy for the cultural achievements of a city or community. Moreover, and this is important for analyzing how culture relates to and interacts with urban creative achievements, they suggest that it is possible to study cultural events in their (urban) context in a systematic way. The LCE approach allows for qualification of events (in addition to quantification) to establish for instance levels of novelty, local embeddedness, social inclusion, and cross-sectoral linkages (depending on the data type). Scholars may also employ it to develop comparisons of (features of) events across time, space, and cultural sectors, while its rich semantic structure also allows for searching internal regularities such as recurrent sequences or causal links between separate events [47].

The LCE-approach thereby allows for a more historical and comprehensive treatment of both the actors involved in 'creative cities' and the relationships between these actors than was hitherto possible, enabling researchers to broaden the research framework in which urban creativity (in past and present) can be studied. Our discussion of the FELIX and ONSTAGE projects showed, for instance, how the evolution of Amsterdam as a creative city cannot be mapped or analyzed without taking into account its inter-local and international connections. Moreover, by analyzing the cultural fabric of urban creativity in linked data structures, these projects make it easier to engage with practices of performing and reception, as well as with the different actors involved. This is important, because we might easily think of Beethoven, Mozart, and Lope de Vega as important artists by definition. But their relevance, in the end, is defined by (sequences of) performative events in cities like Amsterdam.

References

1. Hall, P.: Cities in Civilization: Culture, Innovation, and Urban Order. Weidenfeld & Nicolson, London (1998)
2. Landry, C.: The Creative City: A Toolkit for Urban Innovators. Earthscan, London (2000)
3. Florida, R.: The Rise of the Creative Class: And How It's Transforming Work, Leisure, Community and Everyday Life. Basic Books, New York (2002)
4. Andersson, D.E., Andersson, E., Charlotte Mellander, C.: Handbook of Creative Cities. Edward Elgar Publishing, Cheltenham (2011)
5. Scott, A.J.: The Cultural Economy of Cities. Essays on the Geography of Image-Producing Industries. Sage, London (2000)
6. Scott, A.J.: Social Economy of the Metropolis: Cognitive-Cultural Capitalism and the Global Resurgence of Cities. Oxford University Press, Oxford (2008)
7. Scott, A.J.: Cultural economy and the creative field of the city. Geogr. Ann. Ser. B - Hum. Geogr. 92(2), 115–130 (2010)
8. TotallyMoney: The World's Most Cultural Cities 2017. http://www.totallymoney.com/cultural-cities/?_sp=906870f6-c1dc-4e7b-ab8f-22230937c366.1499415503535
9. O'Brien, P., 't Hart, M., Van der Wee, H. (eds.): Urban Achievement in Early Modern Europe: Golden Ages in Antwerp. Amsterdam and London. Cambridge University Press, Cambridge (2001)
10. Deinema, M.: The culture business caught in place: spatial trajectories of Dutch cultural industries, 1899–2005. Ph.D. thesis, University of Amsterdam (2012)
11. Prak, M., Kloosterman, R.: De relatie tussen plaats en cultuur: Nederlandse culturele industrie vanuit langetermijnperspectief. In: Taverne, E., de Klerk, L., Ramakers, B., Dembski, S. (eds.) Nederland stedenland: Continuïteit en vernieuwing, pp. 195–205. NAi Publishers, Rotterdam (2012)
12. Van Asseldonk, N., Van Mensch, P., Van Vliet, H.: Cultuur in Context: Erfgoeddata in nieuwe samenhang. Reinwardt Academie, Amsterdam (2009)
13. Van Vliet, H., Dibbets, K., Gras, H.: Culture in context: contextualization of cultural events. In: Michael Ross, M., Grauer, M., Freisleben, B. (eds.) Digital Tools in Media Studies: Analysis and Research, pp. 27–42. Transcript Verlag, Bielefeld (2009)
14. Weber, W.: The Great Transformation of Musical Taste: Concert Programming from Haydn to Brahms. Cambridge University Press, New York (2008)
15. Concert Programmes Database. http://www.concertprogrammes.org.uk
16. Programs of the Marshall-Hall Orchestral Concerts 1892–1910. https://digitised-collections.unimelb.edu.au/handle/11343/156
17. Bashford, C., Cowgill, R., McVeigh, S.: The concert life in nineteenth-century London database project. In: Dibble, J., Zon, B. (eds.) Nineteenth-Century British Music Studies, vol. 2, pp. 1–12. Ashgate, Aldershot (2002)
18. Concert Life in 19th-Century London: Database and Research Project. http://www.concertlifeproject.com
19. Wells, V.A.: Concert Programmes Database (review). Notes 68, 145–147 (2011)

20. Day, D.A.: Digital opera and ballet: a case study of international collaboration. Fontes Artis Musicae **61**, 99–106 (2014)
21. Cinema Context. http://www.cinemacontext.nl
22. Internet Movie Database. http://www.imdb.com
23. ONSTAGE (Online Datasystem of Theatre in Amsterdam in the Golden Age). http://www.vondel.humanities.uva.nl/onstage
24. Jautze, K.: ONSTAGE! EMagazine eHumanities Royal Netherlands Academy of Arts and Sciences 6 (2015). http://ehumanities.leasepress.com/emagazine-6/recent-events/onstage
25. Jautze, K., Frans Blom, F., Álvarez Francés, L.: Spaans theater in de Amsterdamse Schouwburg (1638–1672): Kwantitatieve en kwalitatieve analyse van de creatieve industrie van het vertalen. De Zeventiende Eeuw: Cultuur in de Nederlanden in interdisciplinair perspectief **32**(1), 12–39 (2016). https://doi.org/10.18352/dze.10000
26. FELIX (Felix Meritis Programming Database). http://www.vondel.humanities.uva.nl/felix
27. Van Nieuwkerk, M.: Een vergeten repertoire. De concertprogrammering van Felix Meritis in de periode 1830–1888. MA thesis University of Amsterdam (2015)
28. Short-Title Catalogue Netherlands (STCN). https://www.kb.nl/en/organisation/research-expertise/for-libraries/short-title-catalogue-netherlands-stcn
29. International Music Score Library Project (IMSLP). http://imslp.org
30. Berners-Lee, T., Hendler, J., Lassila, O.: The semantic web: a new form of web content that is meaningful to computers will unleash a revolution of new possibilities. Sci. Am. **284**(5), 34–43 (2001)
31. Troncy, R., Shaw, R., Hardman, L.: LODE: une ontologie pour représenter des événements dans le web de données'. In: 21es Journées francophones d'Ingénierie des Connaissances (IC 2010), Nîmes, pp. 69–80, June 2010. http://hal.archives-ouvertes.fr/hal-00487630
32. Shaw, R.: A semantic tool for historical events. In: Proceedings of the 1st Workshop on EVENTS: Definition, Detection, Coreference, and Representation, Atlanta, Georgia, 14 June 2013, pp. 38–46 (2013)
33. Houda, K., Troncy, R.: EventMedia: a LOD dataset of events illustrated with media. Seman. Web J. **7**(2), 193–199 (2016)
34. Peck, J.: Struggling with the creative class. Int. J. Urban Reg. Res. **29**(4), 740–770 (2005)
35. Van Damme, I., De Munck, B., Miles, A. (eds.): Cities and Creativity from the Renaissance to the Present. Routledge, London (2017)
36. Davids, K., De Munck, B. (eds.): Innovation and Creativity in Late Medieval and Early Modern European Cities. Ashgate, Aldershot (2014)
37. Rasterhoff, C.: Painting and Publishing as Cultural Industries. The Fabric of Creativity in the Dutch Republic, 1580–1800. Amsterdam University Press, Amsterdam (2016)
38. Hietala, M., Clark, P.: Creative cities. In: Clark, P. (ed.) The Oxford Handbook of Cities in World History. Oxford University Press, Oxford (2013)
39. Smith, A.: Events and Urban Regeneration: The Strategic Use of Events to Revitalise Cities. Routledge, London (2012)
40. Richards, G., Palmer, R.: Eventful Cities: Cultural Management and Urban Revitalisation. Routledge, London (2010)
41. Bathelt, H., Glückler, J.: The Relational Economy. Oxford University Press, Oxford (2011). https://doi.org/10.1093/acprof:osobl/9780199587384.001.0001
42. Sewell, W.H.: Historical events as transformations of structures: inventing revolution at the Bastille. Theory Soc. **25**, 841–881 (1996)
43. Casati, R., Varzi, A.: Events. In: Zalta, E.N. (ed.): The Stanford Encyclopedia of Philosophy (2015). http://plato.stanford.edu/archives/win2015/entries/events

44. De Boer, V., Oomen, J., Inel, O., Aroyo, L., Van Staveren, E., Helmich, W., De Beurs, D.: DIVE into the event-based browsing of linked historical media. J. Web Seman. **35**(3), 152–158 (2015). https://doi.org/10.1016/j.websem.2015.06.003
45. Exhibitium. http://exhibitium.com/en/project
46. Hutter, S.: Protest event analysis and its offspring. In: Della Porta, D. (ed.) Methodological Practices in Social Movement Research, pp. 335–367. Oxford University Press, Oxford (2014)
47. Tilly, C.: Event catalogs as theories. Sociol. Theory **20**(2), 248–254 (2002)
48. Tilly, C.: Contentious Performances. Cambridge University Press, Cambridge (2008)
49. O'Madadhain, J., Hutchins, J., Smyth, P.: Prediction and ranking algorithms for event-based network data. SIGKDD Explor. Newsl. **7**(2), 23–30 (2005). https://doi.org/10.1145/1117454.1117458
50. Dirksmeier, P., Helbrecht, I.: Time, non-representational theory and the "performative turn"—towards a new methodology in qualitative social research. Forum: Qual. Soc. Res. **9**(2), 1–24 (2008)
51. Hymes, D.: Introduction: toward ethnographies of communication. Am. Anthropol. **66**(6, Part 2), 1–34 (1964)
52. Hyvönen, E.: Publishing and Using Cultural Heritage Linked Data on the Semantic Web. Morgan & Claypool, San Rafael (2012)

Cataloguing Monuments - Some Changes in the Documentary Work of Art Historians in Silesia over the Past 150 Years

Agnieszka Seidel-Grzesińska[✉] and Małgorzata Wyrzykowska

Institute for Art History, University of Wrocław,
Ul. Szewska 36, 50-137 Wrocław, Poland
{agnieszka.seidel-grzesinska,
malgorzata.wyrzykowska}@uwr.edu.pl

Abstract. The aim of this paper is a critical analysis of the process of creating a 'classic' monuments catalog, in the context of the implementation of ICT in the history of art. The starting point for this discussion is an analysis of the genesis, structure and function of the catalog in the form in which it was created at the beginning of the 20th century. Texts and illustrations from the beginning of the 17th century on have been taken into consideration. The key problems to be addressed are: the changes that ICT brought to the work of the documenter and its impact on the methodology of cataloging. The conclusion compares the 'classic' published monuments catalog with databases of similar character.

Keywords: Catalog of monuments · Silesian cultural heritage
Documentary research · Digital humanities resources · Methodology

1 Introduction

In recent decades Information and Communication Technology (ICT) has led to important changes in the research methods of many scientific disciplines, including the humanities. The question is whether it has also had an impact on the implementation of one of the fundamental tasks in the field of art history - the cataloging of monuments. Has the use of ICT influenced the process of data collection and data elaboration, and to what extent? What kind of technologies have provided real support for this type of work? Have they contributed to an increase in the quality of the catalog – that is, the reliability and comprehensiveness of the research? Would it be useful to extend catalog documentation in connection with the availability of new tools such as 3D scanning, digital photogrammetry, LiDAR? Finally there is a question about the future of the 20th century catalog model: should we consider replacing it for some digital solutions?

This paper discusses some changes in the process of cataloguing, undertaken in accordance with the rules formulated by German art historian Georg Dehio (1850–1932), who is considered to be the father of the topographical catalog. These rules became assumptions for his model publication entitled *Handbuch der deutschen Kunstdenkmaeler,* which was prepared in the years 1905–1912 based on the contributions of the Viennese school of art history [4, 5, 19, 28]. This was intended to be a

S. Münster et al. (Eds.): UHDL 2017/DECH 2017, CCIS 817, pp. 34–43, 2018.
https://doi.org/10.1007/978-3-319-76992-9_3

complete handbook of monuments within the area of the German Empire, prepared relatively quickly using modest means and intended for various readers. Based on a similar formula, such catalogs were prepared and published over time for other European regions. Catalogs were intended primarily for informative purposes and the only form of evaluation of the monuments included in the catalog was selection based on the artistic and historical value of the objects. However, as the catalogs were not part of the governmental monument protection system, the selection of material was not determined by legal or financial conditions but was based solely on the expertise of scientists. In 1905 Dehio, in his speech on the protection and preservation of monuments in the 19th century delivered at the Kaiser Wilhelms Universiteat in Strasburg, pointed at the catalog as one of the foundations of monuments protection, which helps to raise consciousness and the importance of monuments. In that way the catalog contributed to the protection of cultural heritage as widely understood [8].

The following ideas were raised when preparing the project *Katalog Zabytków Sztuki w Polsce* (Catalog of Art Monuments in Poland) covering the Lower Silesian counties, undertaken at the Institute of Art History at the University of Wroclaw in Poland under the supervision of Jan Harasimowicz and published by the Polish Academy of Sciences. The project, financed by the National Program for the Development of the Humanities, is scheduled for 2015–2020 within the frame of Tradition (Contract No. 0452/NPRH/H1a/83).

2 Modern Models of Historical Monuments Documentation

In recent centuries several models of monuments documentation have been developed. They are adapted to different types of cultural goods and the circumstances in which they exist. Taking into consideration only the published materials, one can distinguish catalogs of collections and catalogs of exhibitions as a tool for the documentation of works in public and private collections, as well as catalogs of problems, which also include the furnishings and interior decoration of buildings. Distinct forms of documentation were also elaborated for architecture. However, the methodological reflection of such forms of documentation is not an easy task. Trying to define their models, one has to measure both the different traditions of conceptualization of cultural heritage in individual states and its varying legislative contexts in each country.

The question of the differing conceptualization of documentation processes in various countries requires careful attention from the investigator. A similarity in the sound of words in different languages (for example, in English *inventory*, in German *der Inventar*, in Polish *inwentarz*) does not mean their sense is the same. It should be also stressed that modern scientific inventories are not the direct continuation of studies known as inventory or *urbaria* in the late Middle Ages and Early Modern Times. Nevertheless, not going into details, two categories of scientific works describing monuments and other artifacts in situ can be distinguished: the inventory and the catalog. Inventories of monuments are generally divided into two types: topographical and corpora (for example, *Corpus basilicarum christianarum Romae*). The inventory, the most comprehensive and most precise description of monuments, is equipped with the full research apparatus (measurement, description, text and illustrative sources, bibliography, historical context). The objects included in inventories are documented strictly according to a predefined format. As a consequence of this, all items in an inventory are described using the same criteria. The preparation of inventories to be published is extremely time-consuming, requires a lot of work and is very expensive. One example is the inventory of the monuments of the Province of Salamanca prepared from 1903 on and finally published in 1967 [6, V; 10].

Therefore, there was a need to create a model for a handheld publication, which would relatively quickly record the state of ancient monuments located in a particular area, with only brief but professional and reliable information about them. This should be addressed to a wide audience and serve as a guidebook for all interested. [6, VI]. The response to this need became the modern catalog of monuments (German *Denkmaltopographie*) based on the pattern of the previously mentioned publication by Dehio [6, 7, 26, 27]. Over the years in Germany the name of Dehio became the title of a topographical catalog series. According to this pattern there was published, for example, a series of monuments catalogs in England by Nicolaus Pevsner in years 1951–1974 (50 volumes) [24]. Also based on this model is a series of *Katalog Zabytków Sztuki w Polsce* initiated in the 50s of the 20th century.

3   The Special Role of the Catalog in the Protection of Monuments

A key feature of the modern catalog of monuments is the usage of topographical approaches to documentation of cultural heritage. This is a model known even in antiquity (Pausanias, *Description of Greece*). Over time, the description of a particular area, taking into account its geographical features, historical outline and cultural heritage for various reasons considered important, has undergone a series of transformations, resulting in, *inter alia*, the formula of the modern topographic catalog.

To define the scientific modern catalog as a category of description of monuments, it should be emphasized that its basis is the analysis of monuments at the place of their location *(in situ)* and mirroring their state of preservation. The monuments are examined during the field inquiry. The monument's first description is based on the knowledge of a scientist. Another important step is the library and archive inquiry in order to gather written and published sources and their verification. The final stage is the preparation of the notes for each monument according to a certain formula with a precisely specified scope of information provided. The catalog notes ought to be written using a precise conceptual apparatus. The oldest editions of monuments catalogs were limited to text. Illustrated albums with prints were published separately or in additional volumes [e.g. 18]. Over time some layouts and photographic images of monuments were added to the catalog.

These activities can be implemented in various ways, depending on the tools and resources available to the researcher. In the past decades there were many obstacles to reaching the examined monuments. Means of transport were limited. The library and archival inquiries were difficult. Photographic procedures were extremely time-consuming and burdened with a high risk of error. At present digital technologies are being used more and more in order to facilitate the above-mentioned tasks. An interesting example of the above-mentioned transformation is the process of contemporary monument documentation in Silesia, because Silesia is a region in which many problems related to documenting cultural heritage were born due to its geographical location, varying political statehood and dynamic religious situation.

4 Documentation of Silesian Art and Architecture to the Beginning of the 20th Century

The geopolitical location of Lower Silesia resulted in cultural diversity in this area. Through the ages the region belonged among others to Princes of the Piast Dynasty, to the Czech Kingdom, the Hapsburg Monarchy, Prussia and Poland. The art and architecture of Silesia were developed under the influence of various artistic factors, coming from the main artistic centers (such as Italy, Vienna, Prague, Berlin). Therefore the documentation regarding Silesian art and architecture is nowadays dispersed and preserved at many places and institutions. Some resources are gathered at European universities, archives and museums - in Berlin, Dresden, Vienna, Warsaw, Marburg. When cataloging and investigating Silesian architecture it is necessary to pursue research at these places in the search for documents and written sources about the artifacts.

The most important sources for documentation of Silesian historical artifacts are the descriptions of the region undertaken during the Early Modern period and cartographic sources as well as iconographic ones—drawings and engravings. Silesia is a region which had early gained extensive "documentation" of its architecture. The 17th century already brought very inspirational and valuable descriptions of regional monuments. Worth mentioning among them are studies like *Silesiographia* by Nicolaus Henelius, dated from 1613 and taking into account such aspect], s as toponymy, geophysics, nature, history and the description of urban area (cities) [14] and the description of the Duchy of Świdnica i Jawor by Ephraim Nason entitled *Phoenix Redivivus*, prepared in 1667 [21]. The latter source is an example of work focused much more on description of architecture, especially single buildings and their furnishings.

This model was applied in the following centuries as well. From the first half of the 18th century, the best example is the description of Wroclaw curiosities written by Daniel Gomolcke (active 1733–1754). The author was an amateur topographer who wanted to present to the wider public and tourists visiting the city the most important, beautiful and interesting buildings of Wroclaw and the key historical events. Gomolcke, based on his experiences gained when traveling around Europe, had realized the importance of reliable information about the buildings and history of visited towns and villages. He decided to describe, in a scientific way as he stressed, according to historical facts, the most extraordinary and valuable buildings of Wroclaw from his point of view. The buildings were presented mainly in a descriptive manner as the publication was accompanied by only a few prints [11].

In the middle of the 18th century the most distinguished and important Silesian buildings were described and drawn by Friedrich Bernhard Wernher (1690–1776) in his works on Silesia in *Compendio seu Topographia das ist Praesentatio und Beschreibung des Herzogthums Schlesiens* and *Scenographia Urbium Silesiae* and

Perspectivische Vorstellung derer von Sr. Konigl. Majest. in Preußen... allergnadigst concedirten Beth-Hauser A.C. Numerous graphic images of Silesian buildings, towns and villages based on Wernher's colored drawings were prepared and published over the following decades. *Topographia* is an example of a richly illustrated manuscript containing maps, axonometric views of buildings, panoramic views of cities and presentations of single monuments. Wernher was primarily interested in buildings that were distinguished by form or function, mainly noble houses and palaces as well as churches. Of primary importance in the text commentary were historical facts and selected decorative elements and inscriptions. Elements of description or formal architectural analysis were rare, not individualized and rather schematic. Wernher used simple expressions and very general aesthetic notions in his evaluation such as beautiful, graceful, rich [20, 25]. He described some complex iconographic programs, such as Aula Leopoldina in the Jesuit college in Wroclaw (now a university). He was less interested in the authors of the monuments (architects, painters, sculptors), although their names sometimes also appeared on the *Topography* cards. A visible sign that information provided by Wernher was updated were the empty spaces in the manuscripts reserved for drawings that would show buildings which were still under construction. According to those researching Wernher's works and analyzing his aesthetic opinions, it can be acknowledged that he was impressed by fashionable contemporary architecture (mainly Baroque) and was able to capture its specificity and stylistic diversity. As a consequence the selection of palaces and churches chosen by Wernher and the information provided were to a certain degree random and subjective. Nevertheless, Wernher's work is unique due to its complexity and relevance. It is also of great importance for contemporary researchers as a source which combines the description of monuments with illustrative materials [20]. Statistical studies, which appeared from the beginning of the 19th century [e.g. 1, 16], brought a new quality to the field of artifact description. Publications of this type were anticipated by works published at the end of the previous century [17, 28]. These works included, besides the descriptive sections, "catalog" parts, which consisted of basic information, ordered according to *a priori* accepted principles, about the villages and cities in the region.

The origins of the systematic documentation of architectural monuments in Silesia are connected with the activity of Hans Lutsch (1854–1922), educated as an architect, active as the building councillor in Wroclaw and the Provincial Conservator of Silesian Monuments. His five-volume work, published in the 1880s, was devoted to regional monuments and until the present day is an indispensable source for research undertaken on architecture and its furnishings [19]. The scope of his research was focused on architecture and valuable interior decoration. His own artistic preferences were visible in his work. Lutsch took little account of Baroque works, because, unlike Wernher, from his point of view they were too new and did not match his sense of taste. Nevertheless, undoubtedly Lutsch's ambition was to visit all of the documented monuments in person [22].

One of the primary sources in research on urbanism and architecture are old maps. The territory of Silesia was systematically documented by cartographers from the 17th century on. Silesia was included among other regions on Hapsburg military maps dating from 1739. Less than ten years later the next measurement was executed by the Prussian government. Based on the results of this measurement *Krieges-Karte von*

Schlesien was prepared, showing some examples of defensive architecture. Silesia was also included within the frame of a project for the so-called table topographical image *(Urmesstischblaetter)* ordered by the General Headquarters of Prussia, on which work began in 1816. Initially these were handwritten maps, updated frequently and printed from the 1880s. *(Messtischblaetter)*. Today these maps allow us to find the locations of buildings, gardens, parks and cemeteries, monuments either completely ruined or not preserved at all.

Other iconographic documents of great importance for contemporary documentation of Silesian cultural heritage are drawn and engraved prospects of villages and small towns made since the 17th century. Nowadays they are very useful in recognizing and dating monuments, as well postcards [2] and photos, which arose and were published more and more frequently from the last quarter of the 19th century. In the first half of the 20th century most Silesian villages had their own postcards. These are a valuable source of information about their infrastructure including buildings like post offices, schools and inns. They were numerously printed, but simultaneously they were easily exposed to destruction, which makes them at the present a unique source.

The texts and images mentioned above were created as documentation of the up-to-date state of monuments, however over the time they achieved the status of sources. Therefore they required of course, as does every source, a critical approach. Knowledge of their authors, the facts of their lives and interests, allows us to formulate reliable interpretation of such sources. This is now possible thanks to research carried out on them and biographical studies [e.g. 12].

5 ICT in the Process of Monuments Cataloguing

The above-mentioned Early Modern manuscripts, old maps and printings dated before the first half of the 19th century are accessible in single copies in the collections of manuscripts, cartography or old printings at Polish and foreign libraries - partly in larger libraries in Austria, Germany, Czech Republic, France, Switzerland and so on. Access to books published in the 19th and 20th centuries is easier, but usually limited to some volumes in bigger academic centers.

After World War II, Silesia was incorporated into the borders of Poland and these lands became much more interesting for Polish art historians. At that time in Poland, work on the documentation of monuments were carried out within the above-mentioned series of Catalogs of Monuments of Art in Poland. Documentary works regarding monuments in Silesia were indicated in the 1980s and were intensified about 2000. These last projects coincided with the development of humanities web resources, which became very helpful in the process of cataloging monuments in Silesia and introduced a new quality in field research.

Initially very helpful were some digital online catalogs of libraries, which facilitated bibliographic queries. Also useful were aggregation portals such as the German KVK - Karlsruher Virtueller Katalog or the Polish catalog KaRo. Relatively early database systems began to be used to collect bibliographies. One of the most useful tools is the thematic bibliography of the literature concerning the former eastern German territories

- *Bibliographieportal zur Geschichte Ostmitteleuropas* - provided online by the Herder Institute in Marburg.

A new quality in the cataloging of monuments appeared with the development of digital repositories of full text documents and image databases, which facilitate and accelerate research. Thanks to these many primary historical sources are available online: visitations to churches, registers of Medieval documents, the above-mentioned descriptions of regions and their towns. This is especially important when carrying out research regarding monuments in small provincial towns, which until now were out of the scope of scientific interest.

Particularly helpful for researchers are the maps available in GIS (Geographic Information System). This system provides the various layers of mapping of a territory concerning such data as administrative data, functions of buildings, hypsometry and so on (for example the web portal of Lower Silesia created by the Marshal's Office of Lower Silesia). Very practical service is offered by the digital catalog of cartographic collections of the University Library in Wroclaw. This brings together the services of the library catalog, the graphical interface of GIS, and access to the resources of full text documents. In this system are cartographic documents connected with a position on a interactive map. When indicating a certain place one can find a list of bibliographic references in collections connected with this location or even view images of some cartographic documents in the digital library [23].

Besides all this, digitized materials offer some sources of the "born-digital" type, such as the Arch-Inform database, which supports inventory work. They provide extensive comparative material and often access to the most current data and bibliographic indications as well. Nevertheless the biggest challenge for Internet resources is their critical analysis. The guarantee of the quality of digital content is connected with the methodology of the institutions, which are in possession of materials and make them accessible on the Web. That is why the sources shared on the Internet by research institutes, universities and museums are so highly valued. These institutions are responsible for the quality of the material presented and its compatibility with the mapped physical object as well as its description.

6　Conclusions

From the turn of the 20th century, when the formula of the topographic catalog was created, methods of documentation have gradually changed. This was connected, *inter alia*, with the development and spread of photography, then the development of video filming and means of communication. Through the 20th century, the scope of information included in catalogs of monuments was extended and refined; simultaneously photography became, separate from description, a significant part of the documentation.

At the turn of the 21st centuries, the beginning of the dynamic development of digital technology and the World Wide Web opened up some new possibilities in the field of research on cultural heritage. On the one hand, they were related to the development and dissemination of technologies for digitizing and making available online publications, sources and documentation, written and printed (digital photography, 2D scanning, OCR), as well as 3D images of physical (real) objects (for example digital photography and photogrammetry, 3D scanning), while on the other they allowed the creation of completely new methods for collecting and processing information, such as in database systems. Many of these technologies are currently used extensively in monographic research and artifact conservation. They allow the extension of research perspective and change in documentation standards, and support analysis and projects carried out within the frame of conservation work (LiDAR, 3D scanning, photogrammetry, video filming, CAD technology, GIS). VR and AR technologies and so-called mobile technologies have also found usage in popularization and dissemination of knowledge on cultural heritage. Real-time network collaboration makes it easier to maintain contact within larger, diffused research teams.

At the same time, it seems that significant changes in the methodology of the field of catalog editions cannot be observed. The basic rules of documentary work on the catalog - the field inquiry and the inquiry into basic sources - which built the basis for the development of catalog notes, remained essentially unchanged, although digitization has brought a number of new facilities. Thanks to various tools and resources - photo collections, map services and source materials available online within the frame of digital libraries - examination of monuments *in situ* can be better prepared, and with digital photography and video many tasks can be carried out as studio work. With the support of digital online sources the documentation of monuments becomes much more efficient, the results are optimized and can be more easily verified, and the costs of and time spent on monuments documentation are reduced. Some barriers to the accessibility of certain sources, resulting from their uniqueness or stage of preservation, have been eliminated, allowing for more extensive research in the field of literary and graphic materials than in previous decades.

To conclude, it should be noted that the recent edition of *Katalog Zabytków w Polsce* encounters certain critics. On the one hand, the increasingly hermetic nature of the text is criticized for being too complicated and not understandable enough for the nonprofessional reader. On the other hand, some experts perceive inconsistencies in the scope and structure of the information gathered. It is also stressed that the catalog is not as available to the reader as was expected by the founders. Perhaps it is worth considering whether the model of the topographic catalog has been exhausted and ought to be replaced by other forms of documentation. Already nowadays some institutions publish "digital born" repositories of monuments, which are focused on the creation of methodologically consistent monuments database systems in order to create complete, professional but also generally accessible monuments documentation in a particular area. Interesting examples of such services are provided by Landesdenkmalamt Berlin (http://www.stadtent wicklung.berlin.de/denkmal/liste_karte_datenbank/de/denkmaldatenbank/index.shtml) or Landesdekmalamt Hessen (http://denkxweb.denkmalpflege-hessen.de/). Mostly these use opportunities offered by GIS; it should be stressed however that these services primarily do not go beyond traditional photographic and textual documentation, whereas the use of the other technologies mentioned above takes place rather in research projects [e.g. 13] or projects focused on conservation [e.g. 15] and popularization.

Although catalogs offered in database systems undoubtedly provide easy access to information, from the art historian's point of view the most important question will remain the guarantee of the durability of such digital repositories. Studies analyzed in this article, from Henelius to Dehio, were undertaken to prepare the catalogs to illustrate the current state of the preservation of monuments. Over time with changes in the resources of cultural heritage, these studies changed their character to primary source. The key question is then whether for several hundred years we would be able to use the information contained in the digital catalogs of monuments, as we use the works of Henelius, Wernher or Lutsch? How do we intend to safeguard the current state of knowledge for future generations (compare the research thesis of the 3DVisa Project for the Computer-based Visualisation of Cultural Heritage and the initiative of the London Charter for the computer-based Visualisation of Cultural Heritage [3])? Such reflection must follow the implementation of modern catalogs of monuments, so that the effects of these works which are fundamental to the discipline are not lost in the near future.

References

1. Anders, E.: Historische Statistik der Evangelischen Kirche in Schlesien nebst einer Kirchen-Charte, Breslau (1867)
2. Banaś, P.: Orbis pictus: świat dawnej karty pocztowej. Acta Universitatis Wratislaviensis, no. 2773, Wrocław (2005)
3. Beacham, R., Denard, H., Niccolucci, F.: An introduction to the London charter. In: Ioannides, M., et al. (eds.) The Evolution of Information Communication Technology in Cultural Heritage: Where Hi-Tech Touches the Past: Risks and Challenges for the 21st Century, Short Papers from the Joint Event CIPA/VAST/EG/EuroMed. Archaeolingua, Budapest (2006)
4. Betthausen P.: Die kirchliche Baukunst des Abendlandes. In: Kunze, M. (ed.) Augen unterwegs …: Reisebilder. Aquarelle und Zeichnungen von Georg Dehio. Eine Ausstellung des Winckelmann-Museums Stendal, Ruhpolding, 13 Marz 2005–8 Mai 2005, pp. 69–79 (2005)
5. Betthausen, P.: Georg Dehio. Ein deutscher Kunsthistoriker, Munchen (2004)
6. Dehio, G.: Handbuch der deutschen Kunstdenkmaler: Bd. 1. Mitteldeutschland, Berlin (1905)
7. Dehio, G.: Handbuch der deutschen Kunstdenkmaler: Bd. 2. Nordostdeutschland, Berlin (1906)
8. Dehio, G.: Denkmalschutz und Denkmalpflege im neunzehnten Jahrhundert. Rede zur Feier des Geburtstages Sr. Majestat des Kaisers gehalten in der Aula der Kaiser-Wilhelms-Universitat am 27 January 1905, Strassburg (1905)
9. Dehio, G., Bezold, G.: Die kirchliche Baukunst des Abendlandes, historisch und systematisch dargestellt, Stuttgart (1892)
10. Gomez-Moreno, M.: Provincia de Salamanca, Madrid (1967)
11. Gomolcke, D.: Des kurtz-gefaßten Inbegriffs Der vornehmsten Merckwurdigkeiten In der Kayser- und Konigl. Stadt. Darinnen gehandelt wird, Von deren Erbauung, Erweiterung und Bevestigung … Breslau (1733)
12. Harasimowicz, J., Marsch, A. (eds.): Friedrich Bernhard Werner (1690–1776). Życie i twórczość - Leben und Werk, Materiały z międzynarodowej konferencji naukowej zorganizowanej przez Muzeum Miedzi w Legnicy w dniach 21–23 listopada 2002 r., Legnica (2004)
13. Hauck, O.: Das Licht in der Hagia Sophia - eine Computersimulation. In: Daim, F., Drauschke, J. (eds.) Byzanz - Das Romerreich im Mittelalter, Monographien des Romisch-Germanischen Zentralmuseums, Bd. 84, pp. 97–112, 2, 1, Mainz 2010

14. Henel von Hennenfeld, N.: Silesiographia, Hoc est: Silesiae Delineatio Brevis Et succincta: in qua non modo regionis rationem, naturam, cultum, et prouentum, verum etiam ingenia, mores et instituta habitantium formamque Reipubl. tanquam in tabula contemplari licet Breslau (1613)

15. Jaskanis, P.: Prace konserwatorskie w Muzeum Pałacu w Wilanowie po 2003 roku. Conservator's works in the Museum, Palace in Wilanów after 2003, Wiadomosci Konserwatorskie. Conservation News, 26/2009, pp. 390–403 (2009)

16. Knie, J.G.: Alphabetisch-statistisch-topographische Uebersicht aller Dorfer, Flecken, Stadte und andern Orte der Konigl. Preuss. Provinz Schlesien, Breslau (1830)

17. Leonhardi, F.G.: Erdbeschreibung der preussischen Monarchiè, Bd. 1–3, Halle (1791–1794)

18. Lutsch, H.: Bildwerk schlesischer Kunstdenkmaler, Breslau (1903)

19. Lutsch, H.: Verzeichniss der Kunstdenkmaler der Prvinz Niederschlesien, Bd. 1–5, Breslau (1886–1894)

20. Morelowski, M.: Ocalone rękopisy F. B. Wernhera i ich znaczenie dla historii sztuki i kultury Śląska. Wrocławskie Towarzystwo Naukowe/Sprawozdania Wrocławskiego Towarzystwa Naukowego, Dodatek 4, Wrocław (1955)

21. Naso, E.I.: Phoenix redivivus Ducatuum Suidnicensis et Jauroviensis, Der wieder- lebendige Phoenix der beyden Fuerstenthuemer, Schweidnitz und Jauer, Breslau (1667)

22. Ochendowska-Grzelak, B.: Hans Lutsch (1854–1922). Architekt – konserwator zabytków - - badacz architektury. Szczecin (2013)

23. Osowska, A., Przybytek, D.: Georeferencyjna aplikacja inwentarzowo-katalogowa jako przykład zastosowania metod numerycznych w organizacji zbiorów kartograficznych Biblioteki Uniwersyteckiej we Wrocławiu, In: Seidel-Grzesińska, A., Stanicka-Brzezicka, K. (eds.) Dobra kultury w Sieci, Wrocław, pp. 213–223 (2012)

24. Pevsner, N.: Buildings of England, Harmondsworth (1951–1974)

25. Rybka-Ceglecka, I.: Topografia Śląska F.B. Wernera, koncepcja dzieła i jego realizacja. In: Harasimowicz, J., Marsch, A. (eds.) Friedrich Bernhard Werner (1690–1776). Życie i twórczość - Leben und Werk, Materiały z międzynarodowej konferencji naukowej zorganizowanej przez Muzeum Miedzi w Legnicy w dniach 21–23 listopada 2002 r, Legnica, pp. 91–108 (2004)

26. Scheuermann, I.: Tot Gesagte leben langer. Georg Dehio und die gegenwartige Denkmalpflege. In: Dehio, G., Scheurmann, I. (eds.) ZeitSchichten: erkennen und erhalten - Denkmalpflege in Deutschland: 100 Jahre Handbuch der deutschen Kunstdenkmaler, Munchen, Berlin, pp. 68–81 (2005)

27. Weis, M.: Zur Geschichte des Handbuchs der Deutschen Kunstdenkmaler. In: Dehio, G., Scheurmann, I. (eds.) Zeit- Schichten: erkennen und erhalten - Denkmalpflege in Deutschland: 100 Jahre Handbuch der deutschen Kunstdenkmaler, Munchen, Berlin, pp. 60–67 (2005)

28. Zimmermann, F.A.: Beitrage zur Beschreibung von Schlesien, Bd. 1–13, Brieg (1783–1796)

Technical Access

Time and Space in the History of Cities

Andrea Giordano, Isabella Friso, Paolo Borin(✉),
Cosimo Monteleone, and Federico Panarotto

University of Padova, Padua, Italy
{andrea.giordano,isabella.friso,paolo.borin,
cosimo.monteleone,federico.panarotto}@unipd.it

Abstract. This essay deals with the representation of cities focusing on their historical transformations and relying on digital scanning, 3D modeling and Augmented Reality (AR) technologies. The instances shown in it come from a project titled *Visualizing Venice*, an international multi-institutional cooperation now shifting to *Visualizing Cities*. The main challenge of Visualizing Cities is to digitally describe how cities – with their architectures – evolve and change over time using an interoperable 4D digital model linked to external sources, such as historic images. Experiencing the workflow of such a digital model a current lack of interoperability between CAD and GIS systems has emerged. This problem is particularly evident in the transition from digital scanning to a Building Information Model (BIM). This gap must be filled because a representational database, such as a 3D BIM model, helps researchers in representing architectural and urban history in all its phases. It makes the users able to control any kind of information: from recording the current state of an urban environment to the interpretation of historical records; from 3D reconstruction of data to their dissemination at different levels of complexity. This paper shows new methodologies in this field and, relating to historical data, attempts to answer also an important question: what kind of information can we get from paintings that show a city view? Representation methods based on perspective rules offer the opportunity to obtain scientific data on how to implement the BIM model correctly.

Keywords: Venice · CAD · BIM · Restitution of perspective
Drawing

1 Introduction

This paper deals with representations of cities that rely on digital scanning, 3D modeling and digital applications that focus on historical transformation over time. The content of our study is based on a research project entitled *Visualizing Venice*, an international multi-institutional cooperation that was initiated in 2009 between IUAV University (Venice, IT), Duke University (Durham, USA) and University of Padua (Padua, IT). As our research initiative is now shifting to *Visualizing Cities*, our main challenge is how to digitally describe urban and architectural change over time using interoperable 4D digital models linked to external sources, such as historic images. Studying a city means utilizing various types of documentation, such as works of art,

© Springer International Publishing AG, part of Springer Nature 2018
S. Münster et al. (Eds.): UHDL 2017/DECH 2017, CCIS 817, pp. 47–62, 2018.
https://doi.org/10.1007/978-3-319-76992-9_4

architectural and urban documents, construction methods, and various types of representations of architecture and topography. The European Commission considers that a multidisciplinary and integrated approach is needed in order to improve their societal and economic objectives, as well as their impact on public policy. Thus an interoperable 4D model offers an opportunity to integrate heterogeneous data to enable the acquisition of a wide and specific knowledge about a city combined with high quality outputs. The latter include technical drawings; renderings; videos; smartphones applications; 3D printed objects and immersive visualizations. The 4D model embedded with data is the basis for understanding and representing the historical transformations that have occurred over time. As will be discussed in this essay, the integration of other types of sources and representational methods, based on perspectival rules, offers the opportunity to obtain scientific data from paintings and city views that can be correctly utilized within the BIM model. This paper, based on a series of case studies that began in 2009, aims to explain how the research was conducted and to clarify our method by describing their development.

Section 2 analyzes the opportunity for knowledge management with BIM models in order to improve the traditional CAD workflow. Section 3 focuses on the problems that can arise when modeling historical transformation with CAD technology, with specific reference in building narrative tools such as 3D printing and portable applications. Section 4 concerns the information that can be obtained from heterogenous historical data, such as paintings and city views, through the utilization of the rules of perspective and semi-automatic modeling processes to align pictures and BIM model. We provide a specific example in our paper of the use of these technologies in an analysis of Canaletto's painting, *Campo Santi Giovanni e Paolo* in Venice.[1]

2 Managing Digital Modeling to Produce Knowledge

For the well-trained practitioner of 3D modeling software, a digital replication of the appearance of an existing building is a straightforward task. However, such a model depicts only a geometric mimesis of reality. In the field of architectural and urban research it would be more appropriate to create a so-called "in-depth" *mimesis* that reflects the internal consistency between the parts of the model, in order to achieve both figurative and analytical goals. This study starts from the typical issues met in the field of historical reconstruction: a multidisciplinary group of researchers, a wide heterogeneity of primary sources and a limited economic funding. The aim of this section is to demonstrate the advantages of using a BIM-based[2] system to manage effectively a research project that demonstrates changes to cities over time.

A review of the literature reveals the need for the design and use of computational systems to represent architectural information [1]. Such a system has been defined by

---

[1] Andrea Giordano is the author of this section.

[2] Building Information Modeling (BIM) is a digital representation of physical and functional characteristics of a facility. A BIM is a shared knowledge resource for information about a facility forming a reliable basis for decisions during its life-cycle; defined as existing from earliest conception to demolition.

De Luca as an assembly of structured objects, each of which is indicated by a specific taxonomy [2]. Although research groups have already created some of these information systems with the specific purpose of representing significant buildings for the analysis of the work of particular architects [3], the absence of national or international standards has prevented not only the dissemination of their outcomes, but also a guarantee of technological improvement. This fact implies some other concerns, such as the inability to integrate other knowledge management systems, and the challenges of enabling structural, energy and security simulations within the creation of historical models. For instance, the information system created for *Visualizing Venice* was based on a geo-database to catalogue recorded documents, drawings and maps, assigning geographic coordinates whenever possible. This led to the positioning of documents on the historical maps within the GIS environment (HGIS or Historic Geographic Information System) [4]. Unfortunately, the analysis of geometry and information exchanges proved that the HGIS system need a new system to model and manage information at small scales (building, district).

In order to achieve a more effective architectural knowledge system, we changed our approach, creating a BIM for existing buildings (HBIM as Historical BIM).[3] Indeed, two features of BIM models help address the need for the integration of heterogeneous sources and information. The first is its relationality, the ability of each object to match a geometrical reference structure, which organizes the elements in common buildings groups (architectural levels, zoned, grids). With the increasing complexity of the model, it becomes possible to define relational rules among classes of elements: in this way, the user can identify the distinctive constraints of historical buildings [5]. The second important feature of this approach is the option of linking objects to the meta-data [6].

A recent case study, our analysis of the *Chiesa degli Eremitani* in Padua [7], demonstrates the efficacy of a BIM-based breakdown of the model. First, we were able to create a "decomposition framework", in which we could describe the connection between architectural elements, in five object classes: basic elements (walls, roofs, floors) as elements which organize the structure of the model; structural vertical elements (buttresses); ornamental vertical elements; ornamental horizontal or sloped elements; and finally ornamental local elements.

Secondly, we were able to develop a method with which we could isolate individual architectural components by their functional context. A BIM authoring tool is able to automatically create the necessary relations of objects (column-shaft-capital, window-panel-decoration), taking advantage of processes already created for BIM classes and subclasses. A further characteristic of the model is the ability to link information to the second-level breakdown structure: information associated with the main component (i.e. specific window); information associated with a single sub-component (i.e. specific panel of the window); information associated with an assembly of sub-components (i.e. group of panels of windows).

These features represent the geometry of a building and its semantic components in order to evaluate a structure critically, linking historical aspects (such as information

---

[3] The BIM model presents typical features of any CAD representation, thus this paper overlooks them.

about workers, historical phases of objects constructions) with the management of the facility (information about the buildings' condition).

In addition, this chapter presents the advantages of linking BIM to primary sources and using collaborative methods, which demonstrate the expanding opportunities of adopting BIM-methodologies. The relation between a digital model and a survey in the form of point clouds, improves the modeling process. In this sense, the results of two different phases of knowledge structuring – surveying and modeling – become coexistent within the same modeling environment. The point cloud is not only related to the goal of documentation, but also enables analyses, leading, for instance, to the use of algorithms that allow interrelated geometric evaluations. Again, our case study of *Chiesa degli Eremitani* verifies the application of a deviance analyses between vertical walls and the surveyed points. From the management perspective, structural engineers will be easily able to evaluate the out-of-plumb value of the single wall, by means of a distance-mapped representation. At the same time, the point cloud guarantees the geometrical mimesis requirements, as a model that better describes geometrically the existing surfaces, while the BIM model and the documentation about deviance analyses perform the required "in-depth" analysis.

It seems important, in conclusion, to describe the opportunities for the information exchange established by the international standard related to Building Information Modeling. Although these standards are well suited to an AEC (Architecture Engineering and Construction) industry application, they also can be useful in creating an effective exchange of information, for example from GIS to BIM. Another of our recent projects, a reconstruction of the Venetian Ghetto [8], demonstrates how the useful features of a GIS model can be converted to a BIM environment [9]. In particular [4], in this example, we were able to map individual features with IFC classes: land polylines and surveyed point (IfcSite); waterways polylines (IfcSite); building polylines and heights (IfcBuildings, IfcBuildignStorey, IfcWall, IfcRoof) [10]. It is thus possible to develop tools that transfer information, assuring a continuity from GIS to BIM, to avoid reworking and while at the same time preserving quality. This last case study serves to check the BIM framework for further works. Particularly, it has been developed a collaborative cloud-based environment to help users to communicate through the BCF (BIM Collaboration Format) standard [11].[4] Researchers will therefore not need to be versed in using modeling software: they can access all the information through a web-application, insert observations and requests of information or a review, and specify links to the already existing geo-database. The requests are thus linked both to a specific object and to a knowledge base. This process shows a deep change in managing the information related to such projects: future research will specify how to develop the parameters for the accuracy of the hypothetic model in relation to the primary sources [12].[5]

---

[4] The standard links information/change requests to model's components. Consequently, the information exchange occurs without the models transfer, but using common GUID of the IFC file.

[5] The fact that the model represents a new document is a common, established concept within the presented project: the model enables new knowledge in researchers, not only for the general-purpose users. A specific research project is trying to understand the best way to define the accuracy degree of models' parts.

In conclusion, and using as a point of departure earlier research that showed specific needs and issues in reconstructing buildings and districts over time, the author can embed in the Building Information Modeling system an "in-depth" analysis tool to show transformation over time, to manage and collect architectural knowledge for further studies. This method assures the same results already reached by other scholars (see literature reviews presented), adding features about integration and collaboration. Compared with a standard CAD-based procedure (see Sect. 3), in terms of time and software proficiency, the BIM procedure is much more demanding. However, it is possible to use the same model not only for reconstruction but also for managing purposes (for example, by public administration systems, or by the property owners). This double use guarantees an economic advantage for funding historical reconstruction, thanks to the implicit financial value of the model.[6]

3 Digital Modeling to Organize Narratives

This section aims to show problems and opportunities in the production of high quality visual elaborations, by underlining the differences between CAD and BIM models in the graphical elaborations of two different and emblematic case studies. The first one – developed from 2011 to 2015 – involves modeling change in the city of Carpi, focusing on the area inside its historical walls; the second one – which is part of broader *Visualizing Venice* initiative, which initiated in 2012 and still ongoing – aims to analyze some of the most important *campi* (city square) in Venice.

Both examples are based on a similar type of narrative process, in each case starting from the present urban situation, to which we applied a reverse process of time, enabling a demonstration of a series of fundamental historical moments [13]. In approaching these two different projects we produced two different kind of models: a CAD model for Carpi and an interoperable BIM model to analyze the *campi* of Venice. These different choices were selected because of the different purposes and final outputs of the model. There were also divergent complexities in both cases, because the outcomes depend on the correct interpretation of the historical, scientific, graphical and literary data on which to base a critical understanding of the buildings.

Although the CAD ambient is able to produce a model in a high detail level, at the same time it is very difficult to produce drawings can communicate the same level of detail in a correct and clear way.

In spite of the fact that the process of generating a CAD model is often easier than that used in BIM, we have learned from our past experiences we learnt that improving the geometries in a CAD solution is more difficult than the process used during a BIM 3D virtual reconstruction. Indeed, it is often necessary to modify the simple geometries of surfaces during the 3D modeling process. The BIM model allows editing of the surface, modifying only every single parameter, but the same operation is not possible in a CAD ambient. Although it is also possible to insert some textual information into a CAD virtual model, but this kind of information refers only to the representation of a

---

[6] Paolo Borin is the author of this section.

real object and not to the architectural element itself, restricting the operability of the virtual model in the future. Conversely, textual information in a BIM model can be linked directly with architectural standards and this is one of its main characteristics and advantages.

In the example of our work on the city of Carpi, we were able to obtain images that show its historical *forma urbis* and its transformations: our point of departure was an urban survey of the city in its present state from which, going back in time, we were able to show the fourteenth-century conformation of the city. In doing this we moved from the large scale of the entire city to single monuments, in order to study the principal buildings of the city, that face the main square: the castle, the theatre, the portico (a row of similar buildings whose feature is a long porch along their façades), and the church. We showed the results of this research in two different exhibitions in the Castle that communicated our work on the city through architectural and urban drawings, videos of the 3D virtual models, and chalk prototyped models.

The digital 3D models do not aspire to reproduce an exact urban reconstruction in a specific historical moment, but rather aim to represent a scientific analysis of the major changes in the city. The actual trend is to produce parametric models [14] that could not only provide a simulation of the geometrical surfaces but also to get information about the structure of the buildings. In some specific cases, detailed are not necessary for the viewer, and as a result we choose to utilize the simplest software, especially when the representational scale is so large that the viewer would not be able to perceive the architectural details. For example, if the output is a chalk scale model we recommend to use a Rapid Prototyping process basing on a CAD software (Fig. 1a).

Although BIM models permit researchers able to create a digital clone of a real building, with details in a scale 1:1, this level of precision is not useful for we printed a 3D scale models that seek only to create a solid representation of a city. Whereas parametric models provide an exact simulation of walls, floors and ceiling stratifications, this level of detail is not appropriate for the representation of a city, and of course cannot be produced by a 3D printer; in this case, moving from a BIM to a CAD model is preferable.[7] This approach is useful not only when we have to reproduce a specific area of a city, but also when the virtual model is intended as a static visualization of buildings.

For the configuration of the main church in Carpi (Fig. 1b), we have reconstructed the original design of the architect, Baldassare Peruzzi (1481–1537), and developed an app for mobile devices such as tablets and smartphones. By placing a pattern on the floor in the exhibition room, the observer could visualize the 3D virtual model of the original church based on the lost wooden model produced by this early Renaissance architect. The visitor was able to compare this virtual model with other two extant wooden models from the Renaissance, each created for other religious buildings of the area [15]. The goal was to demonstrate the scientific character of the research and enable the observer to compare the virtual reconstruction not only to the three different models, and to analyze their differences and similarities, but also to reproduce the original documents used to reconstruct the lost wooden model by Peruzzi.

---

[7] The team will be able to develop a specific software which, starting from BIM model information it will be able to create the geometry useful also for Rapid Prototyping.

In conclusion, while it is true that today new technologies improve our models and digital databases, thus providing additional information and details, it is not necessarily the case that the quality of the outputs is linked to the quality of the model. These last considerations can be considered as starting points for future researches in the field of architectural and urban representation.[8]

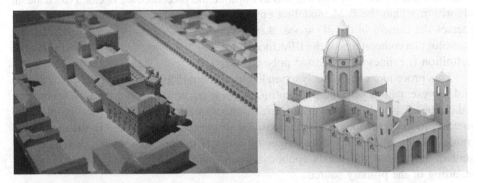

Fig. 1. On the left (a): The chalk model of the Piazza dei Martiri, Carpi. On the right (b): The digital reconstruction of Baldassarre Peruzzi's original design of the Chathedral (Source: I. Friso)

4   Integrating Images in Digital Models: Perspective Parameters and Algorithms Toward a Semi-automatic Modeling

4.1   Introduction and Methodology

The creation of a virtual environment that contains a three-dimensional semantic model, has become an essential tool in integrating different representational methods within one environment [5]. Pictures, paintings and engravings, obtained by a mathematical or optical procedure, include important information to understand cities changes over time. This entails linking the model with primary sources, such as iconographic images and pictures.[9]

As was specified by De Luca, it is essential to build a spatial link between pictures – 2D entities – and tridimensional objects. One approach might be a manual alignment procedure, but this option is time-consuming and is not sufficiently accurate for a scientific environment. A second method estimates the image position, adding it within

---

[8] Isabella Friso is the author of this section.

[9] This application becomes important to find the discontinuity surfaces between original elements (or parts of them) and the in-place reconstructed elements. The correct position of the elements is useful to complete seismic analysis and check construction works' accuracy.

the aligning process of a generic photo-modeling procedure.[10] Unfortunately, photogrammetric modeling does not represent a typical phase in our projects. Moreover, in the case of historic paintings, information becomes relevant after interpretation and understanding of historical and scientific context (see Sect. 4.3). Consequently, the process of restitution of perspective from the image, its reconstruction in a 2D model, completed with a comparison with the 3D model, is a necessary part of the process. In order to increase the performance and to improve the precision, we decided to create an algorithm within the BIM modeling environment (see Sect. 4.2). First, the algorithm locates the camera in the 3D space, then it projects 2D elements of the image on the homologous components of the BIM model, filtering the object by BIM-based semantic definition (i.e. lines are projected only on walls).

This procedure can be easily extended to orthogonal projections (plans, elevations) and representations of building conditions. As a result, the model thereby becomes a catalogue of two-dimensional and three-dimensional objects, linked by simple geometric procedures. Moreover, if the position of the camera is located in the model, the model has the ability to group images by areas of the building, or by element represented, improving the user's (public administration, scholars, and tourists) understanding of the primary sources.[11]

4.2   Case Study: Architectural Elements as-it-was for Rebuilding Eremitani's Church

The *Chiesa degli Eremitani* project [7] is an interesting case study to test the third methodology mentioned above. Once the virtual semantic model of the church is created, the elements of the building can be located in the constructive phases over time, thus enabling a focus on reconstructing from historical sources the portions of the building that no longer exist. The need to reproduce changes in buildings over time entails the challenge of "automatically" relocating precise geometric shapes from the two-dimensional surface of photographic film to a three-dimensional model. In our specific case study, one of the crucial phases of the history of the church was the bombardment of 1944 and its reconstruction in the following years. In order to relocate the damaged portions of the building in a three-dimensional virtual space, the virtual model needed to be divided in two parts: 1: the original building and, 2: the rebuilt structure. This division was important in order to establish the correct location of the irregular profiles of the damaged walls and ruins that can be observed in the historical pictures.

As a point of departure, it was necessary to locate the position of the observer at the center of the projection that generated the image, i.e. the position of the lens and focal direction. For this reason, our method (Fig. 2) relied on the principles of photogrammetry and photo-restitution. The first step consisted in identifying the kind of perspective of the image, that is, whether it was a vertical plane example or an inclined

---

[10] In order to find necessary parameters automatically, this last procedure allows to use commercial products such as Agisoft Photoscan and Bentley Context Capture.

[11] Paolo Borin is the author of this section.

one. We tested this methodology using an image based on a vertical plane: as the parallelism of the vertical edges of the building is always respected inside the image [16].

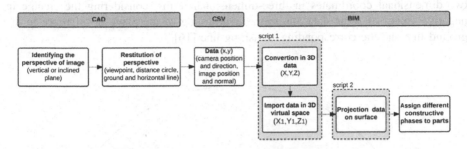

Fig. 2. Workflow of the method we applied (Source: F. Panarotto)

The next steps were to move such a geometric reconstruction in a three-dimensional model (translating 2D drawings into spatial objects) and then to generate In the next steps we moved this geometric reconstruction to a three-dimensional model (thus translating 2D drawings into spatial objects) and then generated a procedure for projecting the texture of the original building on the modeled surfaces. Our studies of the reconstruction of historical perspective systems[12] based on classical methods made possible the identification of the metrical data necessary to generate three-dimensional virtual objects. In order to create some degree of automation in this process of representation it was necessary to assign a proper reference system for the main entities that can be distinguished on the photographic image; this allowed the creation of a correspondence with the counterparts of the virtual three-dimensional space. For this purpose, coordinate points obtained from the restitution of perspective were assigned utilizing a reference system (x, z) having the origin A*, located in the π plane, that is the plane of the photographic image. Considering the example shown in the figure (Fig. 3) and the line A*B*, obtained in the restitution of perspective, performed on a segment of any object identified in the picture (in this case the base of the facade), this dimension can be used as data in order to scale the image and to orient the different reference systems. The data thus obtained were: the coordinates of point A*(0, 0) and the coordinates of point B*(x_{B*}, z_{B*}), the endpoints of the line A*B*; the coordinates of the homologous center V*(x_{V*}, z_{V*}), used for the restitution of perspective; the coordinates of the four vertices R'$(x_{R'}, z_{R'})$, S'$(x_{S'}, z_{S'})$, T'$(x_{T'}, z_{T'})$, U'$(x_{U'}, z_{U'})$, of the surrounding polygon of the image (edge of the image); the distance h between the ground line and the horizon line (observer's height); the distance d of the picture, in the direction z, referring to the origin of the axes at point A*. These detected data were manually transcribed into a CSV file. The next step was to create a script 1[13] that was able to automatically read this data, which allowed the conversion of coordinates of the

---

[12] The restitution of perspective was performed in CAD software, Autodesk AutoCAD®.

[13] Made through a VPL (Visual Programming Language), Autodesk Dynamo®.

points from the two-dimensional system *(x, z)* to the three-dimensional one *(X, Y, Z)*. The script 1 then permitted us to import the data into the virtual space with coordinates (X_1, Y_1, Z_1)[14] contained in the three-dimensional model, operating rotation, translation and an appropriate scale conversion. As noted above, the script 1 initially modified the two-dimensional coordinates in three-dimensional terms, considering the change in negative values of some data due to the overturning of the plane in reference to the ground line and the corresponding vanishing line [16].

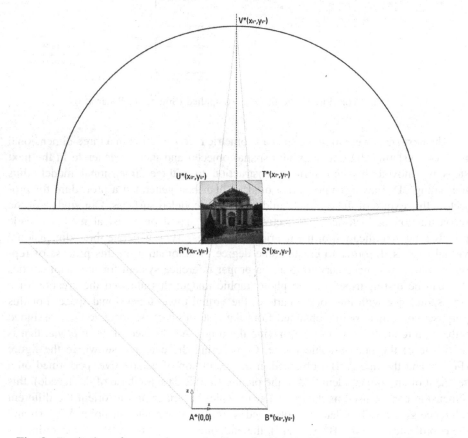

Fig. 3. Restitution of perspective starting from the historical image (Source: F. Panarotto)

The converted coordinates generated: a point A(0, 0, 0), again considered the origin of the axes; a point $B(X_B, Y_B, Z_B) = (x_{B*}, -z_{B*}, 0)$, second point of the straight line taken as reference; a point $V(X_V, Y_V, Z_V) = (x_{V*}, -(z_{V*} -h), h)$, center of view of the lens; the points $R(X_R, Y_R, Z_R) = (x_{R'}, -d, (z_{R'} -d))$, $S(X_S, Y_S, Z_S) = (x_{S'}, -d, (z_{S'} -d))$, $T(X_T, Y_T, Z_T) = (x_{T'}, -d, (z_{T'} -d))$, $U(X_U, Y_U, Z_U) = (x_{U'}, -d, (z_{U'} -d))$, vertices of the polygon containing the image.

---

[14] Reference model in virtual modeling environment, Autodesk Revit®.

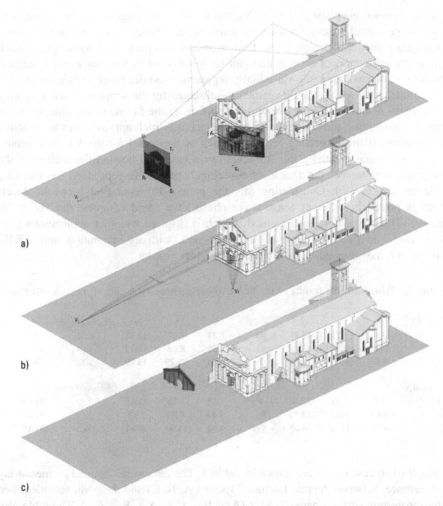

Fig. 4. Processes: a: the import of data obtained from the restitution of perspective into a three-dimensional environment; b: the projection of the data on the model; c: the separation of the 3D model in some objects, which are placed in different construction phases (Source: F. Panarotto)

The script 1 then assigned the coordinate of point $A_1(X_{A1}, Y_{A1}, Z_{A1})$ (first endpoint of the line A_1B_1 previously plotted in the virtual space) to point $A(0, 0, 0)$, which coincides with the segment in the model, corresponding to segment AB in the picture (the base of the facade). The script 1 performed the same procedure for point $B(X_B, Y_B, Z_B)$, whose homologous point was $B_1(X_{B1}, Y_{B1}, Z_{B1})$. Then, reading the length and direction of A_1B_1, the script continued by orienting the whole system and aligning the direction of AB with the direction of A_1B_1, moreover, it scaled the entire system by computing the length ratio between the two lines. Finally, script 1 inserted the image into the correct position, located between the four vertices R_1, S_1, T_1, U_1 (Fig. 4a).

Once the system, consisting of point V_1 (center of view, target) and the image, was placed in the virtual space, it worked by retracing the objects of interest in the picture by tracking points and straight lines. This operation was performed by script 2, which allowed the projection of objects that can be recognized in the image, on a surface. Returning to our example, the slit initially represented on the photographic image was approximated to a set of straight segments; subsequently the script operated assigning the segments of the rectilinear line and the surface of the facade of the church in 3D. Script 2, recognizing the endpoints of each segment (which approximates the fracture line) constructed the projecting beams for each of them and for the V1 view center. These lines, which created a loft surface,[15] were extended beyond the surface of the photograph to intersect the facade of the church pattern to reproduce the cracking profile on it (Fig. 4b). Considering this the pattern of separation between objects (which is placed in different constructive phases) we could complete the 3D model (Fig. 4c). The above-described method, which is inspired by other applications [17–20], is useful in order to achieve our goals, and, with its integration into a BIM environment, has allowed us to achieve satisfactory results.

Table 1. Table with the results of the first two experiences. The unit of measure is meter

REAL	x	y	z	PIC 1	x	y	z	distance/error	d
A	7.4	7.23	13.36	A_{P1}	7.37	7.27	12.38	0.98	37.74
B	6.47	8.69	13.36	B_{P1}	6.35	8.88	12.34	1.04	35.29
C	4.66	11.57	14.85	C_{P1}	4.84	11.29	13.79	1.32	33.53

REAL	x	y	z	PIC 2	x	y	z	distance/error	d
A	7.4	7.23	13.36	A_{P2}	7.38	7.26	13.15	0.22	97.63
B	6.47	8.69	13.36	B_{P2}	6.47	8.70	13.2	0.14	97.52
C	4.66	11.57	14.85	C_{P2}	4.63	11.62	14.81	0.06	97.69

For the two cases these are shown in Table 1. The data were obtained by measuring the difference, between the real fracture[16] (points A, B, C) and the point sets identified by the projection of the image 1 and 2 (A_{P1}, B_{P1}, C_{P1}, A_{P2}, B_{P2}, C_{P2}). The table also shows the distance d between the center of view and the points. Our goal for the future is to increase the number of case studies in order to improve the data. It is clear however that the accuracy of our results is directly proportional to the quality of execution of the manual operations on the initial perspectival image.

This work has not yet been concluded, as in the future the feasibility of this method will be evaluated for perspectival images based on inclined pictorial plane. Our goal is to develop an automatic method that can facilitate the prospective rendering phase and reduce the likelihood of human error.[17]

---

[15] This surface is a cone based on a mixed-line, that is the line that approximates the slot to be rebuilt.

[16] The real fracture was detected by the points cloud obtained from photogrammetry survey.

[17] Federico Panarotto is the author of this section.

4.3   The Relationship Between Document, Sources and Interpretative Models

Digital tools are useful in representing urban change over time because they enable us to study the city in virtual contexts based on the historical data that researchers collect and interpret. Before the advent of these new technologies, the analysis of urban space relied on architectural drawings, paintings, historical cartography and photography. Now, however, we are able to represent architecture at different scales in a virtual world where dynamic and interactive testing are offered by digital tools. This enables us to compare, evaluate and study buildings and their transformation from many different points of view. Particularly important is our new ability to isolate, compare and represent specific topics for urban or architectural analysis, such as streets and passageways, or the transformation of specific areas or single buildings. Another clear advantage of new technologies is that they enable us to transcend the limits of space and time because we can thereby represent the city in relation to utopian projects, destroyed, or transformed buildings. These undeniable advantages, however, also present new types of issues: how can these new techniques of architectural representation be related to archival data? How do they compare with traditional methods? Is it important to place side by side virtual space and canonical representation? What do we lose or gain using new technologies? How can digital tools address our evolving needs in three-dimensional representation?

A case study, taken from the *Visualizing Venice* research initiative [21], helps us to answer these questions through our work on the *Insula di Santi Giovanni e Paolo* in relation to its architectural and urban transformation. The reconstruction of this particular site and buildings was achieved through the use of a painting by Canaletto (Fig. 5), which records the situation of the *Campo* in XVIII century. Canaletto's painting demonstrates the potential of documentary data in 3D virtual reconstruction of historic architecture. The Venetian painter knew the rules of perspective and used a *camera obscura* to paint his famous views of the city. This knowledge of his technical tools allowed us also to apply the rules of perspective to obtain plans and elevations of the represented buildings. However, some elements needed to be taken into account during our reconstruction, because Canaletto often emphasized certain aspects of the city and its monuments. In the specific case of *Campo Santi Giovanni e Paolo*, for example, the artist designed the scene using multiple points of view in order to render a more dynamic view of the area in question. A reconstruction of the buildings, starting from the use of perspective, enabled us to underline Canaletto's visual strategy that gave priority to specific information about the city and its architecture.

The process of modeling and representing historical reality based on archival documentation, paintings and even on objective data obtained through a digital survey of the area, implies a new type of critical consideration for the study of original drawings and scientific measurements, which can lead to the reinterpretation of historical sources in a new light. The challenge is to overcome the inconsistencies that lie behind the iconographical sources and present-day reality. It is often only through the act of "re-creating", utilizing the science of drawing and the knowledge of historians, that these incongruities are revealed.

Combining visual science and experience in the scholarly approach seems to us an operation that improves our understanding of urban space: indeed, it becomes possible to facilitate the understanding of a place and to contribute to the construction of knowledge about it by guiding and controlling the interaction between medium and the observer [22]. Studying a painting by Canaletto emphasizes the multifaceted role of virtual reality, one that has gone far beyond the simple description of the city. On the one hand, the virtual 3D model represents urban conditions and architectural artifacts in their historical context; on the other, the rules of perspective indicate how an artist's pictorial strategy can be the result of the juxtaposition of multiple views and not the outcome location in a position.

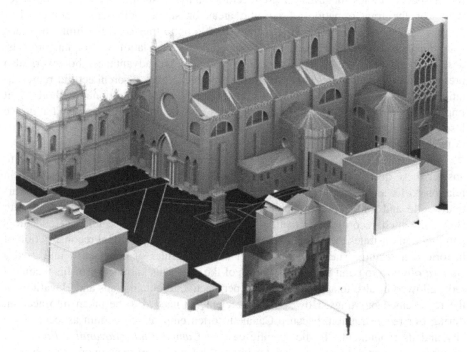

Fig. 5. Digital Reconstruction of the *Insula di Santi Giovanni e Paolo* starting from Canaletto's paint (Source: C. Monteleone)

Digital tools for studying the painting overcome the crystallized moment of a static vision into dynamic and physically interactive "images". This virtual world, spatially and temporally versatile, translates scholarly studies and analyses into compelling 3D reconstructions. The 3D models, in turn, perform a dual function: they are exceptional vehicles for communicating and disseminating the complex mechanisms related to urban change, and they facilitate a new research strategies for the analysis of historical architecture. In contrast to traditional, solitary forms of scholarship, the collaboration of multidisciplinary collaboration in the creation of 3D models opens innovative avenues of interpretation. In this context the new frontiers of architectural drawing and representation provide historians with opportunities to visualize the city, both its past and present, and to undertake scholarly research and disseminate the results in a broader and more dynamic way. Historical and urban transformation over time, dynamically expressed, thus can function as a facilitator of scientific, even complex concepts, immersing the audience – whether generic visitors, scholars or students – in simulative virtual activities that profit from the sense of movement, approximating reality [23]. In the future, researchers, comparing the traditional approach of publication in architectural and urban history – closed and finished – to the new knowledge system triggered by virtual media – open and dynamic – will contribute with their studies and insights towards a more conscious dissemination of the architectural heritage.[18]

5   Discussion

Describing historical transformation of architecture and the city can no longer remain simply a matter of mimesis of reality. Digital technologies, in addition to the emulation of appearances, offer new and stimulating opportunities. This paper shows that the BIM models can represent overlapping transformations of buildings with their current geometries, linking them to documents, such as descriptions, pictures, paintings, drawings, and engravings. The case studies from *Visualizing Venice* and *Visualizing Cities* demonstrate that when the work consists of the 3D modeling and virtual visualization of buildings and the city are set in an interoperable environment, they embody not only an effective means of communication, capable of involving any type of user, but they are also an extraordinary scientific medium available to researchers for conducting their own analyses. In this context we have only considered historical images highly reliable, those that artists have made in accordance with the rules of perspective. Fortunately, irrespective of photographs, perspectival images were very numerous in the past because artists were inclined to utilize geometric science in their art to show that their works were intellectual and not purely mechanical executions. When it is possible, as was the case in Canaletto's painting, to rebuild a specific part of an historic city, we applied the restitution of perspective to have plan and elevation of the painted architecture. In addition, we experimented with digital technologies in order to express the rules of perspective through appropriate algorithms, with the aim of utilizing the 3D modeling phase to facilitate the reconstruction of historical transformation through automatic procedures. The methodology that has been described and applied in this paper is an example of how a synergy between different disciplines and scientific skills can in the future enhance our understanding and the representation of architecture and the city in for both academic and touristic purposes, as well as for the management and improvement of cultural heritage.

---

[18] Cosimo Monteleone is the author of this section.

References

1. Blaise, J.Y., Dudek, I.: Beyond graphics: information. An overview of infovis practices in the field of the architectural heritage. In: Third International Conference Computer Graphics Theory Applications, GRAPP 2008 (2008)
2. Apollonio, F.I., Gaiani, M., Corsi, C.: A semantic and parametric method for 3D models used in 3D cognitive-information system. In: 28th eCAADe Conference Proceedings, pp. 863–872 (2010)
3. De Luca, L., Veron, P., Florenzano, M.: Reverse engineering of architectural buildings based on a hybrid modeling approach. Comput. Graph. **30**, 160–176 (2006)
4. Ferrighi, A.: Cities over time and space. Historical Gis for urban history. In: Handbook of Research on Emerging Digital Tools for Architectural Surveying, Modeling, and Representation, pp. 425–445. IGI Global, Hershey (2015)
5. De Luca, L.: Methods, formalisms and tools for the semantic-based surveying and representation of architectural heritage. Appl. Geomatics (2011)
6. Di Mascio, D., Pauwels, P., De Meyer, R.: Improving the knowledge and management of the historical built environment with BIM and ontologies: the case study of the book tower (2013)
7. Giordano, A., Borin, P., Cundari, M.R.: Which survey for which digital model: critical analysis and interconnections. In: Le vie dei Mercanti, p. 8 (2015)
8. Calabi, D.: Venice the Jews and Europe: 1516–2016. Marsilio, Venezia (2016)
9. van Berlo, L., de Laat, R.: Integration of BIM and GIS: the development of the CityGML GeoBIM extension. In: Kolbe, T., König, G., Nagel, C. (eds.) Advances in 3D Geo-Information Sciences. LNGC, pp. 211–225. Springer, Berlin (2011). https://doi.org/10.1007/978-3-642-12670-3_13
10. El-Mekawy, M.: Integrating BIM and GIS for 3D City Modelling: The Case of IFC and CityGML (2010)
11. BuildingSMART International: BCF intro. http://www.buildingsmart-tech.org/specifications/bcf-releases
12. Vasantrao, K.V.: Need to understand "Uncertainty" in the system development modeling process. In: Proceedings of 2011 International Conference on Communication Systems and Network Technologies CSNT 2011, pp. 619–623 (2011)
13. Monteleone, C.: Verso una delle verità: rappresentare Carpi e le sue trasformazioni. In: Giordano, A., Rossi, M., Svalduz, E. (eds.) In mezzo a un dialogo. La piazza di Carpi dal Rinascimento a oggi, pp. 87–91. Edizioni APM, Carpi (MO) (2012)
14. Carpo, M.: The digital turn in architecture 1992–2012. AD Read, 264 p. (2013)
15. Friso, I.: I problemi sorgono modellando. In: Giordano, A., Rossi, M., Svalduz, E. (eds.) Costruire il Tempio, pp. 52–57. Edizioni APM, Carpi (MO) (2015)
16. Sgrosso, A.: Note di fotogrammetria applicata all'architettura. Lithorapid, Napoli (1979)
17. Dzwierzynska, J.: Reconstructing architectural environment from the perspective image. Procedia Eng. **161**, 1445–1451 (2016)
18. Lordick, D.: Parametric reconstruction of the space in Vermeer's painting "girl reading a letter at an open window". J. Geom. Graph. **16**(1), 69–79 (2012)
19. Yang, H., Zhang, H.: Automatic 3D reconstruction of a polyhedral object from a single line drawing under perspective projection. Comput. Graph. (Pergamon) **65**, 45–59 (2017)
20. EUCLID. http://camillotrevisan.weebly.com/ricerca.html
21. Visualizing Venice. http://www.visualizingvenice.org
22. Wilson, A.: Urban Modeling. Routledge, London (2012)
23. Haydn, T.: Using New Technologies to Enhance Teaching and Learning in History. Routledge, London (2013)

3D Reconstruction of Urban History Based on Old Maps

Hendrik Herold$^{(\boxtimes)}$ and Robert Hecht

Leibniz Institute of Ecological Urban and Regional Development,
Weberplatz 1, 01217 Dresden, Germany
h.herold@ioer.de

Abstract. Digital libraries increasingly provide large amounts of scanned maps. These historical cartographic documents are considered as part of the cultural heritage. In a geographical context, however, old topographic maps are very valuable information sources for tracking land use changes over long periods of time. This chapter presents a methodology for the automated 3D building reconstruction from recent and old topographic maps. The presented methodology was developed focusing primarily on urban research, spatial planning, and a nationwide retrospective land-use monitoring. In the interdisciplinary discourse, perspectives and benefits of the method application in urban history and cultural heritage research and education have been identified and are presented here.

Keywords: Urban history · Historical maps · 2/3D building reconstruction
GIS

1 Introduction

Digital libraries provide not only digitized books and historical photo collections, but increasingly also large amounts of scanned paper maps. These historical cartographic documents are considered as part of the cultural heritage. However, old topographic maps are – from geographical point of view – also very valuable information sources for tracking landscape and settlement changes over long periods of time (e.g. [13, 26, 42]).

This chapter presents a methodology for the automated two- and three-dimensional building reconstruction from recent and old topographic maps. The methodology was developed and is constantly further advanced focusing on urban research [33], spatial planning [24] and a nationwide, retrospective land-use monitoring [28, 34]. In interdisciplinary exchange and discussions, however, we have identified perspectives, interlinkages, and potential benefits of its application in urban history and cultural heritage research and education. In the future, the increasing availability of digital map repositories in both the spatial and the temporal dimension will even foster this interconnection.

The chapter is organized as follows: section two gives a brief overview on topographic maps and their temporal availability. Subsequently, the methodology for the 2D and 3D reconstruction, which is divided in four major processing steps, is presented in Sect. 3:

© Springer International Publishing AG, part of Springer Nature 2018
S. Münster et al. (Eds.): UHDL 2017/DECH 2017, CCIS 817, pp. 63–79, 2018.
https://doi.org/10.1007/978-3-319-76992-9_5

- georeferencing of the maps,
- derivation of 2D building footprints,
- derivation of building types, and the
- 3D building reconstruction.

In the following, some sample application and visualizations are shown (Sect. 4). Section 5 suggests potential benefits as well as limitations of the methodology in the field of urban history research and education. Conclusions and directions for an interdisciplinary research agenda are given in Sect. 6.

2 Old Maps and Temporal Scopes

In a general sense, old maps are referred to all cartographic records such as historical cadastral maps, city plans, and topographic map series. This research primarily focuses on old topographic maps, because of their representational homogeneity and availability over larger areas (i.e. above city, landscape, or even region level). Topographic maps depict the geographic variation of height and shape over the Earth's surface as a two- dimensional representation at a defined cartographic scale [15, p. 479]. In this function, topographic map preserve a scale-depended state of urban and landscape settings at certain points in time. This characteristic makes them an interesting and valuable information source for the geosciences, but also other disciplines such as urban history research and cultural heritage education.

Cartographic records already exist for many centuries. The era of trigonometry-based topographic maps, which are in the focus of this research, started in 1744 with Cassini de Thury's new projection and trigonometric land survey in France [22, p. 22]. Numerous of these land surveys followed all across Europe, for instance the:

- Austro-Hungarian surveys (e.g. Josephine, 1763–1787, at scale 1: 28,800),
- Ordnance Survey (1791–1850, at scale 1 inch: 1mile),
- Gaussian survey (1821–1825, at scale 1: 21,333),
- Prussian survey (1830–1865, at scale 1: 25,800), or the
- Saxonian survey (1780–1806, at scale 1: 12,000)

(cf. [13, 22, 43, 53, 59]). Since that times, European nations and parts of their former colonies have been repeatedly mapped. Digital libraries, but also national mapping agency (e.g. USGS) and individuals (e.g. David Rumsey), increasingly make large map collection online available. To date, the largest meta-collection for old maps is the portal "OldMapOnline" [40], which provides access to many digital map repositories such as the Harvard Library Map Collection, the ETH-Bibliothek Map Collection, the National Library of Scotland, the Saxon State and University Library Dresden, the Land Survey Office Czech Republic, or The David Rumsey Map Collection. A detailed overview of these map repositories is given in [22].

In order to make use of old maps in urban research and spatial planning, the maps have to be georeferenced and objects of interest have to be extracted. These tasks are usually done manually, which is feasible for small study areas. For large-scale and long-term applications, however, hundreds of map sheets need to be manually prepared and analyzed. Hence, research on methods for automated map analysis has a long scientific tradition. For detailed overviews the reader is referred to [8, 22]. In the following, a methodology is proposed for (semi-)automated map georeferencing and the reconstruction of 3D building models based on the extraction of 2D building footprints from maps.

3 Methodology

Digital, i.e. scanned maps are basically digital images. That means, structured information, which can easily be captured by humans, is not readily accessible by computers. Image analysis and computer vision algorithms need to be applied in order to extract useful information such as map coordinates, street outlines, built-up areas, urban blocks, or building footprints. Hence, the methodology for the reconstruction of 3D buildings from old maps comprises several processing steps (see Fig. 1) and methods, which will be described successively in the following.

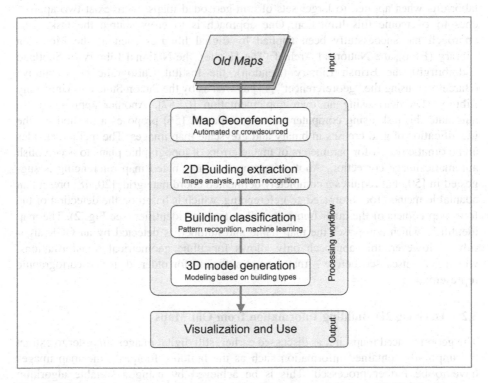

Fig. 1. Methodology and workflow for deriving 3D urban models from 2D historical maps.

3.1   Map Georeferencing

In order to use the topographical content of a map for spatial research and planning, the date of map survey as well as the exact location of the map content have to be known. While the survey date and the approximate location (generally given by a major place name/toponym that is depicted in the map) is usually provided by the digital map repository, the information on the map coordinates and the geodetic projection is only implicitly contained.

There are two principal possibilities for georeferencing. One possibility is to assign coordinates of depicted objects to known real world coordinates or to locations of an already geocoded map using so-called ground control points (GCPs). This approach is advantageous for old, distorted maps because inner-map distortions can be corrected in this way (see for example [38]). However, for larger sets of maps, this georeferencing approach is very laborious and time consuming.

The second possibility is to use the printed or known coordinates of the map corners along with sheet line system for a topographic map series. However, this procedure works usually only for trigonometric survey-based topographic maps, which were described in the previous section. Since the second possibility gets also very laborious when applied to larger sets of non-geocoded maps, there exist two approaches to overcome this limitation. One approach is to crowdsource the task. This approach has successfully been applied by digital libraries such as the Moravian Library (Brno), the Nationaal Archief (The Hague), the National Library of Scotland (Edinburgh), the British Library (London), the Institut Cartografic de Catalunya (Barcelona) using the "georeferencer" [11] as well as by the Saxon State and University Library (Dresden) using an own implementation [6, 57]. Another approach is to automate this task using computer vision techniques. [56] proposes a method for the identification of grid crosses in binary and greyscale map images. The method enables an automatic search for parameters of image errors of topographic plans to accomplish automatic image correction. Another approach to automated map referencing is suggested in [50], but requires a completely delineated coordinate grid. [20, 48] present an adaptable method for automated georeferencing, which is based on the detection of the four map corners of the inner frame as well as the map identifier (see Fig. 2). The map identifier, which comprises the map name and number, is detected by an OCR algorithm. However, this approach only allows for affine geometrical transformations, which – as discussed before – may be not sufficient for older, distorted cartographic representations.

3.2   Deriving 2D Building Information from Old Maps

The georeferenced maps are, as discussed earlier, still digital images. In order to extract the implicitly contained information such as the building footprint, the map images have to be further processed. This is be achieved by using a suitable algorithm depending on the map layout. In order to develop or select an adequate method, it is decisive to analyze the characteristics of the maps under investigation. Compared to other imagery (e.g. natural photographs), maps are based on a structured symbolic graphical model, which generalizes the complex geographical reality. That is, the map

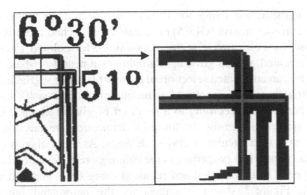

Fig. 2. Map georeferencing by automated detection of map corners and their coordinates using OCR (Source: [20, 48]).

content comprises a limited set of symbols, forms, or colors, for instance, which can be formalized and hence be represented in a computational recognition system.

Depending on the cartographic representation of the building footprint (e.g. solid, hatched, colored), different delineation algorithms need to be used. Morphology-based segmentation using a combination of Mathematical Morphology operators is suitable for delineating footprints in solid, grayscale map representations (as shown in Fig. 3).

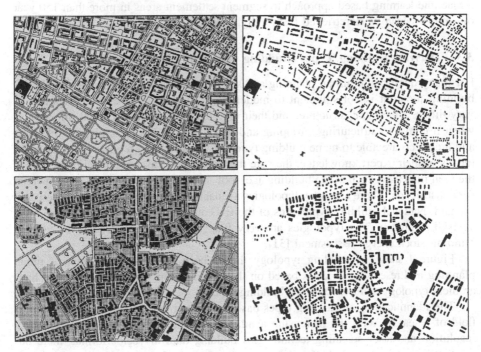

Fig. 3. 2D building extraction from topographic maps (map data sources: TK25 © GeoSN 2006 for the map on the upper left, TK25 © GeoBasis NRW 2005 for the map on the lower left).

Texture-based segmentation using for instance the spatial texture measures of the gray-level co-occurrence matrix (GLCM) is suitable for hatched footprints in grayscale maps. In contrast, for color image segmentation (CIS, for colored footprint representation) an edge-oriented, region growing algorithm or a neural net-based approach are suggested [22]. For an automated selection of the most suitable segmentation algorithm and its parametrization [22] developed a metaheuristic approach, which optimizes algorithms and parameters according to a small set of given reference samples.

A further major challenge for the footprint delineation are the map symbols and lettering (toponyms), in particular in gray-scale maps. As these objects have similar or even identical morphological properties as the buildings representation (in terms of size and form), they need to be detected and removed using OCR and pattern recognition algorithms [21]. Figure 3 shows examples for the automated building footprint reconstruction from a map (on the left) and the extraction result on the right.

For spatial planning, historical demography, and visualization, it might be useful to additionally extract – besides the building footprint retrieval – the historical urban block structure. [36] suggests a model-based approach for the extraction of built-up areas and urban blocks. As this block structure and roads can be considered as mutually exclusive within urban areas, the approach may also be used to approximate the historical street network.

For a use in longer-term studies with large spatial coverage (larger than regions or even nations) it might be more useful not to detect every single building but rather to delineate whole settlement areas and populated places in historical maps. [51] presents a machine learning based approach to segment settlement areas in more than 150 year old maps, which were retrieved from a digital library [56].

3.3 Deriving Building Types (Building Footprint Classification)

For many questions in urban planning and spatial sciences, a reconstruction of the 2D building footprint is not sufficient to model cities' complexity. The buildings can be very different in shape, structure, and their use. Typologies are of central importance, when it comes to structuring, grouping and naming them. For example, city planners and architects are able to name building types by visually interpreting a black plan. By means of their expert knowledge, they are then also able to assign typical properties of the identified type, such as the building age, roof shape or the presumably used material for construction. There are many typologies available in the urban and housing research domain. National building typologies of the EU countries have been developed in the TABULA project. The typologies are very fine-grained and intended to be used in building stock energy assessment [31].

Figure 4 shows a building typology that is been used in the context of urban planning and research, which is based on the classification scheme of [33]. The hierarchical typology differentiates ten building types.

The identification of building types based on topographic data is a relatively new field of research. With the increasing availability of remote sensing imagery in high resolution and laser scanning technologies building data in vector format, there has been an increasing number of activities in recent years. In particular, in urban modeling, the building classification and recognition of urban structures plays an important

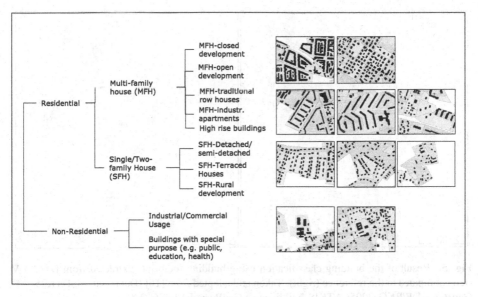

Fig. 4. Building typology (Source: [16]).

role (e.g. [2, 3, 12, 35, 58, 61]. However, even in cartography, building types are important when it comes to identifying specific types of buildings or groups and to generalize them in a specific manner (e.g. [1, 46]). For classifying building footprints, knowledge-based approaches and data-driven approaches can be distinguished. Using a knowledge-based approach, the classification problem can be easily formalized by experts based on existing a priori knowledge. In this case, the model and its model parameters are explicitly entered. Choosing a data-driven approach, the knowledge (e.g. parameters of a classification algorithm) is acquired in a training process where the model parameters are trained automatically based on a given trainings sample.

First knowledge-based approaches have been used in [33, 41, 54], for example. With the increasing complexity (many classes) and the availability of new spatial data sets, data-driven approaches are gaining in importance. The learning strategy can either be supervised or unsupervised. In the case of unsupervised learning, homogeneous groups (clusters) are formed on the basis of characteristics derived from the geodata. The identified clusters need to be interpreted in a subsequent step in order to assign a meaning. The studies [12, 37, 60] follow an unsupervised approach. Supervised classification approaches have been used in [19, 49, 55].

In this research, a data-driven, supervised classification approach is applied that uses methods of pattern recognition and machine learning. The approach is described in detail in [16–18] and consists of the following five processing steps: data preparation, feature extraction, pre-processing, feature reduction and classification. The Random Forest Algorithm [7] has been used as a classification algorithm. Figure 5 shows the result of the building classification for a subset of the City of Halle, Germany, using a topographic map (left) compared to the reference (right). As reference an existing IOER ground truth database on building types was used. The ground truth data were collected

Fig. 5. Result of the building classification using building footprints extracted from DTK25-V (left) compared to the reference (right). Taken and adopted from [16] (Data sources: DTK25-V © GeoBasis-DE/BKG 2005; ATKIS buildings © GeoBasis-DE/BKG 2007).

in an on-site inspection campaign. The classification accuracy by using extracted building footprints from the German topographic map (DTK25-V) was 76.6% [17]. The accuracy refers to the building type classification, not to the extraction of the building footprints. However, the building block geometry and the house coordinate database were also used to support the building classification process. When applying the approach on historical maps, these ancillary information are usually not available.

3.4   3D Building Reconstruction

Investigating and understanding historical settlements requires a realistic 3D representation of the urban landscape using the CityGML standard defined in [10]. In this context, the acquisition of an associated building height is of central importance. This allows for a 3D building model representation in the level of detail 1 (LOD 1). For all buildings, which still exist today, the current building heights can be transferred to the building footprints derived from the old maps by GIS-based spatial matching. Building heights can be used from existing 3D building models, obtained by means of airborne laser scanning, or estimated (e.g. [5, 44]). For historical buildings that do not exist anymore there is the possibility to define typical building heights according to the building type. However, this requires expert knowledge. The process of acquiring building heights can also be supported by other historical documents and photographs (e.g. [32]). In addition to the building height, the buildings can be further described with a roof shape resulting in a 3D building representation in LOD 2, i.e. with differentiated roof structures. For this, current data (in case of existing buildings), or typical assumptions, can be used. Finally, the buildings can be mapped with textures on the roof surfaces and façade for a better approximation of reality. In this case, existing texture databases can be used or created based on the knowledge of typical façade and roof structures as well as the historically used materials.

4   Applications Examples

The proposed approach for the reconstruction of settlements at the building level offers a variety of applications in both spatial research and spatial planning, particularly in the urban context. In addition, the results are also relevant in cartography, urban history, cultural heritage, urban morphology, and architecture. In the following, selected application examples in the context of spatial science and planning are presented.

4.1   Small-Scale Description of the Settlement Structure

The approach offers the opportunity to efficiently generate a very detailed representation of the settlement structure relevant for research and planning. Figure 6 shows the estimated building age as a result of the multi-temporal map analysis by combining

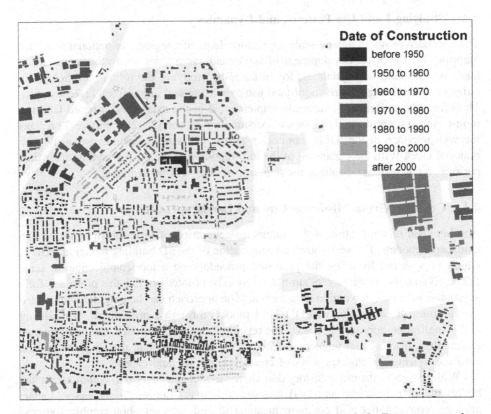

Fig. 6. 2D Reconstruction of building age by multi-temporal map analysis (Data sources: urban blocks and buildings: ATKIS Basis-DLM © LGL-BW 2016; maps: DTK25 © LGL-BW 1950, 1960, 1970, 1980, 1990, 2000, Geoprocessing: IOER, R. Hecht, H. Herold).

current building footprints in vector data with a series of old topographic raster maps at scale of 1:25k. The building age information is an important information for planning renewable energy and assessing the buildings energy consumption (e.g. [9, 47]). Estimated building age can be a valuable indicator for energy consumption, but it has to be combined with data on energetic improvements that have been carried out since a building was erected. Based on the classified building stock and the derived period of construction a number of further planning-relevant data can be extracted on a very detailed level. For example, the floor area ratio can be derived more precisely than without the knowledge of the building type and the construction period. The same applies to the mapping of dwelling and population density [29], since each type of building also has specific characteristics (e.g. apartment sizes, household sizes).

Spatio-temporal modeling of the dynamics of the urban structure, floor space and the population also opens up the possibility to evaluate planning instruments ex-post and studying the effects of land use policy changes on the settlement structure in regional or even national contexts [25]. The knowledge of the building age information can also improve GIS-based models to estimate the material stocks and flows in buildings as a basis for the future mining of metallic and mineral resources [27].

4.2   Studying Land Use Patterns and Dynamics

The approach provides a large-scale application (e.g., at a regional or national level) for mapping the historical development of settlements as a basis for further research on land use and land use dynamics, for instance by studying the urban morphology of cities or determining the drivers of land use expansion and urban sprawl (see e.g. [4]). Therefore, the procedure is currently implemented in the existing web-based land use monitoring system of the IOER (www.ioer-monitor.de, see [24, 28]). Figure 7 presents the web interface of the IOER monitoring system showing the building density on a national level. With the expansion of the information system, e.g. by adding older time periods, a much richer database for scientific studies will be available.

4.3   Creating Virtual Historical City and Landscapes Models

Another field of application is the automatic generation of virtual historical city and landscapes models. Figure 8 shows a visualization of the 3D building model in LOD 1, which is achieved by using the proposed procedure on a topographic map at scale 1:25k. Even if the model is very simple, it has to be pointed out that this process is fully automatic without intervention by a human. The approach can be potentially extended for an automatic derivation of LOD 2 - 4 models through a procedural 3D modeling and visualization approach [14, 45]. The resulting virtual city models can be of interest to scientists from spatial science, architects, and historians, but also to game makers who are looking for efficient ways of creating large 3D landscapes.

With respect to the urban history domain the model can be used to communicate the historical urban structure and land use and also may support "historians to locate, analyze, contextualize and compare meaningful and relevant photographic sources" such as in the UrbanHistory4D project (www.visualhumanities.org).

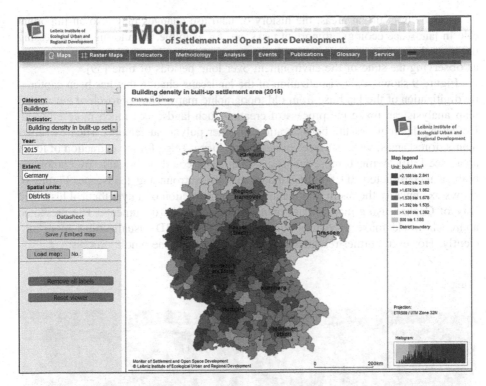

Fig. 7. Screenshot of the IOER-Monitor showing the building density in built-up areas. (Source: [24] based on [28]).

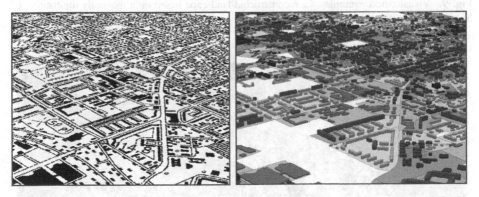

Fig. 8. 3D Reconstruction of a building model of the City of Dresden by deriving building footprints, types and heights based on a topographic map (Map data source: TK25 © GeoSN 2006, Geoprocessing: IOER, H. Herold, R. Hecht, based on [33]).

Besides from urban areas, the history of land use changes play also an important role in landscape ecology. Important tasks are, for example, monitoring and assessing the natural resources, examining the impacts and effects of human intervention as well as observing the state of the environment over long periods of time [59].

Figure 9 shows a 3D visualization of the landscape change that has been captured by digitization of the land use from old topographic maps. The approach of automated map analysis can make the process of creating such landscapes much more efficient. However, this requires the consideration of other polygonal features, such as settlements, forest areas, water surfaces or agricultural areas (e.g., for the extraction of forest areas see [30]). A much more realistic visualization could be possible by combining both, a reconstructed 3D building model and the surrounding landscape. Figure 10 shows exemplarily the result of a manual 3D reconstruction of a hypothetical historical City of Cagliari using maps, aerial photographs and other documents. The presented approach would make a contribution to generate such 3D visualizations more efficiently. However, further research is needed to automate the whole process.

Fig. 9. Visualization example of a reconstructed landscape based on a manually digitization of historical maps (Source: [23] based on [59]).

Fig. 10. 3D historical reconstruction of the City of Cagliari (Source: [52]).

5 Discussion and Reflection

In the previous sections, a methodology and processing results were presented. In the following, potential benefits, but also limitation of the methodology and challenges for the reconstruction and visualization of urban history research are outlined.

5.1 Potentials Benefits and Ideas for the Use in Urban History Research

The interdisciplinary application of the described methodology may offer some benefits for the research and education in urban history, for instance:

- Historical 2D and 3D reconstructions and visualizations over large areas (above city, landscape, or region level),
- Virtual embedding of cultural heritage sites in the 3-dimensional historical urban setting and context (which is typically represented in a lower level of detail),
- Reconstruction and visualization of no longer extant sites and buildings,
- Generation and estimation of historical population distributions,
- Analysis and visualization of historical vistas (i.e. visual axes),
- Visualization of the history of places for architectural planning,
- Visualization of slowly proceeding urban renewal processes,
- Reconstruction of historic relief by contour line detection (e.g. [39]),
- Embedding of the urban history into the historic landscape setting (Figs. 9 and 10),
- Combination with photogrammetric building reconstructions based on historical photographs (e.g., see [32]),
- Combination of the extracted buildings with historical socio-economic, archeological and architectural data.

5.2 Limitations and Challenges for the Use in Urban History Research

The specific use and the detailed scale used in research and education in urban history and cultural heritage poses some limitations and challenges for the use of the described workflow, for instance:

- Temporal limitations for the automated reconstructions, which are restricted to available map survey dates,
- Spatial and temporal uncertainties due to the map making and scanning process, the map lettering and inner-map distortions, particularly in older maps,
- Building reconstruction still limited to maps with colored and textured building footprints, so far not possible for line drawings,
- Automated georeferencing still only works for certain types of maps, for others a crowdsourcing approach may be suitable,
- Results as 3D GIS models, so far no CAD or BIM export possibility,
- To date, restricted to LOD 1 reconstructions; typical façade, roof structures, materials (LOD 2 to 4) not yet available, but suitable for procedural 3D modeling.

Most of these challenges can only be approached and overcome by an interdisciplinary research effort and community. In particular, the methodology could be greatly improved by extracting place-based information from other historical sources and integrating it in the map interpretation process.

6 Conclusions

The chapter has presented methods and perspectives of the automated two- and three-dimensional building reconstruction from old maps for urban history and cultural heritage research. The presented methodology has been developed primarily for urban planning and retrospective land-use monitoring. However, there could be various interlinkages and potential benefits for the field of urban history research identified. The increasing digital availability of old maps in both the spatial and the temporal dimension will even widen and foster this interconnection. For addressing the challenges and overcoming the limitation outlined in the previous section, an interdisciplinary research effort of both disciplines urban history/cultural heritage research and geoinformatics/computer science is necessary. Directions for this kind of a common, interdisciplinary research could be: (1) adapting and improving the extraction and georeferencing methods towards older and larger scale maps or cadastral plans as well as (2) to integrate historical building types in order to improve the quality of 3D reconstruction of past urban landscapes. Improving on this may even widen the spectrum of possible applications in the digital humanities in general.

Acknowledgments. The authors would like to thank federal mapping agency as well as the Saxon State Library for providing the maps. We also want thank the anonymous reviewers for their valuable comments that helped to improve the quality of the paper.

References

1. Anders, K.-H., Sester, M., Fritsch, D.: Analysis of settlement structures by graph-based clustering. In: SMATI 1999 Workshop on 'Semantic Modeling', München, Germany, pp. 41–49 (1999)
2. Banzhaf, E., Höfer, R.: Monitoring urban structure types as spatial indicators with CIR aerial photographs for a more effective urban environmental management. IEEE J. Sel. Top. Appl. Earth Observ. Remote Sens. **1**(2), 129–138 (2008)
3. Barr, S.L., Barnsley, M.J.: A region-based, graph-theoretic data model for the inference of second-order thematic information from remotely-sensed images. Int. J. Geogr. Inf. Sci. **11**(6), 555–576 (1997)
4. Behnisch, M., Poglitsch, H., Krüger, T.: Soil sealing and the complex bundle of influential factors: Germany as a case study. ISPRS Int. J. Geo-Inf. **8**(132), 23 (2016)
5. Biljecki, F., Ledoux, H., Stoter, J.: Generating 3D city models without elevation data. Comput. Environ. Urban Syst. **2017**(64), 1–18 (2017)
6. Bill, R., Walter, K.: Crowdsourcing zur Georeferenzierung alter topographischer Karten: Ansatz, Erfahrungen und Qualitätsanalyse. In: ZfV, vol. 140, pp. 172–179 (2015)
7. Breiman, L.: Random forests. Mach. Learn. **45**(1), 5–32 (2001)
8. Chiang, Y.-Y., Leyk, S., Knoblock, C.A.: A survey of digital map processing techniques. ACM Comput. Surv. **47**(1), 1–44 (2014)

9. Delmastro, C., Mutani, G., Schranz, L.: The evaluation of buildings energy consumption and the optimization of district heating networks: a GIS-based model. Int. J. Energy Environ. Eng. **7**(3), 343–351 (2016)
10. Gröger, G., Kolbe, T.H., Nagel, C., Häfele, K.-H.: OGC City Geography Markup Language (CityGML) Encoding Standard, version 2.0, OGC Doc No. 12-019. Open Geospatial Consortium. http://www.opengis.net/spec/citygml/2.0
11. Fleet, C., Kowal, K.C., Přidal, P.: Georeferencer: crowdsourced georeferencing for map library collections. D-Lib Mag. (2012). https://doi.org/10.1045/november2012-fleet
12. Geiß, C., Taubenböck, H., Wurm, M., et al.: Remote sensing-based characterization of settlement structures for assessing local potential of district heat. Remote Sens. **3**(7), 1447–1471 (2011)
13. Haase, D., Walz, U., Neubert, M., Rosenberg, M.: Changes to central european landscapes – analysing historical maps to approach current environmental issues, examples from Saxony, Central Germany. Land Use Policy **24**(2007), 248–263 (2007)
14. Haegler, S., Müller, P., Van Gool, L.: Procedural modeling for digital cultural heritage. EURASIP J. Image Video Process. **2009**(1), 1–8 (2009)
15. Hendricks, M.D.: Topographic map. In: Kemp, K.K. (ed.) Encyclopedia of Geographic Information Science, pp. 479–481. SAGE, London (2008)
16. Hecht, R.: Automatische Klassifizierung von Gebäudegrundrissen – Ein Beitrag zur kleinräumigen Beschreibung der Siedlungsstruktur. Dissertation, Dresden University of Technology. IÖR-Schriften 63. Rhombos, Berlin (2014)
17. Hecht, R., Meinel, G., Buchroithner, M.F.: Automatic identification of building types based on topographic databases – a comparison of different data sources. Int. J. Cartogr. **2015**(1), 18–31 (2015)
18. Hecht, R., Herold, H., Meinel, G., Buchroithner, M.F.: Automatic derivation of urban structure types from topographic maps by means of image analysis and machine learning. In: Proceedings of 26th International Cartographic Conference (2013)
19. Henn, A., Römer, C., Gröger, G., et al.: Automatic classification of building types in 3D city models using SVMs for semantic enrichment of low resolution building data. GeoInformatica **16**(2), 281–306 (2012)
20. Herold, H., Roehm, P., Hecht, R., Meinel, G.: Automatically georeferenced maps as a source for high resolution urban growth analyses. In: Proceedings of ICA 25th International Cartographic Conference, Paris, France, pp. 1–5 (2011)
21. Herold, H., Meinel, G., Hecht, R., Csaplovics, E.: A GEOBIA approach to map interpretation – multitemporal building footprint retrieval for high resolution monitoring of spatial urban dynamics. In: Proceedings of 4th GEOBIA, Rio de Janeiro, pp. 252–256 (2012)
22. Herold H.: Geoinformation from the Past – Computational Retrieval and Retrospective Monitoring of Historical Land Use. Springer Nature, Cham (2018)
23. IOER   2017a.   http://www.ioer.de/langzeitmonitoring_slr/html/visualisierung/imaps_iframe3D.html. Accessed 18 Oct 2017
24. IOER 2017b. http://www.ioer-monitor.de. Accessed 18 Oct 2017
25. Jehling, M., Hecht, R., Herold, H.: Assessing urban containment policies within a suburban context – an approach to enable a regional perspective In: Land Use Policy (2016, online first)
26. Kienast, F.: Analysis of historic landscape patterns with a geographical information system - a methodological outline. Landscape Ecol. **8**(2), 103–118 (1993)
27. Kleemann, F., Lederer, J., Rechberger, H., Fellner, J.: GIS-based analysis of Vienna's material stock in buildings. J. Ind. Ecol. **21**, 368–380 (2017)

28. Krüger, T., Meinel, G., Schumacher, U.: Land-use monitoring by topographic data analysis. Cartogr. Geograph. Inf. Sci. **40**(3), 220–228 (2013)

29. Kunze, C., Hecht, R.: Semantic enrichment of building data with volunteered geographic information to improve mappings of dwelling units and population. Comput. Environ. Urban Syst. **53**(2015), 4–18 (2015)

30. Leyk, S., Boesch, R., Weibel, R.: Saliency and semantic processing: extracting forest cover from historical topographic maps. Pattern Recogn. **39**(5), 953–968 (2006)

31. Loga, T., Diefenbach, N., Balaras, C., Dascalaki, E., Zavrl, M.S., Rakuscek, A., Corrado, V., Corgnati, S., Despretz, H., Roarty, C., et al.: Use of building typologies for energy performance assessment of national building stocks. Existent experiences in European countries and common approach – First TABULA synthesis report (2017). http://www.buildup.eu/node/9927. Accessed 25 July 2017

32. Maiwald, F., Vietze, T., Schneider, D., Henze, F., Münster, S., Niebling, F.: Photogrammetric analysis of historical image repositories for virtual reconstruction in the field of digital humanities. In: International Archives of the Photogrammetry, Remote Sensing and Spatial Information Sciences, vol. XLII-2/W3, pp. 447–452 (2017)

33. Meinel, G., Hecht, R., Herold, H.: Analyzing building stock using topographic maps and GIS. Build. Res. Inf. **37**(5–6), 468–482 (2009)

34. Meinel, G.: Monitoring of settlement and open space development on the basis of topographical spatial data - concept, realization and first results. In: Core Spatial Databases - From Theory to Practice, Haifa, Israel, ISPRS Archives of the Photogrammetry, Remote Sensing and Spatial Information Sciences, pp. 132–137 (2010)

35. SJM Tech: 3D Historical Reconstruction of the City of Cagliari. 3D render by © SJM TECH (2018). www.sjmtech.net/portfolio/cagliari_storica/

36. Muhs, S., Herold, H., Meinel, G., Burkhardt, D., Kretschmer, O.: Automatic delineation of built-up area at urban block level from topographic maps. Comput. Environ. Urban Syst. **58**, 71–84 (2016)

37. Neidhart, H., Sester, M.: Identifying building types and building clusters using 3D-laser scanning and GIS-data. Int. Arch. Photogramm. Remote Sens. Spat. Inf. Sci. (Part B4) **35**, 715–720 (2004)

38. Neubert, M., Walz, U.: Auswertung historischer Kartenwerke für ein Landschaftsmonitoring. In: Strobl, J., Blaschke, T., Griesebner, G. (eds.) Angewandte Geographische Informationsverarbeitung XIV - Beiträge zum AGIT-Symposium Salzburg 2002, Wichmann, Heidelberg, pp. 396–402 (2002)

39. Oka, S., Garg, A., Varghese, K.: Vectorization of contour lines from scanned topographic maps. Autom. Constr. **22**, 192–202 (2012)

40. OldMapsOnline. http://www.oldmapsonline.org. Accessed 18 Oct 2017

41. Orford, S., Radcliffe, J.: Modelling UK residential dwelling types using OS Mastermap data: a comparison to the 2001 census. Comput. Environ. Urban Syst. **31**(2), 206–227 (2007)

42. Petit, C.C., Lambin, E.F.: Impact of data integration technique on historical land-use/land-cover change: comparing historical maps with remote sensing data in the Belgian Ardennes. Landscape Ecol. **17**(2), 117–132 (2002)

43. Podobnikar, T.: Georeferencing and quality assessment of Josephine survey maps for the mountainous region in the Triglav National Park. Acta Geodaetica et Geophysica Hungarica **44**(1), 49–66 (2009)

44. Prechtel, N.: On strategies and automation in upgrading 2D to 3D landscape representations. Cartogr. Geogr. Inf. Sci. **42**(3), 244–258 (2015)

45. Radies, C.: Procedural random generation of building models based Geobasis data and of the urban development with the software CityEngine. AGIT (2013)

46. Regnauld, N.: Contextual building typification in automated map generalization. Algorithmica **30**(2), 312–333 (2001)
47. Resch, B., Sagl, G., Törnros, T., Bachmaier, A., Eggers, J.-B., Herkel, S., Narmsara, S., Gündra, H.: GIS-based planning and modeling for renewable energy: challenges and future research avenues. ISPRS Int. J. Geo-Inf. **3**, 662–692 (2014)
48. Röhm, P., Herold, H., Meinel, G.: Automatische Georeferenzierung gescannter deutscher Topographischer Karten im Maßstab 1:25000. Kartographische Nachrichten – J. Cartogr. Geogr. Inf. **62**(4), 195–199 (2012)
49. Römer, C., Plümer, L.: Identifying architectural style in 3D city models with support vector machines. In: Photogrammetrie - Fernerkundung - Geoinformation, 05/2010, pp. 371–384 (2010)
50. Rus, I., Balint, C., Craciunescu, V., Constantinescu, S., Ovejanu, I., Bartos-Elekes, Z.: Automated georeference of the 1: 20,000 Romanian maps under Lambert-Cholesky (1916-1959) projection system. Acta Geodaetica et Geophysica Hungarica **45**(1), 105–111 (2010)
51. Schemala, D., Schlesinger, D., Winkler, P., Herold, H., Meinel, G.: Semantic segmentation of settlement patterns in gray-scale map images using RF and CRF within an HPC environment. In: GEOBIA 2016: Solutions and Synergies. Faculty of Geo-Information and Earth Observation (ITC), University of Twente (2016)
52. SJM Tech (2017). http://www.sjmtech.net/old/show_cag_en.html
53. Skokanová, H., Havlícek, M., Borovec, R., Demek, J., Eremiášová, R., Chrudina, Z., Mackovcin, P., Rysková, R., Slavík, P., Stránská, T., Svoboda, J.: Development of land use and main land use change processes in the period 1836–2006: case study in the Czech Republic. J. Maps **8**(1), 88–96 (2012)
54. Smith, D.; Crooks, A.: From buildings to cities: techniques for the multi-scale analysis of urban form and function. In: CASA Working Papers 155. Centre for Advanced Spatial Analysis (UCL), London (2010)
55. Steiniger, S., Lange, T., Burghardt, D., et al.: An approach for the classification of urban building structures based on discriminant analysis techniques. Trans. GIS **12**(1), 31–59 (2008)
56. Titova, O.A., Chernov, A.V.: Method for the automatic georeferencing and calibration of cartographic images. Appl. Probl. - Pattern Recogn. Image Anal. **19**(1), 193–196 (2009)
57. Virtual Map Forum 2.0, SLUB. http://kartenforum.slub-dresden.de
58. Walde, I., Hese, S., Berger, C., Schmullius, C.: Graph-based mapping of urban structure types from high-resolution satellite image objects—case study of the German cities Rostock and Erfurt. IEEE Geosci. Remote Sens. Lett. **10**(4), 932–936 (2012)
59. Walz, U.: Monitoring of landscape change and functions in Saxony (Eastern Germany) - methods and indicators. Ecol. Ind. **8**(6), 807–817 (2008)
60. Werder, S., Kieler, B., Sester, M.: Semi-automatic interpretation of buildings and settlement areas in user-generated spatial data. In: Proceedings of 18th SIGSPATIAL International Conference on Advances in Geographic Information Systems, pp. 330–339. ACM, New York (2010)
61. Wurm, M., Taubenböck, H., Roth, A., Dech, S.: Urban structuring using multisensoral remote sensing data: by the example of the German cities Cologne and Dresden. In: Joint Urban Remote Sensing Event, Shanghai, 8 p. (2009)

Systematization

Accessing and Using Digital Libraries in Art History

Christina Kamposiori[1](✉) ⓘ, Claire Warwick[2], and Simon Mahony[1]

[1] Centre for Digital Humanities, University College London, London, UK
christina.kamposiori.11@ucl.ac.uk
[2] Department of English Studies, University of Durham, Durham, UK

Abstract. Over the past decades, the increase in the use of digital resources and the growth of research conducted in digital environments has transformed academic scholarship. The goal of this paper is to highlight the importance of understanding user behavior and needs for building digital libraries and resources that have a positive effect on the whole scholarly workflow. For this purpose, the art historical discipline will be used as a case study; by employing an ethnographic approach to the study of scholarly habits, we managed to uncover the requirements that scholars in the field have in terms of accessing and using digital libraries. The complex information behavior of art historians as well as the challenges they often face when interacting with digital resources make them a great example to demonstrate the impact that digital libraries and archives can have on the research process.

Keywords: Digital libraries · Digital resources · Information behavior
Art history · Access · User requirements · Research · Teaching

1 Introduction

Technological progress and mass digitization of information resources have brought large changes to traditional scholarship in the Arts and Humanities during the past fifty years. Never before was there such breadth of information and services available for scholars to use; most importantly, though, such developments offer the advantage of not only speeding up the research process, but also for enabling innovative research inquiry. Therefore, as the employment of digital resources and methods in the Arts & Humanities increases, so does the necessity to understand scholarly behavior and provide digital infrastructure tailored to the needs of these researchers.

The emergence of digital libraries and archives has greatly facilitated the need of Arts & Humanities scholars for finding diverse types of information (especially secondary literature); thus, accessing and using a variety of digital resources have become a standard step in their daily work routine. Regarding art history, it is no surprise that most of the previous studies examining the practices of scholars in the field [e.g. see 6, 22, 32] have focused on the ways they look for information. This can be easily justified if we consider the importance that the initial stages of research have for the whole research process; for example, the seeking and discovery of accurate information plays a key role in producing reliable and credible results.

© Springer International Publishing AG, part of Springer Nature 2018
S. Münster et al. (Eds.): UHDL 2017/DECH 2017, CCIS 817, pp. 83–101, 2018.
https://doi.org/10.1007/978-3-319-76992-9_6

However, there is little research on the criteria upon which art historians' decisions are made when choosing specific digital resources as well as the impact these have in the whole research process. Against this background, we aim to explore how art historians access and use digital resources for the purposes of research and teaching as well as identify the challenges they meet and needs they have. More specifically, the questions we aim to address in this paper are:

- Why do scholars choose particular resources over others for accessing the material they need?
- What are the challenges faced when accessing and interacting with digital resources?
- What effect can digital resources have on different stages of the research process?

Managing to answer these questions could foster significantly our understanding of art historical practice; this knowledge, in turn, could be applied to the creation of better digital resources and tools to support research and teaching in the field. Before presenting our results to illustrate our argument, though, it is necessary to provide some background details with regards to the information objects employed in art history as well as the practices that scholars follow in order to find the information they need. This will contribute to the building of a more detailed picture of art historians' profile as users of digital resources and libraries.

2   Information Behavior in Art History

2.1   The Discipline and Its Information Objects

Concerning the discipline of art history, scholarly behavior and researchers' needs is a subject that has been under examination for more than twenty years; though, even today, the needs of art historians seem insufficiently satisfied by digital technologies. According to recent studies [11, 36, pp. 19–22], art historians are still considered to be hesitant towards the adoption of technology, while many researchers are not convinced about the positive effect such technologies can have on their research.

However, this issue can be better understood if we consider several factors that characterize the field and make the employment of digital technologies for research purposes especially challenging. Firstly, the extensive list of subjects studied – many times interdisciplinary in nature – and methodological approaches employed by art historians today frequently require the use of a wide array of information objects (e.g. textual, visual and multimedia) in order to successfully answer a project's research questions. On the other hand, the different career stages of scholars, the various degrees of digital literacy as well as the difficulties often faced by researchers when using digital material - such as access problems, low image quality, copyright issues, cost [also see 13, p. 2, pp. 9–11, 18, p. 6, p. 33, p. 40, 36, pp. 33–34] - can significantly impact the use of digital services and tools in research and teaching. Despite the challenges, though, art historians have started developing a greater reliance on digital resources [6, p. 30].

Thinking about the information objects used most frequently by scholars in this area, it is worth noting that, from the foundation of the discipline, art history has developed a close relationship with art objects; art objects tend to play a key role in art historians' research even when they are not the central topic under examination [also see 3, pp. 7–11, p. 7, p. 94, 8, pp. 120–123]. Yet, although art objects play a principal role in art historical research, information objects in the field are not confined to artworks.

Instead, the information objects necessary for the art historical inquiry consist of an array of resources which complement, substantiate or even sometimes replace the works of art. These have conventional and digital form and they can be textual, visual and multimedia; mainly, they consist of the primary and secondary resources collected from libraries, archives and museums throughout the world. This wide variety of material has also been highlighted by several authors, such as Case [10, pp. 73–74] and Palmer et al. [28, p. 18], who argued that historians' collections can be of the most diverse type, as they collect and study various resources, from archival and visual material to toys and objects related to the time and place of their project's subject; it is worth noting that Palmer et al. [28], in particular, reached this conclusion after examining the collecting habits of researchers in several humanities and sciences discipline.

Of particular significance, though, for the field are the rare books and manuscripts and the visual material, which are considered necessary for the successful conduct of research in art history. More specifically, these information objects acquire additional value if the original art object is lost or difficult to access, as well as when the research subject itself places the art object in a secondary role; for example, when the main subject is the biography of an artist [also see 3, pp. 14–15, pp. 22–31, 8, pp. 122–123, 13, p. 3].

In the digital age, the places where art historians look mostly for the necessary information objects include various digital libraries and archives; databases with visual or other documentary material; digital journals and books; online thesauri, indices and dictionaries; discussion lists, various sites, relevant blogs and online communities [13, p. 3, 20, p. 7, 31, pp. 735–750]. Harmsen [19], in 1996, argued that as the online material increases so will the level of importance that digital resources have for art historical research. Yet, although the use of digital resources has been significantly increased since Harmsen's observation and art historians consider them to be a standard part of their daily work routine, later studies [e.g. see 32, pp. 40–41, 36, pp. 33–34] showed that this does not necessarily indicate a greater degree of importance when compared, for example, with conventional resources; factors such as copyright or the quality of material available can affect their usefulness for scholars' work and, thus, their degree of importance.

Hence, it is widely known that scholars in the field still rely greatly on the conventional material for their research and teaching practice. According to Rose [32, pp. 37–38], digital resources were more likely to be treated as secondary material than to constitute the basic information object. However, she noted that this preference occurs more due to habit and a feeling of insecurity about digital technologies than indifference about the possibilities they can offer. A similar attitude applies towards the original work of art and its visual surrogates. Generally speaking, there is a strong desire to distinguish the original artwork from its reproductions [3, pp. 11–12, 29, p. 40]. Moreover, the emergence of digital visual surrogates has not managed to substitute the necessity to visit and examine the artwork in person [e.g. see 32, p. 37]. In particular, as lack of access, poor quality and copyright issues are problems art historians have to face frequently when dealing with digital images, the physical examination of the object seems unavoidable [e.g. see 13, pp. 9–11].

Nevertheless, despite the difficulties met, visual surrogates obtain further value and can be treated as primary information objects if the original artwork is lost or inaccessible [as in 3, pp. 14–15]. Also, they are valuable tools for publishing and teaching in art history, as well as for the analytical method of iconography where the comparison between visual representations of art objects is the main concern [e.g. see 3, pp. 19–20, 7, pp. 94–96, 8, p. 123]. Regarding digital images, more specifically, some of the recent studies in the field [6, p. 30, 22, pp. 53–54] have found an increase in their use compared to previous years, suggesting that scholars in the visual arts may have started trusting digital resources. In contrast to previous studies [14, p. 5, 32, p. 39], the results of Larkin's [22, pp. 53–54] research showed a new level of comfort with digital images in art historical scholarship. In particular, more than one third of the participants in her research agreeing to own a digital image collection were art historians. Yet, it should be noted that there are not many recent studies after 2010 documenting how the behavior of art historians has developed towards digital resources, along with the reasons behind it, an issue we aim to explore through this paper.

2.2 Seeking for Information

According to Palmer et al. [28, pp. 9–10] searching for research material can be a rather complicated activity for scholars. In art history, the beginning of the research process and, therefore, the seeking of the needed information, is to a great extent linked with the scholar's intuition and memory. These two qualities, which are associated with connoisseurship, apply especially to the case when research starts from the examination of the artwork. Brilliant [8, pp. 121–122], for example, noted that scholars in the field, after mainly relying on their visual memory to examine a work of art, attempt to search for related information objects.

In fact, artworks can often inspire the initiation of the art historical research process through enabling the discovery of the research subject and the generation of research questions. These questions, then, in combination with the experience of the researcher lead to the searching of the required material. At this point, it is worthwhile mentioning briefly the concept of inspiration and how it enables information seeking. A similar behavior with that encountered in art historians can actually be found in architects as studied by Makri and Warwick [24]. According to the authors [24, p. 1758], who examined the information seeking and use behavior of architects, one basic characteristic of the discipline, in general, but also of the behavior of scholars was creativity; for example, students in their research mentioned how the discovery of particular resources in their field inspired them with ideas for their current or future projects. Thus, it was argued [24, pp. 1767–1768] that the electronic resources and systems which are intended to support this type of behavior should be designed to enhance this fundamental quality of the research in the field.

One of the frameworks that Makri and Warwick [24] used for identifying and analyzing this type of behavior in architects was Shneiderman's Genex framework [34, pp. 119–124] which is considered appropriate for understanding creative information work. This framework includes four creative activities with regards to information - collect, relate, create and donate - and potential tasks associated with them [in 24, p. 1750]. Shneiderman, though, suggested that these activities are non-linear and creative work may entail going back to previous stages when required or include repetitive tasks [in 24, p. 1750].

However, the relevance of this framework for this paper lies in the fact that art history is a highly creative discipline, which as we said before uses art works not only as information objects but also as a source of inspiration. Therefore, from the perspective of Shneiderman's framework, it can be argued that the gaining of information from artworks - information that work as inspiration drive for information seeking at the initial stages of art historical research - can constitute a task that belongs to the collect activity. An additional remark here may be that this particular role of artworks as inspiration for further information seeking should be taken into account when designing digital tools and services for supporting art historical scholarship.

Continuing with the examination of the first stages of the research process in art history, Bailey and Graham [2] suggested that the types of information objects required each time for conducting a project in the field, as well as the way the research will continue, are determined by the research subject. At this early stage of research, Bakewell et al. [3, p. 111] argued that every possible resource may prove useful. However, when art historians start looking for information to support their research questions, they have to deal with a variety of difficulties. As mentioned earlier, the diverse information objects that scholars need are usually scattered all over the world; thus, travel becomes an inevitable part of the research process in the discipline. Yet, although digitization of information and the provision of online access to material have not yet managed to replace this need to travel, they have considerably reduced the time to seek and discover the necessary resources [also in 32, p. 40].

Regarding the practices employed for finding information, chaining and browsing are those preferred in the discipline. In fact, this is one of the reasons why Beaudoin [5, pp. 34–35] argued that art historians' information seeking behavior matches Mann's [25] 'Subject or Discipline Model' and 'Library Science Model' of information seeking as well as Bates' [4] 'berrypicking' model. According to these models, the great reliance on libraries for browsing material and the use of bibliographies, citations, indices and abstracts for tracking resources are among the characteristics fitting art historians' information seeking behavior.

To begin with, chaining is a significant information seeking activity in art historical research and it is usually carried out through, principally, textual resources such as books, articles, bibliographic catalogues, references and footnotes [also see 8, p. 126]. In addition, art historians prefer to use chaining not only for finding relevant research material, but also for staying up to date with the latest news in their field [2, p. 752]. In the digital environment, various databases, such as indices and online catalogues, have been designed to meet these specific needs [12, pp. 225–226, 31, pp. 737–741].

Regarding browsing, it tends to be a popular activity among Arts & Humanities scholars and has been traditionally conducted in libraries around the world. Brockman et al. [9, p. 13] argued that this is because printed versions of books and journals are to a great degree suitable for browsing and easy to use. Yet, it is well known that art historians are especially interested in browsing databases containing digital surrogates of artworks; in fact, they constitute one of the primary places of interest for searching visual material.

Also, this activity, as Palmer et al. observed, differs from the other information seeking activities; 'browsing tends to be open ended with the searcher looking through a body of assembled or accessible information' [28, p. 13]. Furthermore, as browsing

> [...] tends to be broad and flexible, scholars encounter materials that would not be found through searching or chaining, and the new information may stimulate unexpected and fortuitous intellectual connections [28, p. 14].

In that way, browsing enables serendipitous discovery [see also 12, pp. 217–218, 28, p. 14], a valuable aspect of information seeking to bear in mind when designing digital tools and services for enabling information searches.

Finally, networking and informal communication with colleagues are practices that are commonly employed across Arts & Humanities to discover information. Regarding art history, Stam [35, pp. 28–29] referred to the communication between colleagues in the field as the 'invisible college', constituting an important part of the information seeking behavior of art historians. Being in the digital age, these activities are supported by a range of tools and services. E-mail, discussion lists, forums, blogs, online conferencing services and other online communities are some of the digital tools and services that enhance these activities and, thus, scholars' information seeking [e.g. see 7, pp. 99–100, 18, pp. 5–6, 20, p. 4].

3   Methodology

This study employed an ethnographic approach to the study of scholarly practices by conducting semi-structured, in-depth interviews with twenty art historians as well as observation of their physical and digital personal information collections in order to identify the particular needs they have when they build them. We argue that personal collections, being at the core of art historians' workspace [also see 23, pp. 23–25], are an important starting point for understanding behavior and practices that are difficult to study otherwise, due to the private nature and the various personal criteria applied.

For the purposes of this project, single face-to-face and Skype interviews with twenty art historians were conducted. These took place from June 2013 to October 2013 and, in terms of format, they were semi-structured, based on an interview guide, while each of them lasted approximately one hour. The interviews were recorded with the written consent of the participants and then transcribed using the Express Scribe software. Moreover, the interviewing phase included, when possible and with the interviewees' consent, observation of the interviewees' personal physical and/or digital collections. Again, when possible, gaining photographs of scholars' collections constituted a part of the observation process.

Regarding the profile of the research participants at the time of the interviews, sixteen were based at UK institutions, while two scholars were based in Europe and another two outside of Europe. Eleven of the participants were female and nine of them male, whereas age was not a prime concern for this study. Moreover, it is worth stating that their technical skills varied from advanced to basic. Also, the interviewees were at different career stages and, thus, they ranged from established academics to PhD students, early career researchers as well as independent scholars.

We were particularly interested in creating a pool of interviewees consisting of two groups; one where scholars worked on commonly studied areas (e.g. various areas of European art, like Renaissance art) or employed traditional art historical methods (e.g. stylistic analysis, historical investigation) and another where the topics examined (e.g. non-Western art, digital art) or the methods employed (e.g. quantitative, digital) were considered less traditional. Yet, it should be mentioned that this categorization was based on the premise that the practices of scholars in the first group (twelve scholars in this study) had been frequently examined by previous studies in the field while the behavior and needs of those in the latter (eight scholars in this study) had been less studied before [also see 32, p. 37]. Identifying any similarities and differences between these two different groups of scholars could provide a better insight into the needs that art historians in different areas of the field have in terms of resources, tools and services.

Thus, the eras the interviewees explored through their projects ranged from the 14th century to today, including Byzantine art, medieval art, Renaissance, contemporary and modern art, 3D documentation of material cultural heritage, and art history education. As a result, there was large diversity in terms of the objects of study in scholars' work; these ranged from actual objects (e.g. paintings, sculpture, manuscripts) and monuments (e.g. churches) to historical and other issues in relation to art and its artists, such as arts education and the creation of guidelines and standards.

When the transcription phase was completed, and before the analysis stage, the transcripts were sent to the participants who confirmed the accuracy of their content. The analysis of the interviews was conducted using the NVivo software for qualitative research and the transcripts were coded according to a grounded theory approach. We started with axial coding, through identifying themes, categories and sub-categories in the data as well as specifying their properties. Then, selective coding was considered necessary for creating links between the different themes and categories and refining the codes until the issues raised during their analysis were of satisfying quality and depth and could be used to answer the study's research questions. The analysis procedure was complemented by the memos (reflective notes) that were kept during the coding process and the photographs and the notes taken during or after the observation which worked as a method for achieving triangulation, and thus, more accurate results.

To conclude, it may be useful to note that a theoretical framework consisting of empirically tested information behavior models was used to analyze the interview and observation data. The models that enabled us to develop a sound understanding of art historians' information behavior included Ellis's [15] features of information seeking, along with the additional features presented by Meho and Tibbo [26]. Ellis's and Meho and Tibbo's models, in particular, were useful for identifying the distinctive behavior of art historians in terms of the way they look for information during the initial stages of their research. Furthermore, Kuhlthau's Information Search Model (ISP) model [21], which is concerned with the cognitive aspects of information seeking, was valuable for understanding the reasons behind certain decisions that scholars made when interacting with digital resources and facilitated our exploration of the scholarly practices that follow information discovery. Shneiderman's framework, on the other hand, enabled the interpretation of our data concerned with the creative interactions of scholars with information. Finally, given the fact that we used scholars' personal collections of information to examine how art historians collect, use and manage information for research and teaching, Palmer et al.'s [28, pp. 16–19] scholarly activities and primitives were fundamental for examining the practices (gathering and organizing) related to the building of personal collections.

4 Results

4.1 Accessing Digital Material

Generally speaking, many of the interviewees participating in this project tended to start their research online [as also in 1, p. 282] or from their personal collections and the material they had usually at their home office; then, if considered necessary (based on the factors and criteria that will be discussed later), would choose to visit specific resources in person. Regarding the information seeking practices followed by art historians in this study, it can be argued that chaining and browsing were the two most commonly employed. Also, colleagues constituted an important part of the initial stages of research, from the understanding of the topic under study to the finding of the necessary information, especially in the cases where scholars were faced with challenges during its discovery and access.

Thinking about the types and formats of the information objects utilized by art historians in this study, they were to a great extent similar to those from previous studies [e.g. see 31, pp. 734–735, 32, p. 37]. Yet, since some of our interviewees were conducting non-traditional research, non-common types of information objects were also employed, such as 3D models and visualizations, mailing lists, or internet artworks which often raised different issues and requirements when compared to those more traditionally employed (as it will be shown later). Although the diversity of resources used for research and teaching in the field of art history was something that, to a large extent, was expected, there are several issues with regards to this finding that are worthwhile discussing further.

Firstly, it should be highlighted that the original artworks and other objects of study in their original form - these could include monuments, manuscripts, Japanese hand-scrolls - the primary resources, such as archival material, and visual surrogates (physical or digital) were the information objects with the greatest significance for these scholars, confirming in that way several earlier studies whose findings were presented earlier [e.g. see 3, 5, 7, 13]. For instance, as Participant 04 (categorized as conducting traditional research) clearly explained, an art object or an image could provide the inspiration for kick-starting the actual research on a project.

> Personally, I tend to start with objects or images. So, an interest will often be sprung by looking at an image - often online just because it's easy to access - either in an image library or normally a museum website. [Participant 04]

This quote brings to mind Makri and Warwick's [24, p. 1758] finding about the inspirational effect that information had on the work of the postgraduate architecture students in their study. By using Shneiderman's Genex framework [34, pp. 119–124] to interpret the data collected in our study, we were able to suggest that art history, as in the case of architecture, is a highly creative discipline; in fact, as scholars reported, information found online could trigger new ideas for current and future projects.

Continuing, many of the art historians in this study tended to be aware of, at least, the main places they had to visit (digital or physical) to find information related to their work. This behavior, which was mostly based on previous experience and habit, was complemented by other information seeking practices (e.g. consulting colleagues) in order to eliminate the chances of missing other useful resources they were not aware of. Yet, knowing where to start looking for information that is relevant to one's topic did not necessarily mean that the process to access it was easy. More specifically, travelling was a choice many had to make for consulting not only primary resources, but secondary as well. Participant 08 (categorized as conducting non-traditional research), who was researching 19th century Japanese painting, had, amongst other places, to visit Japan, since part of the information needed was not accessible in any other way.

> And so, I've got all of that in Japan because it's very hard to get those books here. [...] I'm reading as well manuscripts, handwritten books, as a sort of social context. [Participant 08]

This issue generates questions regarding the extent to which information resources available online - even when including secondary material - meet the needs of scholars in the various sub-disciplinary areas of art history, like non-Western art. Actually, the art period a project was looking at, the geographical focus of its subject (e.g. non-Western art) or the fact that the topic under investigation may have not been researched before were often connected to issues of availability of resources, conveniently accessible to scholars.

Another interesting aspect of the findings in terms of the online places visited in the context of research was the fact that social media and social networks (specifically Facebook, Twitter and YouTube) proved places where scholars researching particular topics could find information that was hard to find anywhere else. This could include documentary videos, interviews and other oral history types of information about people, objects and practices which could be discovered either through searching or by asking relevant community groups. Yet, although there are several studies focusing on humanists' behavior [e.g. 30, 33], there is limited understanding of how social media, social networks or blogging are used by art historians in the context of the research process, e.g. during information-seeking, which is a topic worth examining further in future research.

Concerning the digital collections used by scholars in the field of art history, it may be worth noting that only one of the interviewees referred to any of the large, collaborative, European online initiatives which enable the discovery of primary and secondary material. In this one case, Participant 09 (digital art historian) referred to Europeana Regia (containing manuscripts); however, the brief commentary below suggested that the design of the resource might not fit the needs some of the art historians interested in manuscripts might have.

The ways you can search are very limited and it's very rare actually to find a project that has been created with the end user in mind. [Participant 09]

Despite the challenges, digital resources and services were useful when scholars did not have a concrete idea of the kind of information they were looking for or where exactly to find it. Participant 17 (digital art historian) shared the reasons why they find particular resources helpful under such circumstances.

There are bodies of work that I remember even if I don't remember about exactly how I'm going to find them or where they are. Resources like Rhizome are really useful because for a long time they archived a lot of Internet artworks. So that's a good cause of call which is as similar as it gets to going to an art gallery because I can look of an artwork in that archive but I can also more often than not find discussion that surrounds that artwork. [Participant 17]

Thinking further about the reasons why scholars may prefer to start their research on a project online, apart from the lack of geographical limitations, it seems that the possibility of a serendipitous discovery that such a choice may entail is considered an important factor. For example, Participant 04, while talking about image search, underlined the fact that using Google Images may lead to unexpected findings.

Normally, it's museum websites. [...] But I suppose Google Images throws up stuff that you might not have known otherwise. [Participant 04]

Also, Participant 03's (categorized as conducting traditional research) account of the way they look for material on the Web may suggest that serendipity can influence the material that is going to be collected in the context of a research project.

I mean, there are a lot of these very early texts, these are Victorian texts, all do these seem to be often on the Web somewhere, but I don't intend to go looking for them now. If they come up, I'll go for them [unclear]. But I don't tend to go looking for them. [Participant 03]

Concerning the issue of serendipity, more specifically, several studies have looked into its role in scholarly practice and examined whether it can be supported by information systems. For instance, Foster and Ford [16] studied serendipity in the context of the information seeking behavior of interdisciplinary scholars (including Arts & Humanities) and suggested that further examination is needed in order to understand that phenomenon which, as they argued, is '[...] a difficult concept to research since it is by definition not particularly susceptible to systematic control and prediction' [16, p. 337].

Thinking about the findings presented here, several of the art historians provided examples illustrating the fact that serendipity can be experienced not only through the use of conventional formats, but through the use of digital services as well. More specifically, it can be argued that the issue of serendipity was more likely to occur during the first stage of information seeking when scholars attempted to investigate a topic. On the other hand, encountering interesting information was more difficult during the later stages of research when scholars were looking for more specific and focused information to support and enhance their argument. Also, the fact that some areas of research were found to benefit from a larger pool of online resources cannot be overlooked when considering the possibilities of discovering information serendipitously. Yet, given the limited information available with regards to this aspect of information behavior of art historians, further exploration will certainly prove valuable for increasing the positive impact that digital resources can have on research and teaching in the field.

4.2 Using Digital Resources

4.2.1 Criteria for Choosing Resources

In this section, the aim is to present the factors which influenced scholars' behavior when choosing resources to use as well as the actions that followed the discovery of information, highlighting the impact that digital resources and libraries can have on the research process. To begin with, convenience was one of the issues that influenced researchers' decisions with regards to which places to visit and it was often associated with easy access to digital and physical resources provided by the places where the scholars worked or studied.

On the other hand, and particularly when the place they were based did not offer a good variety of resources, scholars tended to visit other places which were either geographically close to them or were considered worth visiting for particular reasons. In the latter case, the most common reason was the degree to which the material that could be found at a specific library, museum or archive (physically or digitally) was relevant to the topic researched or taught; the accessibility of this material, especially in relevance to cost (due to travel or copyright issues); breadth and quality of material; and reliability of source.

Considering the visual resources, in particular, although the factors described previously applied in this case as well, accessibility in relation to cost incurred by copyright reasons and quality of material available were often two of the most important criteria scholars took under consideration when looking for related material. Thinking about reliability as a factor for choosing the resources to be consulted and the material to be used and quoted in the context of research or teaching in the field, art historians participating in this study explained their criteria for trusting information. Based on our findings, trusting the author or the institution providing the information were the two paramount criteria for scholars when deciding upon the resources to be consulted and used. Other criteria included trusting the publisher or particular resources frequently used in academia (e.g. JSTOR). Additionally, previous experience and intuition often came up as the researcher's tools when evaluating the trustworthiness of a resource.

However, there were some cases where the above criteria were not enough in order to judge the reliability and quality of a resource. For instance, according to Participant 07 below (categorized as conducting traditional research), language can pose its own challenges when scholars attempt to make related judgements.

> I think I had a specific challenge like anyone who is working across languages and working across different areas of scholarship. Spanish scholarship is very different. The approach to scholarship is very different than in the English language and I think I struggled with that at first because it's not my first language and it's hard to tell from the quality of writing; that's often a good gauge in a sense that someone is writing comfortably about something and you can get a sense of it. [...] But I didn't have that advantage with Spanish. [Participant 07]

In the case of this participant, it is worthwhile underlining the connection between the interdisciplinary nature of research and the challenges posed by it, such as those described in terms of language, which inevitably increases the degree of complexity when looking for information and, thus, may imply particular information needs. As Palmer and Neumann [27, p. 107] argued, translation can complicate information seeking and gathering as well as other scholarly practices (e.g. reading) and, therefore, there is greater necessity to understand the information practices and needs of scholars in the Arts & Humanities conducting interdisciplinary research. Furthermore, research projects examining non-traditional topics such as internet art, which may require the consultation of non-traditionally used resources (e.g. mailing and discussion lists) may lead to alternative methods for confirming the reliability of such information; in the case of Participant 17, a method for checking the trustworthiness of the discovered material was to contact the responsible people (e.g. artists).

> In terms of trusting resources, I suppose because I studied Internet Art, a lot of material that surrounds Internet Art, a lot of the online mailing list based discussion was not especially deliberately falsified; there were lots of text based stands where artists were using discussing spaces to create alternative histories. [...] So, it's harder for me to assume that something is valid just because it exists, like I can't say 'Oh, it's in a book, therefore the publisher and various other people have agreed to this'. So I probably then got a lot of the time to go and talk to the people who were involved. [Participant 17]

Finally, aspects of the design of a resource, such the way digitization has been conducted or its interface, and the experience it offered, as a result, to the user was a factor influencing scholars' information behavior. Participant 09, based on their experience with online collections containing digitized material, gives an example of potential problems that can be encountered when using a digital resource, while Participant 03 explains why they avoid using particular resources.

> I mean, I have a manuscript in Rome. It's held in another library, not in the Vatican, and they have digitized their collection, but for some reason that I'm still trying to understand they have digitized only the decorated part of the page. So, basically I get a decorated initial and I cannot read the text. [...] There are choices that have been made online that to me are completely absurd. [Participant 09]

Therefore, such issues were not only the reasons some scholars preferred to consult an art object in person, but they could also constitute factors influencing their decisions as to which resources to use more generally.

4.2.2 Gathering Information

Thinking about art historians' behavior after the discovery of information, Palmer et al. [28, p. 16] highlighted our limited knowledge around practices such as the gathering and organizing of information, along with any patterns in scholarly behavior. Gathering particularly can be challenging to study; the reasons why scholars decide to gather specific information the moment they discover it as well as in what fashion they collect it are details that are difficult to capture. However, the analysis of the interviews brought up several issues regarding the actions of scholars after information discovery.

Generally speaking, art historians in this study collected any material they considered of importance for the purposes of their projects at that time or in the future; this finding is in accordance with earlier studies about Arts & Humanities scholars' gathering habits [e.g. see 28, pp. 16–17]. Yet, the design of this study and the employment of relevant information behavior models enabled the identification of a pattern in their gathering behavior not previously recorded. Starting with Kuhlthau's Information Search Model (ISP) [21, pp. 366–368], and comparing the behavior of the art historians' participating in this study to the different feelings, thoughts, actions and tasks associated with each stage of the model,[1] it was decided that the *exploration* and *collection* stages would constitute our main focus. This is because these stages and their properties were most relevant to explain the patterns identified in our data and, more specifically, the fact that our participants' gathering behavior tended to consist of at least two main phases (see Table 1 below). Although in Kuhlthau's model the gathering of information takes place only when the user has developed a certain confidence in their topic and, thus, it is naturally more focused, art historians in this study began gathering material much earlier, at the time resembling Kuhlthau's exploration stage (when uncertainty is more common).

Table 1. The gathering phases and their characteristics

Characteristics	Exploratory gathering (1st phase)	Focused gathering (2nd phase)
Action	Seeking & gathering relevant information	Seeking & gathering focused information
Task	Investigate/explore the topic	Build/enhance the research argument (often during writing)
Stage of research	Early	Progressed
Type	Non-selective	Selective/discriminate
Intensity	High	Low
Information amount	Large	Small
Feelings	Uncertainty/frustration	Sense of direction
Effect on personal collections	Creation & initial organisation of information	Further information organisation/re-structuring

Indeed, apart from being conducted in the context of exploring a new topic at the beginning of research, this first phase of gathering was often a result of the feelings associated with the obstacles (e.g. frustration due to limited access) encountered during the information seeking process (corresponding to Kuhlthau's exploration stage), making the need to gather as much as possible (digitally and physically) more intense. Then, a more focused gathering phase was identified which often took place at a more progressed stage (after reading and during writing) of the research (especially in the cases where projects lasted for a long time) and it bore similarities to Kuhlthau's

---

[1] The stages included in the ISP model are: initiation, selection, exploration, formulation, collection, presentation. Each stage has associated feelings, thoughts, actions and tasks and can be found in Kuhlthau [21, p. 367].

collection stage. Yet, as Kuhlthau argued, it is possible for users to gather information during various stages of the research process based on their particular behavior and needs, while entering the writing stage as well as conducting an initial organization of the collected material may enable them to develop this more focused approach which leads to a second phase of gathering [21, pp. 368–369].

Therefore, after using Kuhlthau's ISP model to closely examine the behavior of art historians that followed the discovery of information and identifying the impact that the challenges associated with digital resources can have on this process, a variation of the model was suggested. This should include an additional gathering task at the exploration stage called Exploratory Gathering which will follow the Exploratory Information Seeking conducted beforehand. Moreover, the second gathering task (with the same characteristics as the one described in the model) can be named Focused Gathering and will come after the Focused Information Seeking.

This finding was also examined from the perspective of other information seeking studies which include aspects of information collection in their models (e.g. information gathering, information managing), such as Shneiderman's framework (2000) or Meho and Tibbo's [26] extended version of Ellis's information seeking model. More specifically, based on the assumption that there are two - at least - distinct stages of information seeking (of different nature and with different purpose) preceding the different gathering phases, we can then talk about repetitive tasks or a need to go back to a previous stage and, hence, refer to Shneiderman's framework [34, pp. 119–124]. Shneiderman suggested that non-linearity or repetitive tasks can be part of the information seeking behavior in creative areas while users can have different needs during these tasks. Having argued that art historical practice could be characterized as creative, especially in terms of its interaction with information, these observations suggest that art historians have different information needs during the different phases of their information seeking and gathering activities. This finding constitutes an addition to our current knowledge about the information seeking and gathering behavior of art historians and should be taken into consideration when designing digital resources and tools to support scholarship in the field.

Finally, if we consider art historians' behavior during the exploratory stage in more detail (as noted previously), gathering information indiscriminately early in the research process can pose information management challenges for scholars later in their research and have an impact on other scholarly activities (e.g. reading, writing). As discovered in this research, scholars often had to take action with regards to the management of the collected material, and sometimes even discard information, in order to be able to use it effectively. This observation, then, brings to mind Meho and Tibbo's [26, p. 584] argument about information managing; even though it is not considered an actual information seeking task, information managing is an essential activity in the cases where personal collections play an important role in the research process (as in the case of the art historians in our study), since it can affect other scholarly practices and tasks conducted in the context of research, such as information retrieval (in personal collections). Thus, understanding that the problems that art historians face with regards to the use of digital resources can have an impact on different stages of the scholarly workflow is a necessary step towards meeting their needs and improving the research process.

5   Discussion

To begin with, it is necessary to re-state that previous studies' findings on the limited access to useful resources, such as good quality visual information, that their participants were experiencing [e.g. 17, 32] were again validated in this research. Despite the progress that digitization projects have made over the years and the increase in the availability of online material, it became evident that scholars lack digital access, particularly to primary resources and good quality, open access visual material.

More specifically, interviewees in some areas of study, such as Asian and Japanese art, faced greater difficulty in finding these types of material online; unsurprisingly, the availability of digital resources on the Web tended to be greater in areas dealing with Western art of particular popular eras (e.g. Renaissance art, 18th and 19th century art). It should be highlighted that the call to conduct such an examination was first mentioned in Rose [32, p. 41] and has not been explored by other studies looking at the information practices of art historians since then. Also, it should be noted that research focusing on modern and contemporary art would be significantly enhanced by resources which could bring material useful to researchers (e.g. material already available on the Web) together in one place; given that these areas are constantly being shaped by new research, scholars need to be continually updated with regards to new material in their areas of interest. Moreover, since research on the areas described earlier (Non-western art, modern and contemporary art) has been found to be on the rise [see, for example, 23, p. 17], issues of accessibility to resources that meet these art historians' needs become more pressing.

Given the issues stressed so far, it was inevitable that easy access to material (including costs of copyright) would be one of the primary criteria for the research participants when choosing resources to access online and use. The institutions where most of them were based or other easily accessible and frequently visited places (e.g. libraries, museums, archives) were some of the key access providers to material relevant to scholars' projects which had also earned their trust. Previous experience with a resource (or similar resources) and the researcher's intuition were also influential factors when deciding which resources to visit virtually or physically.

Also, it should be highlighted that the problems often faced when interacting with digital resources during these first stages of research were found to affect the gathering behavior of scholars in the field. Thus, art historians often felt the need to collect as much material as possible at the beginning of a project; yet, gathering information indiscriminately early in the research process (from the exploratory stage) could pose challenges for scholars later in their research (e.g. information management) and have an impact on other scholarly activities, such as reading, writing. The variation of Kuhlthau's [21] model presented here aimed to highlight the different needs that art historians can have during different stages of the research process and suggests that digital resources should be built accordingly to meet their requirements.

Thinking about other criteria for choosing resources to use, it is worth further highlighting the issue of language which constituted a consideration for scholars who often researched on highly interdisciplinary topics across the Arts & Humanities. Actually, whenever the gathering of this type of material was regarded as essential for the purposes of a project, the challenges posed could affect other information and scholarly practices; for example, the information seeking process could be postponed until the attainment of the required language skills. Given that art history is a highly interdisciplinary field in terms of topics studied and methods employed, it became clear in this study that barriers posed by language could influence the research process, an additional issue to take into account when creating resources targeted to art historians in the digital age.

On the other hand, there were cases where participants reported gaining inspiration to start researching on a topic through finding images in places such as digital libraries. In fact, this possibility of a serendipitous discovery was one of the reasons that many of these art historians preferred to start their research online. Thus, it is worth highlighting the positive effect that access to good quality digital resources (e.g. image libraries) can have on initiating the research process, through enabling the identification of a topic or triggering further information seeking activity. Managing to facilitate serendipity through the provision of appropriate tools and services will significantly enhance scholarship in the field.

Moreover, the use of social media and social networks as resources for finding information related to a research project was a discovery not encountered in previous studies looking at the information practices of scholars in the field. Although art historians were generally hesitant towards the use of these types of resources, they were keener to employ them when there was a general lack of resources in their area of study or when they constituted the only way to find out about specific information. However, despite the frequent study of the use of these services - especially for scholarly communication purposes - in other areas of the Arts & Humanities [e.g. see 30, 33], there has been little research examining the different uses and the impact of these types of digital media and services on art historical scholarship.

Finally, it is worth closing by mentioning again some of the participants' comments about the apparent interpretative choices that had been made to the content of specific digital resources or to the searching problems encountered due to the way that the material was classified and catalogued. In fact, as became evident through the interviews, such editorial choices could reduce the usefulness of the digitized content for scholars, who would then look for another resource online or, if possible, visit the resource physically. Therefore, incorporating scholars' (as the potential users) views early on in the digitization process (e.g. through understanding their needs), providing essential information about some of the core choices that have been made during the building of a digital resource as well as gaining user feedback about aspects of the interface design, will not only increase its usefulness for scholars and earn their trust but can also prove beneficial for the longevity of this resource.

6   Conclusion

To conclude, the results of this study suggested that scholars in the field become increasingly aware of the effect that digital technologies can have on their work, from the seeking of the information to the analysis of their data. Additionally, it became apparent that, although they tend to employ a wide range of resources in their daily work routine, the different behavior and needs of the various sub-disciplinary groups remain understudied. However, by using scholars' personal collections of information as a starting point for exploring how they access and use digital resources in research and teaching, we managed to uncover aspects of disciplinary scholarly practice rarely discussed before.

More specifically, the finding concerning the impact that the design of a digital resource (beyond its searching capabilities) can have on whether scholars in the field would use a specific resource was an issue that has not been raised before. Also, social media have started to emerge as places where art historians' actively look for information, especially when they face problems accessing other resources; given that our awareness around art historians' engagement with social media is limited, this finding furthers our knowledge of this aspect of scholarly research. Moreover, at least two different stages of information seeking were found to occur in the course of a project where scholars had different information needs during each of them, a new discovery which has direct implications for digital resource design. Lastly, by employing of Kuhlthau's [21] ISP model as the basis for building this argument, we achieved to extend and vary it.

Overall, the findings presented in this paper have enhanced our understanding of some of the core information practices associated with the discovery of information and the steps that follow this; in that way, they contribute to our knowledge about the requirements that art historians have at the early stages of research and beyond as well as the criteria upon which their decisions are made when interacting with digital resources and libraries, which have been underexplored. Finally, this paper has hopefully brought to the fore issues for consideration for information professionals and other scholars interested in understanding and supporting art historical scholarship with appropriate tools and services in the digital age.

References

1. Antonijević, S., Cahoy, E.S.: Personal library curation: an ethnographic study of scholars' information practices. portal: Libr. Acad. **14**(2), 287–306 (2014)
2. Bailey, C., Graham, M.E.: The corpus and the art historian. In: Thirtieth International Congress of the History of Art. Art History for the Millenium: Time, London, UK, 3–8 September 2000. International Committee for the History of Art (CIHA) (2000). https://unites.uqam.ca/AHWA/Meetings/2000.CIHA/Bailey.html
3. Bakewell, E., Beeman, W.O., Reese, C.M.: Object, Image, Inquiry. The Art Historian at Work. J. Paul Getty Trust, Los Angeles (1988)
4. Bates, M.J.: The design of browsing and berrypicking techniques for the online search interface. Online Rev. **13**(5), 407–424 (1989)
5. Beaudoin, J.: Image and text: a review of the literature concerning the information needs and research behaviors of art historians. Art Doc.: J. Art Libr. Soc. North Am. **24**(2), 34–37 (2005)
6. Beaudoin, J.E., Brady, J.E.: Finding visual information: a study of image resources used by archaeologists, architects, art historians, and artists. Art Doc.: J. Art Libr. Soc. North Am. **30**(2), 24–36 (2011)

7. Beeman, A.: Stalking the art historian. In: Shields, M.A. (ed.) Work and Technology in Higher Education: The Social Construction of Academic Computing, pp. 89–102. Lawrence E. Earlbaum, Montclair (1995)
8. Brilliant, R.: How an art historian connects art objects and information. In: Stam, D.C., Giral, A. (eds.) Linking Art Objects and Art Information (1988). Library Trends **37**(2), 120–129
9. Brockman, W.S., Neumann, L., Palmer, C.L., Tidline, T.J.: Scholarly Work in the Humanities and the Evolving Information Environment. Digital Library Federation and Council on Library and Information Resources, Washington, D.C. (2001)
10. Case, D.O.: The collection and use of information by some american historians: a study of motives and methods. Libr. Q. **61**(1), 61–82 (1991)
11. Cuno, J.: How art history is failing at the internet. The Daily Dot (2012). http://www.dailydot.com/opinion/art-history-failing-internet/
12. Dallas, C.: Humanistic research, information resources and electronic communication (1998). http://pandemos.panteion.gr:8080/fedora/objects/iid:773/datastreams/PDF1/content
13. Durran, J.: Art history, scholarship and image libraries: realizing the potential of the digital age (1997). http://www.scribd.com/doc/3799275/Art-History-Scholarship-and-Image-Libraries-Realising-the-Potential-of-the-Digital-Age
14. Elam, B.: Readiness or avoidance: e-resources and the art historian. Collect. Build. **26**(1), 4–6 (2007)
15. Ellis, D.: Modeling the information-seeking patterns of academic researchers: a grounded theory approach. Libr. Q. **63**(4), 469–486 (1993)
16. Foster, A., Ford, N.: Serendipity and information seeking: an empirical study. J. Doc. **59**(3), 321–340 (2003)
17. Greenhalgh, M.: Art history. In: Schreibman, S., Siemens, R., Unsworth, J. (eds.) A Companion to Digital Humanities. Blackwell, Oxford (2004). http://bit.ly/1XdB1Jr
18. Grindley, N.: What's in the art-historian's toolkit? In: A Methods Network Working Paper. AHRC ICT Methods Network, UK (2006)
19. Harmsen, L.: The internet as a research medium for art historians. The Art History Research Centre (1996). http://harmsen.net/ahrc/essay.htm
20. Kamposiori, C., Benardou, A.: Collaboration in art historical research: looking at primitives. Kunstgeschichte, Open Peer Rev. J. (2011). http://www.kunstgeschichte-ejournal.net/157/
21. Kuhlthau, C.C.: Inside the search process: information seeking from the user's perspective. J. Am. Soc. Inf. Sci. **42**(5), 361–371 (1991)
22. Larkin, C.: Looking to the future while learning from the past: information seeking in the visual arts. Art Doc.: J. Art Libr. Soc. North Am. **29**(1), 49–60 (2010)
23. Long, M., Schonfeld, R.C.: Supporting the changing research practices of art historians. ITHAKA S+R (2014). http://www.sr.ithaka.org/research-publications/supporting-changing-research-practices-art-historians. Accessed 30 Apr 2014
24. Makri, S., Warwick, C.: Information for inspiration: understanding architects' information seeking and use behaviors to inform design. J. Am. Soc. Inf. Sci. Technol. **61**(9), 1745–1770 (2010)
25. Mann, T.: Library Research Models: A Guide to Classification, Cataloging and Computers, pp. 9–56. Oxford University Press, Oxford (1993)
26. Meho, L.I., Tibbo, H.R.: Modeling the information-seeking behavior of social scientists: Ellis's study revisited. J. Am. Soc. Inform. Sci. Technol. **54**(6), 580–587 (2003)
27. Palmer, C.L., Neumann, L.J.: The information work of interdisciplinary humanities scholars: exploration and translation. Libr. Q. **72**(1), 85–117 (2002)
28. Palmer, C.L., Teffeau, L.C., Pirmann, C.M.: Scholarly information practices in the online environment. Themes from the literature and implications for library service development. Graduate School of Library & Information Science (GSLIS), Center for Informatics

Research in Science & Scholarship (CIRSS), University of Illinois at Urbana-Champaign. OCLC Research, Dublin, Ohio (2009). https://www.loc.gov/item/lcwa00095544/

29. Promey, S.M., Stewart, M.: Digital art history: a new field for collaboration. Am. Art 11(2), 36–41 (1997)

30. Quan-Haase, A., Martin, K., McCay-Peet, L.: Networks of digital humanities scholars: the informational and social uses and gratifications of Twitter. Big Data Soc. 2(1), 1–12 (2015)

31. Reed, M.: Navigator, mapmaker, stargazer: charting the new electronic sources in art history. Libr. Trends 40(4), 733–755 (1992)

32. Rose, T.: Technology's impact on the information-seeking behavior of art historians. Art Doc. 21(2), 35–42 (2002)

33. Ross, C., Terras, M., Warwick, C., Welsh, A.: Enabled backchannel: conference Twitter use by digital humanists. J. Doc. 67(2), 214–237 (2011)

34. Shneiderman, B.: Creating creativity: user interfaces for supporting innovation. ACM Trans. Comput.-Hum. Interact. - Special issue on Hum.-Comput. Interact. N. Millenn. Part 1 7(1), 114–138 (2000)

35. Stam, D.C.: The information-seeking practices of art historians in museums and colleges in the United States, 1982–83. Ph.D. thesis, Columbia University, US (1984)

36. Zorich, D.M.: Transitioning to a digital world: art history, its research centers, and digital scholarship. Report to the Samuel H. Kress Foundation and the Roy Rosenzweig Center for History and New Media, George Mason University (2012). http://www.kressfoundation.org/news/Article.aspx?id=35338

Virtual Reconstruction as a Scientific Tool:
The Extended Matrix and Source-Based Modelling Approach

Emanuel Demetrescu[✉]

CNR-ITABC, Istituto per le Tecnologie Applicate ai Beni Culturali,
Via Salaria, km 29.3, 00015 Monterotondo, Rome, Italy
emanuel.demetrescu@itabc.cnr.it

Abstract. The focus of this paper is to highlight what are the major theoretical issues of virtual reconstruction in archeology (black-box effect, palimpsest-effect, role of accuracy) and explain how the Extended Matrix approach was designed to respond to these specific needs. The Extended Matrix (EM) is a tool that extends the stratigraphic approach to the recording and managing of the *re-constructive record*: one of the goals of this research is to prove that the stratigraphic method, intended as chronological reading of a spatial context, is able to compose a complete and multidimensional *re-constructive record* through the EM. This approach can improve the quality of virtual reconstructions non only for scientific purposes but also in the industry of Virtual Museums and Digital Libraries.

1 Introduction

Sometimes the virtual reconstruction is used as a final phase that synthesizes the results of an archaeological research. In other cases, it is considered an effective solution for the communication of the intermediate steps of an ongoing project. Finally, it is even carried out without a complete and accurate scientific study because sometimes a suggestive representation of the past seems to be considered "sufficient" for a "general public of non-experts". These scenarios, despite the fact that they can result in very different outputs from a scientific point of view, can generate confusion if they are not correctly recognized. This situation contributes to a widely diffuse perception of the virtual reconstruction as an "aesthetic" endeavor more than a scientific tool (*see* Sect. 3.2).

The focus of this paper is to highlight what are the major theoretical issues of virtual reconstruction in archeology (black-box effect, palimpsest-effect, role of accuracy, *see* Sect. 3) and explain how the Extended Matrix (EM) approach was designed to respond to these specific needs. The EM offers a standardized work-flow and visual tools for analysis, synthesis, data visualization, and publication that are based on the stratigraphic method (temporal reading of a spatial context), and it can be a convenient solution to compose a *re-constructive record* (*see* Sect. 4).

© Springer International Publishing AG, part of Springer Nature 2018
S. Münster et al. (Eds.): UHDL 2017/DECH 2017, CCIS 817, pp. 102–116, 2018.
https://doi.org/10.1007/978-3-319-76992-9_7

2   Related Work

Despite the fact that the practice of virtual reconstruction has a long tradition [17] (*see* Sect. 3.1) and that different digital tools and approaches to record the data provenance have been proposed in the last few years[1] [1,14–16], there is not a shared standard for the documentation of the *re-constructive record* in archeology. There is an approach based on CIDOC-CRM that uses the Cultural Heritage Modeling Language (CHML) [9,10]: unfortunately the CIDOC-CRM has some limitations because it is implemented to describe physical objects and is not intended to describe more abstract and fuzzy concepts like in the case of virtual reconstruction. Other approaches are based on the CHARM abstract reference model and use the ConML language [2,7]. The Extended Matrix language [3,4] is similar to the ConML but is specifically intended to organize data along a time-line, is focused in a meta-data drawing approach trying to simplify the ingestion steps, and is specifically oriented to include the granularity of the stratigraphic record into the *re-constructive* one.

3   Theoretical Issues of Virtual Reconstruction in Archaeology

3.1   The Problem of Reconstruction

Virtual reconstruction is an archaeological/architectonic matter that began a digital matter only in the last decades. Virtual (from the Latin term *virtus*), is a synonym for "potential" and expresses the likelihood of a certain artifact having existed in the past. The reconstruction is not only a digital matter: it started long before the introduction of the computer [17]. The theory of reconstruction in archeology/architecture is well testified by the *Envois de Rome de la Académie de France* (*see* Fig. 1).

The reconstruction pipeline (Fig. 3) starts with the collection on the field of all the information about a monument (survey or excavation). Alongside the activity on the field, all the sources available (ancient drawings, photos, information from very similar contexts) are collected. All these information are stored and organized in a convenient way in the so called *dossier comparatif* [8, p. 322]. The next step is the use of the *dossier comparatif* for the creation of the *eidotipi* (sketches or technical drawings on paper or by means of digital tools [13]) where the hypotheses in the mind of the researcher can be fixed before starting to model in 3D space. The 3D model, in this schematic, seems to be the last step, the output of the whole process. The introduction of digital techniques in archeology stimulated some interesting improvements allowing to use the modeling step as a simulation of the reconstruction. Let us have an example (Fig. 2) from an archaic temple [11]: in the case of the *simae* on the top of the temple, it is possible to make a digital anastilosys using real objects acquired during the 3D

---

[1] For a critical review about data provenance strategies and data granularity in archaeological virtual reconstruction *see* [3, pp. 43–44] and [4, pp. 501–502].

Fig. 1. Virtual reconstruction of the Tabularium in Rome from the XIXth century (Envois de Rome de la Académie de France).

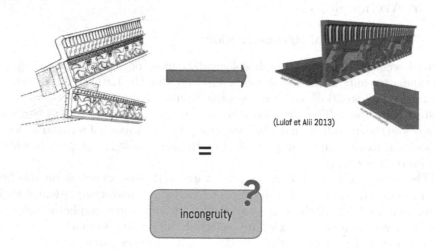

(Lulof et Alii 2013)

incongruity

Fig. 2. Example of incongruity occurence during a 3D reconstruction (*see* [11]).

survey. These elements are placed inside a source based model as a reference during the 3D content creation. During this simulation, something "goes wrong": it is not possible to place it inside the 3D model. It simply does not fit in place like a "wrong" block of a 3D puzzle. Here there is an "incongruity" and, as a result, the 3D reconstruction hypothesis has to be changed. The simulation acts like a test of the quality of the reconstruction: the researcher has to modify something in the *dossier comparatif*, the *eidotipi* or just has to search more (or different) sources.

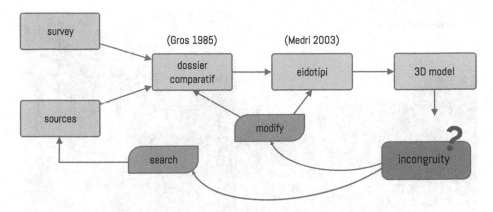

Fig. 3. Archaeological theory in virtual reconstruction.

3.2   Reconstruction is Part of a Scientific Research

When a researcher is dealing with a lacunose system (i.e. a broken ionic capital), it is impossible to interpretate it (and, in some cases, even to describe it) without visualizing in the mind the intact, original object. The reconstruction is part of the research from the earliest stages; it influences the reasoning, the interpretation, and the generalizations which will emerge in the synthesis of the research. For that reason, the reconstruction can be considered a scientific tool able to improve the understanding of a context or phenomenon. A scientific reconstruction is first of all a matter of creating a validated content.

A transparent publication of a re-constructive study can improve the scientific quality of a research and can enable the possibility of the re-use of the "raw" *re-constructive record* in future scientific researches as well as a standardized adoption in several digital outputs like the Virtual Museums or the Digital Libraries.

3.3   The Black-Box Effect (Gap in the Communication
of the Reconstruction Process)

In the case of the reconstruction of the *Templum Pacis* at Fig. 4 the link between the archaeological remains and the source-based model is not easy to figure out.

The process behind the reconstruction is unreadable, it results in a *black box effect*: looking to a 3D reconstruction, several doubts emerge about what is real and what is an invention. It is not clear what is sure, certain and what is just an hypothesis or an "evocative" representation. This happens because in archaeological research, the 3D model is often considered a tool with which to synthesize and convey different elements, each with varying degrees of reliability.

Fig. 4. Templum Pacis, Rome (reconstruction E. Demetrescu, CNR-ITABC).

3.4 The Palimpsest-Effect and the Complexity of an Archaeological Context

Every archaeological/architectonic context shows a stratification of changes and modifications on its surfaces that represents its "history". This phenomenon is the *palimpsest* effect (*pàlin-* again *pseptòs* wrote: wrote again, re-wrote). Let us take an example: it is not enough to take in consideration "a building" in the heritage domain. There are, in the same construction, remains of different "buildings" from different epochs (*see* Fig. 5). In order to enable a reconstruction of a specific epoch it is mandatory to ideally remove all the non coeval physical elements. The same process has to be done with a 3D reality-based model: it is a *digital palimpsest* and has to be segmented using the stratigraphic approach in order to make a virtual reconstruction of a given epoch.

3.5 Scientific Accuracy and 3D Digital Content in Cultural Heritage

As in Fig. 6, the 3D content in cultural heritage can be divided, according to the creation process, into *reality-based modeling* (the digital acquisition through 3D survey of existent archaeological contexts [18]) and *source-based modeling* (virtual reconstruction of "lost" archaeological contexts [3, p. 43]). In the first case the "accuracy" of the model has a *quantitative approach* and can be expressed in real units of measure (i.e. 2 mm) while in the second case the accuracy has a *qualitative approach* and can *not* be expressed in real units of measure since it derives from a blending of different sources (with different reliability degree). In this two scenarios, the digital provenance follows completely different paths.

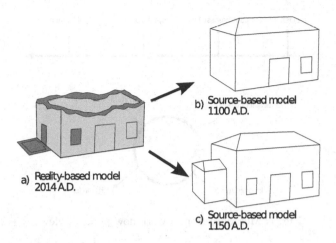

Fig. 5. Palimpsest effect. Every reality-based model can result in different virtual reconstructions, one for each epoch identified in the Extended Matrix.

Meta-Data for Reality Based and Source Based Models. A widely recognized way to annotate the processes behind the creation of 3D models is through a meta-data description. There are however some differences between the reality-based and the source-based approach (*see* Fig. 7). In the first case the steps follow discrete scenarios and has a objective, "closed output" which is not intended to be modified in the future. In the second case, the process is iterative and results in an "open output" that will be likely re-discussed in the future.

In the last fifteen years, several tools have been developed in order to track and manage the information connected to the reality-based models creation. Solid semantic tools like CIDOC CRM or CHARM are present and several shared meta-data schema permit interoperability and dissemination of information.

Some solutions can be derived from these robust 3D survey annotation tools but it is important to take in mind that they are meant to track mainly the digital life of the models, not the archaeological interpretation processes behind the

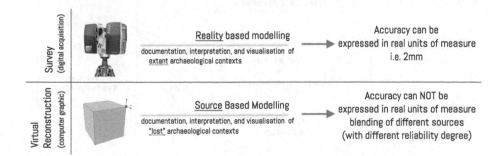

Fig. 6. Accuracy in reality and source based models.

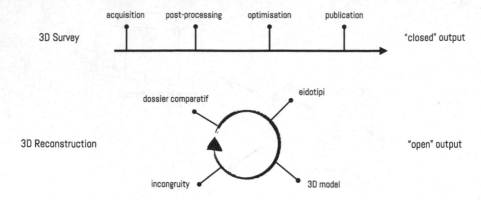

Fig. 7. Metadata from a work-flow point of view

reconstruction: in the case of the annotation of the file creation work-flow, we are able to describe life-cycles of 3D models but there are not standards to annotate the sources used (and the way they are combined together) in order to describe the processes of reconstruction. CIDOC CRM is intended to describe physical collections more than abstract concepts like "virtual" (potential) presence.

It is important to take in mind that in the field of meta-data annotation there are two parallel approaches: (a) the description and

> "[..] management of the life cycle of digital resources, from data creation and management to data use and rights management" ([6, p. 124])

(b) the creation of the re-constructive record (or description of the virtual asset) that is digital-agnostic.

In the first case, the digital source chain description describes events that happen at the time of the research (day of creation of a 3D model using a 3D

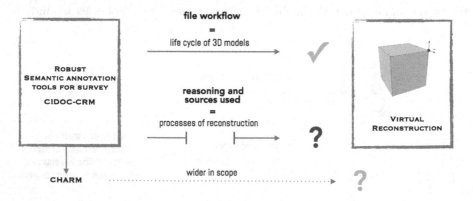

Fig. 8. Semantic tools for reality based models and their applicability to virtual reconstruction

software, the model has been created by the researcher X, etc.). In the second case the historical content chain describes potential (virtual) events happened in the past (construction of a wall, destruction of part of the same wall, first restoration of the wall) (Fig. 8).

4 The Use of the Extended Matrix for the Virtual Reconstruction

The Extended Matrix [3–5] is a formal language with which to keep track of virtual reconstruction processes. It is intended to be used by archaeologists and heritage specialists to document in a robust way their scientific hypothesis. It organizes 3D archaeological record so that the 3D modeling steps are smoother, transparent and scientifically complete. The EM offers a standardized work-flow (*see* Fig. 10) and visual tools for analysis, synthesis, data visualization, and publication. Starting from a stratigraphic reading of masonry (Building Archeology), all the sources used in the reconstruction are provided along (and integrated) with the 3D model. Considering the stratigraphic record as a starting point for the reconstruction process, it is possible to maintain coherence with the level of documentation used during the excavation or the interpretation steps in Building Archeology. The EM (Extended Matrix) has its specific 3D reference in the so-called proxy model, along with the "representation model" (*see* Fig. 9). EM, in combination with 3D models, stores the stratigraphic relations, and enables data-driven representation through computer graphic techniques. All the meta-data are stored in an XML compliant format (GraphML) that permits a graphical data modeling approach and human readable representation of relations and properties (a difficult aspect in meta-data creation is the ingestion process). The XML stores all the reconstruction steps, both the sources used (3D models provenance) and the reasoning involved. It enables a convenient dissemination of the whole 3D reconstruction process for scientific publications, belonging 3D models released as Digital Libraries or inside Virtual Museums.

Fig. 9. Proxy model and representation model related to the II century AC epoch of the Great Temple at Sarmizegetusa.

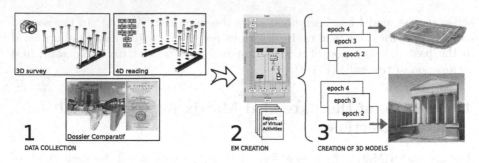

Fig. 10. Production work-flow, from data collection to 3D visualization.

The EM is continuously in development and used in several archaeological researches inside the VHLab of the CNR-ITABC Institute in order to be validated against different scenarios and expanded in its functionalities. Recently, the version 1.1 [4] has introduced a complete support for 3D representation of the validation workflow. Next releases will include software tools (in development) and new solutions for semantic data integration (Open Linked Data, Thesauroi, etc.) and Graph-DB solutions.

4.1 Filling the Black Box Effect Through a Finer Data Granularity and a Standard for Publication

The complexity of the evidences and reasoning behind a virtual reconstruction is a challenge for the standardization of annotation tools.

In literature, one of the most common solution in the management and visualization of reliability is what is generally known as the "generative layers with query-able elements". This approach consists in the segmentation of the model based on the typology and the supposed "degree of certainty" of the sources used in the reconstruction (usually represented with a color scale). It has been tested with different solutions and terminologies, but has not resulted in the creation of a common standard (for a critical state of the art about the methods to validate virtual reconstructions, *see* [3, pp. 43–44] and [4, pp. 501–502]).

All these approaches have a common granularity: the source typology used for the reconstruction hypothesis. Current limitations in the annotation of virtual reconstruction mainly concern this data granularity: in the "source-granularity approach", a reconstruction hypothesis (Fig. 11(a)) is usually segmented (Fig. 11(b)) according to a single source typology (i.e. evidences, analogies - in square brackets). It is a fact that each segment of a reconstruction is not based on a single source but on different sources blended together (i.e. evidences + analogies + general rules - in curly brackets). More, it is possible to state that every source is connected to and validates a specific property (height, width, shape, etc.) of a virtual stratigraphic unit. In Fig. 11(c) and (d) the "property-granularity approach" of the EM provides the details of the sources (and corresponding properties) for each SU.

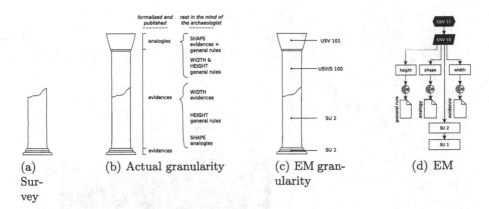

Fig. 11. Current limitations in virtual reconstruction granularity and the EM approach

Publishing a Reconstruction Using the EM. The publication of the reconstructive record involve standardized tools inside the EM work-flow (Fig. 10). The dataset can include more than one reconstructed phase (i.e. roman times, medieval times, etc.). Every epoch is described as a section or chapter and inside this timespan, the Stratigraphic Units and the Virtual Stratigraphic Units are explained as part of Virtual Activities. Every Virtual Activity comes along with a Report of virtual activity, a discursive text that puts into words the reasoning behind the stratigraphic reading and the hypothesis (*see* the Great Temple of Sarmizegetusa in the II century AC at Fig. 12). Every virtual activity is presented with the corresponding portion of EM graph, sections and plans illustrating the *proxy model* and the *representation model* (*see* Fig. 13). The description of virtual activities focuses on portion of the monument/context as likelihood was in the past. They can be integrated with the standard description of activities in the classical publication of an archaeological excavation. In Fig. 14, the site of the great Roman basin found during the excavation for the new Underground of Rome (Metro C) under the scientific direction of Rossella Rea (Superintendence of Rome), is documented both as an excavation (remains found in green) and as a reconstruction hypothesis (in red).

4.2   Managing the Palimpsest Effect: The Stratigraphic Approach and the Matrix of Harris

A very common equivocacy about stratigraphy is that it concerns just earth strata or remains. *Stratigraphy is the grammar used by the Time to write itself on physical elements.* The importance that archaeologists grant to the stratigraphy is directly connected to the need to have a tool as much "wide" as possible in term of semantic representation: dealing with a brush stroke on a canvas (painting stratigraphic annotations from an x-ray image), trees on a landscape, deposits of earth, architectonic elements or graffiti carved in a painted wall, the tool used is the same: the SU. It has a wide scope: it means "result of an action"

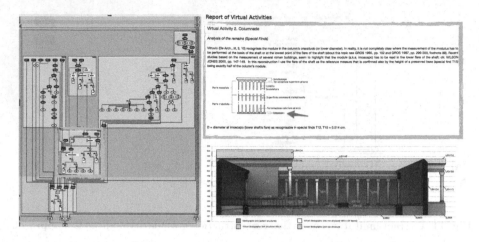

Fig. 12. Extended Matrix with virtual activities (highlighted in grey), report of virtual activities, and proxy model of the Great Temple at Sarmizegetusa in the II century AC.

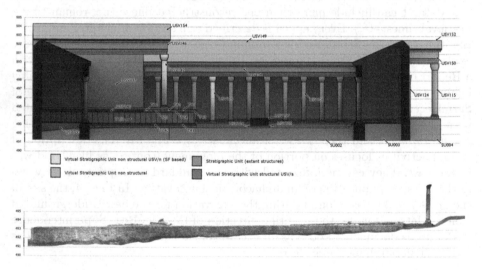

Fig. 13. Proxy model (II century AD) and 3D survey of the Great Temple at Sarmizegetusa.

and it is intended to be applied to every cultural element on a chronological timeline (*see* Figs. 15 and 16). These actions can be natural (earthquake interface of destruction, a tree, an interface of a flooding from the near river) or anthropic (a foundation, a lintel, the decoration of a lintel etc. . .). An interesting thing is that the SU, despite the fact that it can refer to different objects, can have always a precise and actual 4D representation (time and geometry).

When a stratigraphic system results to be intricate, an important step is to reduce its complexity without loosing information.

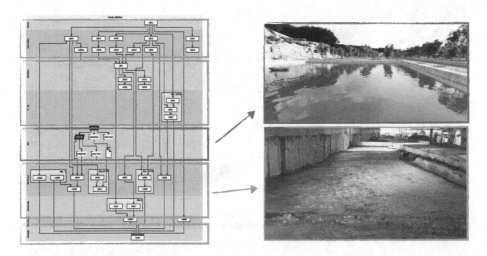

Fig. 14. Extended Matrix, representation model (red) and the state of the site at the time of the excavation. (Color figure online)

A very common way to do this is through the use of the Matrix of Harris, an oriented graph that annotates the chronological relationships between elements (after-before). In the archaeological domain, this is the finest level of granularity about a monument/context.

4.3   Visualize Data Through Graph Based Structures (EM)

In the last years there is and increased adoption of graph databases, especially in scenarios where the connections between the information is a valuable aspect. The visualization of data through graph-based visual structures is the main approach used in data visualization, but has been scarcely involved in the field

small elements   mosaics/paintings   archaeological excavation   architecture/3D survey   vegetation

Fig. 15. Scenarios of application of the stratigraphic reading.

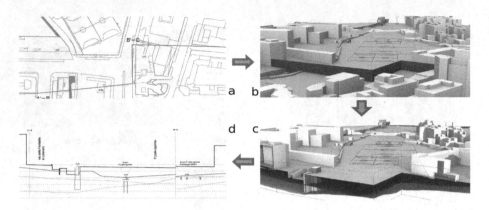

Fig. 16. Extensive reconstruction of stratigraphies at urban scale, Rome

of cultural heritage. Apparently in this domain the elements have a better and more compact representation in forms and tables. When it comes to representing strongly interconnected information (linked data), such as in the case of virtual reconstructions, visual graph databases allow for better adherence to the scientific record [12], better visual appeal, improved effectiveness (for the aesthetic principles for information visualization [19]), and reduced complexity. According to the Steno's vision, every complex system "written" in the historical language of nature has to be studied in its smaller parts and in their mutual relationships. The reciprocal connections between sources, reasoning, and virtual hypothesis can be stored and analyzed within a graph database framework. Unfortunately, a widely diffuse approach to graph databases involves liquid data visualization without the use of a codification for the spatial distribution of the nodes (like in the case of the EM where the y axis is the time-line).

A Schema-Less Database Approach. The Extended Matrix is a semantic graph that leads to a schema-less data model: the reconstructed objects and their descriptive elements are heterogeneously fitted into space and time, in a way that better suits the incompleteness of the historical record. The descriptive elements (EM nodes, *see* [3]) are used as a modular grammar to compose the final description of the reconstruction process (data-driven re-construction). Let's look at an example: I could describe a USV using just the property "material" (i.e. a wooden lintel) because it is the only re-constructive value I am confident in. Meanwhile, in the case of other USVs I may declare more properties, each of which can be validated by different sources. There is no predetermined schema: each USV has its own unique node tree (whiting a common EM data structure) which describes and validates the USV itself.

5   Conclusions

This paper presents a stratigraphic approach to the scientific validation of the virtual reconstruction: the Extended Matrix work-flow. The stratigraphic reading enables the collection of a coherent re-constructive record while the paradata nodes of the EM allow the annotation of the re constructive process. This approach can improve dramatically the use of virtual reconstruction non only for scientific purposes but also in the industry of Virtual Museums and Digital Libraries. In order to better define the innovations of the EM, some key concepts about the classical archaeological theory in virtual reconstruction (black-box effect, palimpsest-effect, role of accuracy) and about the connections between technologies and cultural heritage (meta-data, digital formats, and granularity) are highlighted.

6   Future Works

The Extended Matrix is under active development and has recently reached the 1.1 version with full support to 3D representation.

- In the future, a support for different, self excluding reconstruction hypotheses will be added. In the case where there are more than one possible hypothesis, the EM will help to represent and compare them.
- The scenarios of use of the EM will be categorized with the aim to clarify the limits of applicability in certain typologies of context.

References

1. Apollonio, F.I.: Classification schemes for visualization of uncertainty in digital hypothetical reconstruction. In: Münster, S., Pfarr-Harfst, M., Kuroczyński, P., Ioannides, M. (eds.) 3D Research Challenges in Cultural Heritage II. LNCS, vol. 10025, pp. 173–197. Springer, Cham (2016). https://doi.org/10.1007/978-3-319-47647-6_9
2. Apollonio, F.I., Giovannini, E.C.: A paradata documentation methodology for the Uncertainty Visualization in digital reconstruction of CH artifacts. SCIRES-IT-Sci. Res. Inf. Technol. 5(1), 1–24 (2015)
3. Demetrescu, E.: Archaeological stratigraphy as a formal language for virtual reconstruction. Theory and practice. J. Archaeol. Sci. 57, 42–55 (2015). http://www.sciencedirect.com/science/article/pii/S0305440315000382
4. Demetrescu, E., Fanini, B.: A white-box framework to oversee archaeological virtual reconstructions in space and time: methods and tools. J. Archaeol. Sci.: Rep. 14, 500–514 (2017)
5. Demetrescu, E., Ferdani, D., Dell'Unto, N., Touati, A.M.L., Lindgren, S.: Reconstructing the original splendour of the House of Caecilius Iucundus. A complete methodology for virtual archaeology aimed at digital exhibition. SCIRES-IT-Sci. Res. Inf. Technol. 6(1), 51–66 (2016)
6. Felicetti, A., Lorenzini, M.: Metadata and tools for integration and preservation of cultural heritage 3D information. In: 23rd International CIPA Symposium, pp. 118–124 (2011)

7. Gonzalez-Perez, C., Martín-Rodilla, P., Parcero-Oubiña, C., Fábrega-Álvarez, P., Güimil-Fariña, A.: Extending an abstract reference model for transdisciplinary work in cultural heritage. In: Dodero, J.M., Palomo-Duarte, M., Karampiperis, P. (eds.) MTSR 2012. CCIS, vol. 343, pp. 190–201. Springer, Heidelberg (2012). https://doi.org/10.1007/978-3-642-35233-1_20

8. Gros, P.: Hercule à Glanum: Sanctuaires de transhumance et développement urbain. Gallia **52**, 311–331 (1995)

9. Hauck, O., Kuroczyński, P.: Cultural Heritage Markup Language (2014)

10. Kuroczyński, P., Hauck, O., Dworak, D.: 3D models on triple paths - new pathways for documenting and visualizing virtual reconstructions. In: Münster, S., Pfarr-Harfst, M., Kuroczyński, P., Ioannides, M. (eds.) 3D Research Challenges in Cultural Heritage II. LNCS, vol. 10025, pp. 149–172. Springer, Cham (2016). https://doi.org/10.1007/978-3-319-47647-6_8

11. Lulof, P., Opgenhaffen, L., Sepers, M.: The art of reconstruction documenting the process of 3D modeling: some preliminary results. In: Proceedings of International Conference on Digital Heritage, pp. 333–336 (2013)

12. Mazumdar, S., Petrelli, D., Elbedweihy, K., Lanfranchi, V., Ciravegna, F.: Affective graphs: the visual appeal of linked data. Semant. Web **6**(3), 277–312 (2015)

13. Medri, M.: Manuale di rilievo archeologico. Roma-Bari (2003)

14. Münster, S., Kröber, C., Hegel, W., Pfarr-Harfst, M., Prechtel, N., Uhlemann, R., Henze, F.: First experiences of applying a model classification for digital 3D reconstruction in the context of humanities research. In: Ioannides, M., Fink, E., Moropoulou, A., Hagedorn-Saupe, M., Fresa, A., Liestøl, G., Rajcic, V., Grussenmeyer, P. (eds.) EuroMed 2016 Part I. LNCS, vol. 10058, pp. 477–490. Springer, Cham (2016). https://doi.org/10.1007/978-3-319-48496-9_37

15. Münster, S., Niebling, F.: Building a Wiki resource on digital 3D reconstruction related knowledge assets (2016)

16. Pfarr-Harfst, M.: Typical workflows, documentation approaches and principles of 3D digital reconstruction of cultural heritage. In: Münster, S., Pfarr-Harfst, M., Kuroczyński, P., Ioannides, M. (eds.) 3D Research Challenges in Cultural Heritage II. LNCS, vol. 10025, pp. 32–46. Springer, Cham (2016). https://doi.org/10.1007/978-3-319-47647-6_2

17. Piccoli, C.: Visualizing antiquity before the digital age: early and late modern reconstructions of Greek and Roman cityscapes. Analecta Praehist. Leiden. **47**, 225–257 (2017)

18. Remondino, F., Rizzi, A.: Reality-based 3D documentation of natural and cultural heritage sites-techniques, problems, and examples. Appl. Geomat. **2**(3), 85–100 (2010)

19. Tufte, E.R., Graves-Morris, P.: The Visual Display of Quantitative Information, vol. 2. Graphics press, Cheshire (1983)

Creating Suitable Tools for Art and Architectural Research with Historic Media Repositories

Kristina Friedrichs[1](✉), Sander Münster[2], Cindy Kröber[2],
and Jonas Bruschke[3]

[1] Institut für Kunstgeschichte, Julius-Maximilians-Universität,
Am Hubland, 97074 Würzburg, Germany
kristina.friedrichs@uni-wuerzburg.de
[2] Medienzentrum, Technische Universität Dresden, 01062 Dresden, Germany
[3] Lehrstuhl für Informatik IX - Human-Computer Interaction,
Julius-Maximilians-Universität, Am Hubland, 97074 Würzburg, Germany

Abstract. Due to the ongoing digitization, digital libraries are used more and more by art and architectural historians. Nevertheless, the design of those platforms does not necessarily meet the expectations and user requirements of the scholars. This is especially valid for digital libraries dedicated to historic media such as photography. In this article, we aim to analyze the user community in a first step, in order to see from which fields of interest they come and how far developed their computer affinity is. In a second step, the user requirements of the scholars will be examined, specifically with regard to research questions of architectural history. Based upon those observations, in a third part a possible technical solution will be proposed that could facilitate the work with digital libraries as well as the research process. A case study on the question of the correlation between urban development and the perception of the city will give a further validation of the analytical parts, showing the deficits of yet existing digital libraries and highlighting starting points of further research support.

Keywords: Digital libraries · User requirements · Research tools

1 Introduction

Digital libraries host a continuously increasing number of digitized and natively digital photographs, maps and plans – material that ranks among the main sources for art and architectural historic research. Due to the ongoing digitization, several repositories providing historic media have been developed by the institutions which own the original material, such as libraries, archives or museums. But as the scope of those institutions differs from the needs of the researchers, the extensive digital libraries often do not meet the expectations and requirements of the scholars. Therefore, it is necessary to take a closer look at the art history research process, to identify user groups and their specific needs in order to develop ideas for a technical support through digital libraries. Such support solutions can help to identify the relevant sources, analyze and contextualize them, or compare them with the historical original. Thus, not only the process of finding sources, but also their examination can be fostered.

© Springer International Publishing AG, part of Springer Nature 2018
S. Münster et al. (Eds.): UHDL 2017/DECH 2017, CCIS 817, pp. 117–138, 2018.
https://doi.org/10.1007/978-3-319-76992-9_8

The main focus of this article is to

- Analyze the user groups within the community dealing with cultural heritage, in particular art and architectural heritage researchers
- Identify the user requirements concerning their work with digital libraries
- Suggest a possible technical support for the research on historic visual media
- Validate the findings through a specific research example from the field of urban history.

Therefore, the article will be divided into four parts, each one of them dedicated to the questions enumerated above.

2   A Scope of Users in the Field of Art and Architectural Heritage

2.1   Who are Users?

The actual benefit of applications for users highly depends on usability, suitability and efficiency of the technical solutions [8]. In order to develop and improve tools and applications for visual media research, the demands of the stakeholders need to be identified and distinguished. Therefore, an identification of the target group that relies on images for research is the first step. They will give the relevant insight to e.g. their research abilities, habits and needs as well as the actual motivation, i.e. their research questions and features they value as useful.

Archives and image repositories are usually accessible by everyone for a variety of purposes. Sweetnam provides a general overview of the users of archives which serves as the first narrowing of the target group: (a) professional researchers, (b) apprentice investigators, (c) informed users and (d) general public [1].

The dedicated purposes for accessing archives and repositories are (a) scientific research, (b) pedagogical application and (c) study of historic sites [2]. Our focus in this article is solely on professional researchers as by project design, in particular scholars who place a strong emphasis on media, such as images for their work. Other target groups were examined in another recent study [3].

What else do we know about scholars in the field of art and architectural heritage research? As investigated via a survey involving contributors of major international conference series on digital cultural heritage between 1990 and 2015 [4], a majority of researchers in that field is European and in particular Italian, followed by Germans and Greek (cf. Fig. 1). That provides a clue on information cultures and infrastructure, esp. for technical equipment, literacy or habits of dealing with digital information [cf. 5].

With regards to their disciplinary background, a majority of survey participants are humanists. The high ratio of researchers in that field stood in contrast to our former investigations, where especially the ratio of researchers in computing was much higher [6]. Within the humanities cohort, a majority of around 90% are archaeologists, followed by art historians (cf. Fig. 2). The low number of art and architectural historians found by this survey may be caused by the fact that they rarely publish on international podia [cf. 7]. With regards to methods used by participants of the survey, in particular

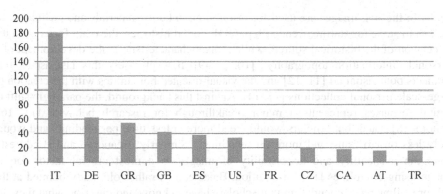

Fig. 1. Nationality (online survey, top 10 out of n = 693)

statistical analysis, computer vision or 3D modelling are of relevance. Vice versa, data of relevance is primarily image and large scale point or polygon data as well as geo-located data and shapes (by GIS) and textual data.

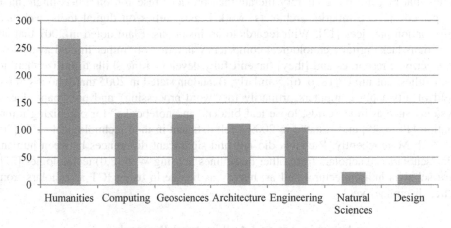

Fig. 2. Disciplinary background (online survey, n = 782)

2.2 Information Search and Retrieval Behavior in Art and Architectural History

How do scholars cope with information and in particular media repositories? Beside the multidisciplinary nature of a community dealing with art and architectural heritage research, many investigations on this topic focus on scholars from arts, architecture and humanities. The meta-analysis by Tenopier on the informational behavior of scholars maintains that the informational behavior [8], and thus also the research process, differs clearly between scholars in different disciplines. Since visual elements and images are important sources for ideation and reflection both in fine arts & architecture and art & architectural history studies, a specific question is about differences between these fields. In the arts, images are used for inspiration, to know materials and techniques as well as to strive for starting trends [9, p. 683]. For art histories, the main focus is on the discussion of the historical source, while a main characteristic is the development of a personal "information topography" [10, p. 49]. It is precisely this last aspect that connects both visual art [11, 12] and the visual-oriented humanities with the creation of large-scale personal collections [13, 14]. Against this background, the paradigm shift to digital resources represents a major breakthrough for research behavior [15, 16]. Tenopir [8] stated that scholars would "read more in less time per reading" and would "rely less on browsing and more on searching". Similarly, Beaudoin and Brady estimate the availability and accessibility of images as a most crucial factor for all image-using disciplines [13]. In addition, Bates et al.'s rather old study pointed at the still prevailing recommendation that scholars have to know and describe what they are searching for by text [15].

2.3   Computer Affinity of Art and Architectural Research Scholars

Since the ICT literacy of scholars from the field of computing is undoubted, previous research draws an uneven picture for other disciplines: For art creating scholars, Mason states that they are more "library-literate than previous research on artists might have suggested" [17]. Similarly, architects' work heavily relies on digital tools, web and information practices [13]. With regards to art historians, Elam noted in 2007 that art historians lack digital technological competency in terms of "rather limited awareness of electronic resources and [they] haven't fully developed the skills to utilize them to their fullest potential" [18, p. 6]. Similarly, Beaudoin stated in 2005 that scholars in the field of arts apply computers primarily for "word processing" and use "paper-based systems such as index cards, loose-leaf binders, and notebooks" for organizing information [19, p. 35] and – stated in 2009 – felt deficient in their technological skills [20, p. 295]. More recently, Pscheida did not find significant differences between humanities scholars and scholars from other disciplines in using Web (2.0) technologies [21]. Are scholars in architectural and art history as literate in using ICT as scholars from other disciplines yet?

2.4   Information Usage in Art and Architectural Research

How do scholars in art and architectural research cope with digital approaches? Especially among scholars in the humanities, in particular art history, there is much discussion [22–25] if there are novel technology-enabled research approaches, where the use of technology raised "new types of research questions" or fostered "new analytic techniques" [26, p. 42]. With specific regards to the importance of images for shaping research, Long stated that scholars are "deeply influenced by the primary sources that they are exposed to during their research process" [26, p. 18]. By empirical means, image users typically seek required images by "following a path that is familiar to them" [20, p. 286] as well as use "subject terms (concept-based for theme, and object-based for thing)" for searching (unfamiliar) repositories [20, p. 297].

3 Identification of User Requirements

The observation that new computer functions are often based upon familiar operating principles is also valid for historic media repositories. Today's vast digitization movement, which started shortly after computers were available to offices, originally aimed at making inventory lists digitally available and therefore accelerate administration. The actual object (e.g. item, image, and book) was not part of that advancement. Disciplines such as art and architectural history were aware of the digitization progress and called out to acknowledge and use the additional value digital images and visualizations hold for their work [35]. Increasing the digitization of historic images as well as objects and information eventually leads to more content available for investigation, the possibility as well as the need for more cross-analyses and more accessible knowledge which needs to be structured and shared [36].

Nevertheless, art and architectural historians, and thus the users, are rarely involved in the conception of digital media platforms. Especially when it comes to gathering and providing access, archives, libraries and museums are responsible for the digital data.

Many scholars relying on visual media note that currently online search for images and information is "counter-productive" due to the large amount of irrelevant data they come across, or due to their limited technical abilities [13]. The degree of search expertise certainly has an influence on research progress and results [31] as well as the implementation of suitable applications and tools for filtering and handling. A lot of the existing tools for searching platforms and applications stem from computer science and neither meet the needs of scholars from humanities [37] nor consider their behavior and skills. Several issues with solutions have been identified that drive users away. Confusing interfaces, difficulties with navigating or searching as well as unsatisfactory content due to e.g. incompleteness or poor quality have been named by users [30]. Unnecessary high numbers of mouse clicks or downloads of browser plugins in order to access information from online media repositories were also noted to be annoying [38].

What may be the functionalities suitable to support research with historical media repositories? User requirements, expectations and behavior should be considered early in a project that aims to develop a good solution. A multi-method user study should involve the user's perspective from the beginning, e.g. when identifying functionalities, and not just at the usability testing stage of a prototype, when the possibility of alteration is limited. This is meant to ensure that new solutions will actually be used, and the project would not have been a waste of resources.

Common requirements of the users may be an ease of understanding concerning the data and knowledge, the development and improvement of tools for accurate search/research as well as an intuitive navigation and interface [2].

Someone vaguely familiar with the object he is interested in is usually in need of a straightforward introduction to the data and topic [39] as well as possibilities to select further material without getting discouraged by an overload of information.

In contrast, scholars will put emphasis on adherence of scientific standards, a thorough documentation through the supply of metadata and the possibility for collaboration and cross-disciplinary work through e.g. annotation. A closer look at research behavior reveals a distinct difference between scientists as well as engineers and scholars from humanities. The first two rely heavily on recent studies and findings whereas the scholars from humanities often reinterpret old sources and revise findings of other scholars [38]. Therefore, sources for humanities research keep their relevance even after years.

3.1 Search and Retrieval

Two different cases of usage are significant for humanities scholars in e.g. art history who carry out a search for digital content within a repository. Either, they are looking for certain content (e.g. a painting usually searched for through the title or artist) for display purposes [40] so they know very well what they need, or they are looking for material connected to their research topic and are not aware of what they will come across.

Several different search approaches support the access for repositories. Most notable are browsing of the content as well as keyword-based or content-based search. Browsing through pictures represented by thumbnails is acknowledged as a thorough way to access an image database [41], and people like to use it for inspiration as well as research [40]. It is very time-consuming considering the amount of digitized pictures image repositories offer today, but is close to the natural search behavior within humanities, where cross-referencing and following footnotes is standard [30]. A more strict and systematic access of image repositories is carried out through a keyword-based search. This calls for the translation of visual needs into text [42]. Some name keyword-based systems as the only successful ones [43] but a search with multiple terms quickly becomes challenging [1]. The keywords for the search have to correspond with the metadata of the content. Hence, a good metadata account and knowledge of it is essential for the success. Also, a structured vocabulary and thesaurus would be beneficial [44]. There are different information the metadata can cover: descriptive, structural, administrative, and information of preservation as well as rights management [45]. A content-based image retrieval relies on the automated analysis of features (e.g. color, texture, shape) and the comparison of image data itself [46]. Automated lower-level feature-based image content analysis can be carried out by a machine but the higher-level semantic content of images still requires human interaction [47] and is usually of more interest for humanities scholars.

In general, a search query addresses two issues: irrelevant items have to be left out in order to maintain a considerably quick review of the results, and relevant items need to be pointed out to ensure an undistorted perception of the data [48]. In computer science, this is referred to as precision and recall, and it becomes even more relevant with the growing amount of digital content.

In order to further narrow down search results, many digital archives offer advanced search functions. Studies have shown that these filter options do not get much attention [49], and a simple Google-like search box is much preferred [30]. However, additional information such as time and location may be used to access media repositories in a GoogleEarth or GoogleMaps-like way [1]. Cognitive load may be reduced by presenting related material in space and time [50], and the context can be grasped more easily [51]. Additionally, a search resembles a content browsing that does not necessarily need keywords.

The search and retrieval step is an essential part of the research process by providing evidence and sometimes revealing new insights. Hence, storing or saving of search results is important not only in order to further use the retrieved material, but also to validate the research process including search and retrieval for argumentation [1]. The obvious solution is to have users register and create a user account when working with the repository. Thus, users can save search queries and material in their personal folders and know their data and findings to be safe [52]. However, a repository user registration at initial access may be counter-productive as it drives away users who first want to assess the quality of its content [3]. Applying a lower threshold in the way of a "shopping cart" function that saves data temporarily on the computer could be a solution. Downloads or bookmarks expect the user to structure the information for further use. Especially a quick and reliable data download in order to use it with other software (e.g. Photoshop and ESRI) for analysis is needed [53]. With the growing technical possibilities and amount of data, support for efficient search and retrieval should be of relevance to repositories [53].

3.2 Manipulation, Interaction, Visualization

Further handling of the data, especially images, is usually done for effect, display, analysis [30] and to produce evidence for research [46]. Zooming has been identified as the essential feature when working with images, together with the enhancement techniques for noise reduction, adjustment of sharpness, brightness color and contrast [38]. General manipulation can be carried out by cropping, using color calibration and correction [46] and even histogram analysis [54]. Some of these effects can be achieved with the help of the software Photoshop, but actual research on image processing aims to develop automated or semi-automated procedures for image manipulation [46]. Thus, the sorting of images, recognition of patterns or features and highlighting within images can support research [30]. Another research approach aims at grouping sets of images for comparison through combining them [40]. Previous steps for such an analysis might be image registration, recognition and segmentation [46]. Consequently, the perspective investigation of paintings becomes possible as does the comparison of 3D wireframe models and photographs [24].

Users as well as the repositories themselves have become aware of the possibilities that collaborations hold, such as peer-to-peer collaboration as well as crowd sourcing [30]. Through comments, feedback and annotation the community is able to further complete the data, but also review research, link different information and engage in quality-assuring discourse. This of course requires the system to ensure control over data access that users provide [53]. Users have to specifically release information for review and also integrate different media for reference.

4 Towards a 4D Web Environment

While the automatic semantic indexing is quite evolved for textual documents [55], it is far more difficult to unlock semantics from images. Images can be indexed by extracting color, texture, and shape features, so images with similar characteristics can be queried [56]. But these content-based image retrieval (CBIR) methods do not extract any semantic information that are interesting to humans. In recent years, machine learning and deep learning techniques have evolved to bridge the gap between "low-level pixels captured by machines and high-level semantic concepts perceived by human" [57]. These techniques, however, need huge training datasets and are very restricted to the data they have learned. There is also some degree of probability to detect and associate wrong features [58]. Processing historical photographs is even more difficult as there is less information available due to the lack of color features.

The ARTigo project [59] chooses another approach: the process of indexing the images is wrapped into an online game, where users can interact with images of artworks. The users' semantic footprints are processed and used to annotate these artworks. Also non-experts can contribute to this so-called "social tagging" approach, so terms that are used by professionals might be missing.

The mentioned methods and approaches strive to enhance the content description of images in order to improve the search results in image repositories. These methods, however, are far from perfect and do not have the capability to determine the creator and dating of an image. The inputs by professionals will still be indispensable.

For historical photographs, an important annotation is the place, where the photograph was taken. However, this annotation is often restricted to the town or city. A more detailed position would be beneficial to users with a less keyword-centered investigation aim in mind or those, who want to get an overview of historical images for a point of interest. Providing spatially and also temporally oriented images in combination with advanced searching and 2D/3D exploring techniques, helping users to navigate to a point of interest, could ease this search process. These oriented images and their visualization in 3D space offer new potentials in supporting historians in their research. Especially in urban areas, where a lot of historical images concentrate, the change of architecture and building situation over time is interesting for experts as well as locals or tourists.

An appropriate application, which offers an intuitive access to those image repositories via suggested features and a 3D city model, is considered to be an enrichment for the scientific community and tourism. As wide accessibility is a modern-day prerequisite, such an application should be a web-based solution.

4.1 State of the Art

While the idea of spatially searching for images is not very new, the combination with 3D city models has not yet been much elaborated. As preliminary work, existing solutions are identified. Challenges and state-of-the-art approaches to aspects that will be central to the proposed application are discussed. The implications will have an influence on a future implementation.

2D map applications. One way of exploring spatially oriented images is the use of interactive 2D maps. Google Maps/Earth and Flickr are just two examples of apps that allow searching images by location. However, these images have to be located by the contributing users and are usually just a modern way of photo albums. Modern handheld devices might even automatically geo-tag taken pictures, but particularly with regard to historical images the respective location has to be reconstructed.

There are a few online platforms which implement interactive 2D maps and focus on historical images, where museums and archives can provide collections of photographs. Users can geo-tag these images [60, 61] or upload own images [62]. Comparison to an equivalent today's view can be realized by contributing re-photographs of the same spot [63], matching the nearest Google Street View location [64], or matching modern photographs by manually stitching several corresponding points [65]. At popular places with many picture entries, the image representations (or markers) are usually clustered to retain clearness.

All of these platforms are implementing Google Maps, OpenStreetMap, or similar map services. However, maps can only visualize the location and orientation of an image or rather the corresponding camera, but not the elevation or tilt. The transfer to Google Street View only works, if the photograph has been taken on a street. References to historic building situations are missing as these maps show only the current state of building. Also, there are not any advanced features available, which would support experts in their research.

Time-varying 3D city models. Introducing the third dimension to such viewers can enhance the visualization of images in relation to the depicted object. The user is not restricted to an orthogonal top view on a map, but can also navigate in custom angles and take up the position and orientation of the camera, respectively the photographer. The user may obtain a more detailed understanding of the distribution of the taken photographs, and a more subtle access to understanding the photographer's intention becomes possible. Additionally extending the map with a 3D model of the area of interest can moreover enhance the understanding of the building situation and show from where the photograph was taken [66]. Such 3D models of urban areas can be either retrieved from city departments [67] or automatically reconstructed from huge amount of (touristic) photos from the internet, i.e. via Structure-from-Motion [68, 69]. However, these models are focused on present buildings and serve as comparison to the historic state of construction.

A 3D city model representing the historic urban situation and visualizing historical images from several decades clearly has to deal with the time-varying aspect of buildings, which may appear and disappear over time. Hence, the representing 3D models need to be equipped with the construction dates, e.g. beginning and end of the building's existence. By using a time slider, the user may navigate through the different versions of the 3D city model.

There are many similarities to Samuel et al. [70]. Though, their primary focus is on the documentation of the change in urban landscape. The individual 3D models are linked to images and other documents that document the construction, demolition, and modifications of the real world objects. The documents are spatially oriented and visualized in a 3D city model, too. Virtually, they aim for similar solutions approaching from a different perspective. Schindler and Dellaert [66] also aimed for the exploration of vast collections of historical photographs via a time-varying 3D city model. Unfortunately, their approach remained as a prototype dating back to around 2008.

Visualization of uncertainty. The 3D city models representing the current building situation will be most likely quite complete and accurate. If they are presented in a low level of detail, it is not due to lack of information, but more for reasons of abstraction.

3D models representing past city structures are reconstructed either manually from a variety of sources or semi-automatically from historical photographs using photogrammetric methods [71]. Either way, it might not be possible to reconstruct those historic buildings accurately. This uncertainty needs to be indicated to the user. Otherwise, it might be assumed that given structures are fact, which might be wrong.

In the field of cultural heritage and digital 3D reconstruction, this matter is of high significance. There are many approaches, how to index and visualize uncertainty, respectively reliability. The methods reach from transparency, wireframe rendering [72], and different levels of details to color-coding the elements [73]. A combination of multiple methods is also possible [74]. The amount of the uncertainty depends on the quality of the sources and knowledge that lead to the reconstruction. These methods can be applied to manually reconstructed 3D models. Due to these issues we suggest the transfer of extensive repositories of historical media and their contextual information into a digital 3D model, but without having to interpret and thus eventually to distort them. The basic method in order to reach this goal is an approach via photogrammetry.

The generation of 3D models from historical photographs using photogrammetric methods is a semi-automatic process [71]. Due to the limited amount and quality of the images, the results may be incomplete and inaccurate. As this is mainly an automatic process, there is no manual interpretation of the sources. To indicate those 3D models according to their accuracy as well, methods need to be developed to evaluate these 3D models according to their precision or deviation.

Usability concerns. As pointed out earlier, usability is an important aspect that should not be neglected. Applications designed without reference to user requirements remain unused or unappreciated [30]. The proposed application needs to approach the gap between a professional usage by experts and a rather simple exploration by non-experts. It is also important to adopt established features and techniques, to which the users are used to. So, keyword faceted search are not replaced, but extended by spatial and temporal exploration.

The navigation in three dimensions is another challenge, as more degrees of freedom are possible. User studies showed that especially people who are not used to 3D environments, e.g. new-to-3D users, "can get into navigation trouble very quickly [...] and once in trouble, have a hard time getting back to known, comfortable viewing state" [75]. This can result in frustration and rejection of the application. A possible fallback to a top view with simple panning and zooming navigation might solve this problem. Preferably, advanced navigation tools that pick up new-to-3D as well as experienced users should be adopted to ensure a good usability for everyone [75].

The visualization itself is also part of the usability. The presented architecture and 3D content need to be properly communicated to the user to prevent misconceptions. This includes the clear differentiation of 3D models representing the modern and historic building situation (cf. Visualization of uncertainty). The images and their 3D representatives populating the scene can cause confusion, too. They are usually displayed as textured planes, sometimes enhanced by a pyramid of vision to indicate the orientation (Fig. 3). At places with a high density of images, however, they can occlude, overlap, or intersect each other. But the orientation and exact position are only interesting when viewing at close range. Looking from further away, the images can have an offset to their position, always face the user's camera, and be automatically arranged to prevent occlusion [76].

Many photographs have been taken on ground level. When viewing the 3D city model from even further away, those images would be hidden in the streets and hard to spot. In such case, they should be floating above the buildings. In general, the visualization of the images needs to be dynamically adapted depending on the user's view. If those visualization techniques are not sufficient enough, the images need to be additionally clustered or weighted and filtered in an appropriate manner.

Fig. 3. Spatially oriented images in 3D city model (prototype)

4.2 Consequences

With a future web-based application in mind, existing approaches and technologies covering diverse aspects were reviewed. Most existing solutions rely on 2D map services. They are easy to integrate into webpages, they provide map material and satellite imagery from the whole earth, and their APIs offer extensive geospatial functionalities. However, the provided maps only show the current situation. The extension with the help of 3D city models is considered to be beneficial in regard to a better identification of the region of interest and a better understanding of the urban building situation and the photographer's position. Because the historic building situation can differ a lot from the current situation, those 3D city models should be time-varying. Due to lacking material, it is, however, possible that only parts of a city can be reconstructed. It needs to be clearly indicated to the user, which 3D models represent the modern building situation and which the historic one. This also applies to uncertainty and inaccuracy of reconstructed historic buildings.

These aspects have to be heavily considered during conceptualization and implementation of the application. Very technical aspects have been left out at this point.

Once the basic features will work, the application can be extended to be a more advanced research environment to help art and architectural historians to answer their research questions.

5 User Requirements – A Case Study

In accordance with the needs pointed out above, an example from the area of urban history will be given on the following pages. It will show the practical challenges when working in this field and name requirements that become relevant in correlation with the question researched.

The chosen example deals with the urban history of Dresden during the 20th century. The interest in this case is twofold: First, and this is the starting point, how did the city develop during this period? Which buildings were erected in which time, when were certain structures built, renovated, changed or lost? Are there areas with strong transformations or, in contrast, more stable areas? For Dresden, this is especially important against the backdrop of the severe damages caused during World War II that led to extensive rebuilding measures. This part has already been researched thoroughly, so that many facts of the development are already known [77–79]. Of course, several knowledge gaps do still exist.

The second part of the research concentrates on what is not the factual evolution of the urban tissue, but the internal perception of the city [80]. For our example, this could concern questions like: Which mental images can be traced? Commonly named among those images are "Dresden as Baroque city of culture" [81], "Dresden destroyed in the war" [82] or "Dresden as city of the Socialist progress" [83, 84]. Furthermore, it can be asked whether there are specific times and places related to internal pictures? Which buildings supported the formation of certain concepts? In return, was the factual city influenced by those mental ideas?

The research is undertaken by means of digitized historic photos, provided on the platform of the Deutsche Fotothek (DFD), and thus gives a practical validation of the user requirements enumerated above. As the standards of the DFD are comparably high [3], the searching tools and given metadata as well as cross-references and the possibility to contribute to the archive's data often already meet the desires of an architectural historian. Still, there is room for improvement as can be shown by the following case study.

5.1 Improving the Search Process

As said above, the main difference between art history research and other disciplines consists of the mainly visual character of the sources instead of texts and words. If we look at image repositories, it becomes clear that already the search for visual sources can be problematic as the scholar needs to verbalize what they are looking for [85].

For example, searching a specific building may pose some challenges: special buildings such as castles, churches, opera houses and so on are simply searchable by their proper name. But an ordinary house does not necessarily have a proper name – so another approach might be searching for its address or special structural features. If we look at the example of Prager Straße 12, a building in one of the most important streets in Dresden, the results of a search undertaken do not explicitly show the building. They show the street as a whole, they depict festive occasions in this street, they also refer to people that had lived in this place, but none is exclusively dedicated to this building (Fig. 4).

Fig. 4. Search results for "Prager Straße 12", none of them showing the building in question

As the building did not have notable distinguishing marks, such as inscriptions or architectural singularities, the search is likely to be restricted to scrolling through the results whose metadata is loosely related to the place. When examining the hits, it becomes obvious that their metadata is focused on other information: date and author of the historic photo, even date and name of the digitization, the city, the name of the street, special characteristics such as the type of a building, whether people are depicted in the photo, the mention of special occasions, and so on. For example, a picture showing the socialist rebuilding process of the Prager Straße in the 1960s gives the following information: place = "Dresden", quarter = "old city", name of the picture = "Prager Straße", tagged with = "workers", "building industry", "underground engineering". Furthermore, the type of building is determined as "public building" and "playground" – depicted is the construction of a public fountain.

At this point the problem of finding adequate sources turns out to be a striking one. One solution could consist in basing the search on the principles of time and space – and thus overcoming the search which is only based on words. In some image repositories the linking to Google Maps is already applied, while the temporal component is covered by an interactive timeline. A further investigation on the technical possibilities could lead to a significant improvement in this sector as the limitations of a verbalized image search might be overcome to a certain extent.

5.2   Collecting Facts

Most image repositories restrict their services to searching only, while the collection of sources and facts is left to the scholar.

Primarily, this concerns the retrieval of sources that is often limited to screenshots or low resolution downloads. Thus, the investigator has to find their own system of cataloguing and storing the visual data. Personal (offline) collections are the outcome of this research setting [3].

But also, the systemization during the search process is limited, either to a specific topic or to a certain time layer. If we take another look at our example of Dresden, we might be interested in searching photographs of the old market square (Altmarkt) together with the adjacent church of the Holy Cross (Kreuzkirche) and how this place was perceived by photographers of different personal and political backgrounds. By typing in the two keywords, 329 results will be displayed (as per June 2017). In a second step, we may limit the results to photos from the years 1945 to 1960 by using the offered timeline, narrowing down the results to 119 hits. In a third step, the photographer might be selected from a displayed list (Fig. 5). The results deriving from this search procedure are already quite satisfactory. Nevertheless, on the DFD platform it is not possible to bookmark a number of photos. The functionality of a shopping cart does exist – for ordering high resolution scans. But this organizational tool does not allow the comparison of images, for example of different photographers, in order to trace their specific view on the cityscape.

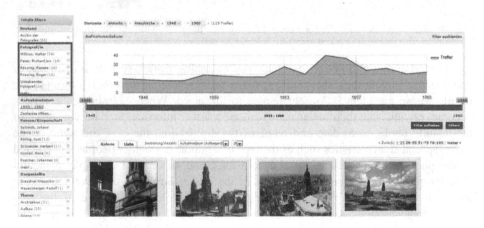

Fig. 5. Possibilities of filtering the results

Even if there are image repositories that already include such a tool, they mainly belong to the museum sector and do not usually focus on architectural history. It might also be interesting to add own material or sources from other platforms, additional photographs, maps and plans for example – a functionality that is not offered in any image repository yet and would certainly require a personal account.

5.3   Supporting the Analysis

When looking at the support of the analysis process, several needs became obvious during the case study: First, the possibility of comparing the sources, second, the numerical examination of the photographs, third, the content-related interpretation of the pictures and fourth, the integration of research output.

Starting with the first point, it would be important for the examination of Dresden's urban history to compare pictures from different times to trace the development of the architectural structures. A chronological example is the investigation of the Altmarkt during the pre-war years, when the general architecture did not change a lot, but when the advertising signs and inscriptions had a huge fluctuation, giving us an idea of the economic evolution of the city's historic center. Visual comparison, e.g. on a split screen, but also the overlaying of photographs are of interest for the scholarly work. A linkage to old historical maps and architectural planning would allow a further analyzation of data in this field.

As for the statistical evaluation of photographic material, questions of how frequently which buildings were taken pictures of can be answered. Does for example during socialism the perception differ between the baroque (but feudal) heritage and the large housing estates which were ideologically supported by the authorities? Did the royal buildings by then receive less photographic interest than the quarters with the newly built prefabricated high-rise blocks? This could lead to a deeper understanding of the perception of the urban tissue and its evolution during the 20th century.

At this point, also the content-related analysis becomes important, as a mere numerical examination does not take into account the artistic freedom and the individual background of each photographer. For example, the photographer Walter Möbius (1900–1959) was bestowed by the predecessor institution of the DFD to take pictures of Dresden's cityscape [86]. His interest was a pure documentary one, leading to a realistic, dispassionate imagery, as shown in the example of the Palace in the Great Garden of Dresden (Großer Garten) (Fig. 6 - left side). In contrast, the truly artistic work of Richard Peter senior (1895–1977) clearly reflects his left-leaning political attitude, even if he was not a member of the SED (Socialist Unity Party of Germany) [87, 88]. He often arranged diligent workers, portrayed in a slightly pathetic way, in the foreground of the urban setting and also chose the architectural subjects according to his main interest, the socialist rebuilding of a new Dresden (Fig. 6 - right side). At this point, the analysis of the historical, personal and political background of a photograph is of highest interest for the question of the city's perception. This could be supported by technical means, for example through individually applicable tags that facilitate a statistical examination.

The last point mentioned above concerns the scientific discussion. First, during the process of collecting facts, it becomes obvious that the metadata of the digital material may be false or imprecise. On the one hand, there are existing possibilities to report back such information to the image repositories, in most cases via e-mail, as it can be done in DFD. A real discussion on the other hand, for example by giving annotations and allowing other scholars to comment on them, is not possible.

Fig. 6. Left: Walter Möbius (1946) Palais im Großen Garten – photographic documentation of the damages of World War 2 (SLUB, DFD – df_hauptkatalog_0037776), Right: Richard Peter sen. (1947) Clearance of the ruins in the center of Dresden (SLUB, DFD – df_ps_0000336_003)

6   Implications

What are high level implications of our investigations for the tool creation?

- *Multilinguality:* Implications derived from our investigation are that the community is mainly situated in European countries – against this background, the provision of tools in the mother tongue language of addressed researchers is of relevance [27, p. 6].
- *Multidisciplinarity:* Since the community dealing with art and architectural research includes many different disciplines and approaches, varying epistemic demands, skills and habits as well as terminologies have to be obeyed [cf. 28, 29].
- *Differing levels of expertise:* Since tools are often developed with the expert user in mind, usability issues may be another hurdle for those with less advanced ICT skills, who want to use specific "academic" tools [30].
- *Enhance accessibility and findability:* As named by many reports [27, p. 7] [20, p. 294], findability and accessibility of resources as well as the digitization of objects are the most critical challenges for media repository users.
- *Raise content quantity:* Recent studies have stated a heavy use of generic search engines such as Google [31, 32], even if various repositories exist that are specifically addressed to scholars in art and architectural heritage [33]. The limited depth and width of content was named as a major obstacle in the use of media repositories as image databases [20, p. 301].

7   Conclusions

In addition to our considerations, a recent study of more than 100 digital image repositories has shown that existing online archives do not necessarily meet the requirements of art and architectural history scholars [3]. Major problems were identified such as

- the lack of good search tools and filters,
- inconsistent and incomplete metadata,
- absence of cross-references, norm-data or supplementary literature,
- poor resolution of the images as well as,
- unclear indications of the user rights.

Although larger platforms, such as the Deutsche Fotothek (German Photographic Collection) [34], do already perform well in the applied categories, many recommendations towards an improvement can yet be given.

A thorough user involvement to assess the user's needs and knowledge is essential. This can preferably be done through a multi-method user study involving formal user surveys (e.g. fieldwork observations, focus groups, questionnaires) as well as software and interface usability tests [30]. It has become clear that the users' requirements evolve over time because they acquire new knowledge and skills [89]. The interaction that can be asked of a user depends on their level of expertise [50] and the willingness to adopt new methods [13]. Regular usability tests ensure intuitive usage and navigation, especially for new-to-3D users. Good concepts and methods need to be developed to present the spatially oriented images in the 3D scene to the user. Depending on their view, the visualization of the images should dynamically adapt to prevent confusion.

Furthermore, some researchers may not be used to obtain and study media through the same interface and may not trust the solution [89] without thorough documentation.

References

1. Sweetnam, M.S., Agosti, M., Orio, N., Ponchia, C., Steiner, C.M., Hillemann, E.-C., Siochrú, M.Ó., Lawless, S.: User needs for enhanced engagement with cultural heritage collections. In: Zaphiris, P., Buchanan, G., Rasmussen, E., Loizides, F. (eds.) TPDL 2012. LNCS, vol. 7489, pp. 64–75. Springer, Heidelberg (2012). https://doi.org/10.1007/978-3-642-33290-6_8
2. Barreau, J.-B., Gaugne, R., Bernard, Y., Le Cloirec, G., Gouranton, V.: Virtual reality tools for the west digital conservatory of archaeological heritage. In: Proceedings of 2014 Virtual Reality International Conference, p. 4. ACM (2014)
3. Münster, S., Kamposiori, C., Friedrichs, K., Kröber, C.: Image libraries and their scholarly use in the field of art and architectural history (2017, submitted article)
4. Münster, S.: The many faces of digital heritage research… A survey on topics, researchers and cultures. Paper presented at the ISPRS Annals of the Photogrammetry, Remote Sensing and Spatial Information Sciences (XXV International CIPA Symposium), Ottawa (accepted paper)
5. European Commission: Measuring Digital Skills Across the EU: EU Wide Indicators of Digital Competence (2014)
6. Münster, S., Ioannides, M.: The scientific community of digital heritage in time and space. In: Guidi, G., Scopigno, R., Torres, J.C., Graf, H. (eds.) 2nd International Congress on Digital Heritage 2015, Granada (2015). ISSN 978–1-5090-0048-7/15

7. Hicks, D.: The four literatures of social science. In: Moed, H.F., Glänzel, W., Schmoch, U. (eds.) Handbook of Quantitative Science and Technology Research: The Use of Publication and Patent Statistics in Studies of S&T Systems, pp. 473–496. Springer Science & Business Media, Dordrecht (2006). https://doi.org/10.1007/1-4020-2755-9_22

8. Tenopir, C., King, D.W.: Electronic journals and changes in scholarly article seeking and reading patterns. D-Lib. Mag. **14**(11/12), 1–13 (2008)

9. Hemmig, W.: An empirical study of the information-seeking behavior of practicing visual artists. J. Doc. **65**(4), 682–703 (2009). https://doi.org/10.1108/00220410910970302

10. Bakewell, E., Beeman, W.O., Reese, C.M., Schmitt, M.: Object, Image, Inquiry: The Art Historian at Work. Getty Art History Information Program, Santa Monica (1988)

11. Cobbledick, S.: The Information-seeking behavior of artists: exploratory interviews. Libr. Q.: Inf. Commun. Policy **66**(4), 343–372 (1996)

12. Visick, R., Hendrickson, J., Bowman, C.: Seeking information during the creative process-a pilot study of artists (2006)

13. Beaudoin, J.E., Brady, E.: Finding visual information: a study of image resources used by archaeologists, architects, art historians, and artists. Art Doc. **30**(2), 24–36 (2011)

14. Long, M.P., Schonfeld, R.C.: Preparing for the future of research services for art history: recommendations from the Ithaka S+R report. Art Doc.: J. Art Libr. Soc. North Am. **33**(2), 192–205 (2014). https://doi.org/10.1086/678316

15. Bates, M.J., Wilde, D.N., Siegfried, S.: Research practices of humanities scholars in an online environment: the Getty online searching project report no. 3. LISR **17**, 5–40 (1995)

16. Hersey, D., Calhoun, S., Crowley, G., Krentz, J., Grafe, M.: Understanding the Research Practices of Humanities Doctoral Students at Yale University. Yale University, Yale (2015)

17. Mason, H., Robinson, L.: The information-related behaviour of emerging artists and designers. J. Doc. **67**(1), 159–180 (2011). https://doi.org/10.1108/00220411111105498

18. Elam, B.: Readiness or avoidance: e-resources and the art historian. Collect. Build. **26**(1), 4–6 (2007)

19. Beaudoin, J.: Image and text: a review of the literature concerning the information needs and research behaviors of art historians. Art Doc.: J. Art Libr. Soc. North Am. **24**(2), 34–37 (2005)

20. Beaudoin, J.E.: An investigation of image users across professions: a framework of their image needs, retrieval and use. Drexel University (2009)

21. Pscheida, D., Minet, C., Herbst, S., Albrecht, S., Köhler, T.: Use of Social Media and Online-Based Tools in Academia. Results of the Science 2.0-Survey 2014, Dresden (2014)

22. Heusinger, L.: Applications of computers in the history of art. In: Hamber, A., Miles, J., Vaughan, W. (eds.) Computers and the History of Art, pp. 1–22. Mansell Pub, London (1989)

23. Kohle, H.: Digitale Bildwissenschaft. Glückstadt (2013)

24. Drucker, J.: Is there a "digital" art history? Vis. Resour. **29**(1–2), 5–13 (2013). https://doi.org/10.1080/01973762.2013.761106

25. Bentkowska-Kafel, A.: Debating digital art history. DAH-J. **1**, 50–64 (2015)

26. Long, M.P., Schonfeld, R.C.: Supporting the changing research practices of art historians. Ithaka S+R (2014)

27. Digital Methods and Practices Observatory Working Group DARIAH-EU European Research Infrastructure Consortium: European survey on scholarly practices and digital needs in the arts and humanities (2016)

28. Cetina, K.K., Reichmann, W.: Epistemic Cultures, pp. 873–880 (2015). https://doi.org/10.1016/b978-0-08-097086-8.10454-4

29. Knorr-Cetina, K.: Scientific communities or transepistemic arenas of research. A critique of quasi-economic models of science. Soc. Stud. Sci. **12**, 101–130 (1982)
30. Warwick, C.: Studying users in digital humanities. In: Warwick, C., Terras, M., Julianne, N. (eds.) Digital Humanities in Practice, pp. 1–21. Facet Publishing, London (2012)
31. Kemman, M., Kleppe, M., Scagliola, S.: Just Google it. Digital research practices of humanities scholars. In: Proceedings of Digital Humanities Congress 2012 Studies in the Digital Humanities Sheffield: HRI Online (2014)
32. Gregory, T.R.: Under-served or under-surveyed: the information needs of studio art faculty in the Southwestern United States. Art Doc.: J. Art Libr. Soc. North Am. **26**(2), 57–66 (2007). https://doi.org/10.1086/adx.26.2.27949470
33. Chen, C.J.: Art history: a guide to basic research resources. Collect. Build. **28**(3), 122–125 (2009). https://doi.org/10.1108/01604950910971152
34. Mösch, K.: Exemplarische Sicherung deutscher Bildgeschichte 1945-1960: Bedeutung des Massendigitalisierungsprojekts der Deutschen Fotothek (SLUB Dresden) (2009)
35. Simon, H.: Kunstgeschichte im digitalen Informationszeitalter–Eine kritische Standortbestimmung (2007)
36. Schuller, G.: Designing Universal Knowledge. Lars Müller Publishers, Baden (2009)
37. Dudek, I., Blaise, J.-Y., De Luca, L., Bergerot, L., Renaudin, N.: How was this done? An attempt at formalising and memorising a digital asset's making-of. In: Digital Heritage, 2015, pp. 343–346. IEEE (2015)
38. Maxwell, A.: Digital archives and history research: feedback from an end-user. Libr. Rev. **59** (1), 24–39 (2010)
39. Maina, J.K., Suleman, H.: Enhancing digital heritage archives using gamified annotations. In: Allen, R.B., Hunter, J., Zeng, M.L. (eds.) ICADL 2015. LNCS, vol. 9469, pp. 169–179. Springer, Cham (2015). https://doi.org/10.1007/978-3-319-27974-9_17
40. Hastings, S.K.: Evaluation of image retrieval systems: role of user feedback. Libr. Trends **48** (2), 438 (1999)
41. Besser, H.: Visual access to visual images: the UC Berkeley image database project. Libr. Trends **38**(4), 787–798 (1990)
42. Pisciotta, H., Brisson, R., Ferrin, E., Dooris, M., Spink, A.: Penn state visual image user study. D-Libr. Mag. **7**(7/8), 169–196 (2001)
43. Elgammal, A.: Human-centered multimedia: representations and challenges. In: Proceedings of 1st ACM International Workshop on Human-Centered Multimedia, pp. 11–18. ACM (2006)
44. Giral, A.: Digital image libraries and the teaching of art and architectural history. Art Libr. J. **23**(04), 18–25 (1998)
45. Lopatin, L.: Library digitization projects, issues and guidelines: a survey of the literature. Libr. Hi Tech **24**(2), 273–289 (2006)
46. Terras, M.: Image processing in the digital humanities. Digit. Human. Pract. **71**(10), 71–90 (2012)
47. Tikka, P.: Image Retrieval: Theory and Research. MIT Press, Cambridge (2006)
48. Datta, R., Joshi, D., Li, J., Wang, J.Z.: Image retrieval: ideas, influences, and trends of the new age. ACM Comput. Surv. **40**(2), 1–60 (2008). https://doi.org/10.1145/1348246.1348248
49. Rieger, O.Y.: Search engine use behavior of students and faculty: user perceptions and implications for future research. First Monday **14**(12) (2009)
50. Cook, M.P.: Visual representations in science education: the influence of prior knowledge and cognitive load theory on instructional design principles. Sci. Educ. **90**(6), 1073–1091 (2006). https://doi.org/10.1002/sce.20164

51. Chandler, P., Sweller, J.: The split-attention effect as a factor in the design of instruction. Br. J. Educ. Psychol. **62**(2), 233–246 (1992)
52. Avancini, H., Straccia, U.: User recommendation for collaborative and personalised digital archives. Int. J. Web Based Commun. **1**(2), 163–175 (2005)
53. Normore, L.F., Tebo, M.E.: Assessing user requirements for a small scientific data repository. Proc. Assoc. Inf. Sci. Technol. **48**(1), 1–4 (2011)
54. Borghesani, D., Grana, C., Cucchiara, R.: Surfing on artistic documents with visually assisted tagging. In: Proceedings of 18th ACM International Conference on Multimedia, pp. 1343–1352. ACM (2010)
55. Manning, C.D., Raghavan, P., Schütze, H.: Introduction to Information Retrieval. Cambridge University Press, New York (2008)
56. Vassilieva, N.S.: Content-based image retrieval methods. Prog. Comput. Softw. **35**(3), 158–180 (2009). https://doi.org/10.1134/s0361768809030049
57. Wan, J., Wang, D., Hoi, S.C.H., Wu, P., Zhu, J., Zhang, Y., Li, J.: Deep learning for content-based image retrieval: a comprehensive study. In: Proceedings of 22nd ACM International Conference on Multimedia, Orlando, Florida, USA, pp. 157–166. ACM, New York (2014). https://doi.org/10.1145/2647868.2654948
58. Llamas, J., Lerones, P.M., Zalama, E., Gómez-García-Bermejo, J.: Applying deep learning techniques to cultural heritage images within the INCEPTION project. In: Ioannides, M., Fink, E., Moropoulou, A., Hagedorn-Saupe, M., Fresa, A., Liestøl, G., Rajcic, V., Grussenmeyer, P. (eds.) EuroMed 2016. LNCS, vol. 10059, pp. 25–32. Springer, Cham (2016). https://doi.org/10.1007/978-3-319-48974-2_4
59. Wieser, C., Bry, F., Bérard, A., Lagrange, R.: ARTigo: building an artwork search engine with games and higher-order latent semantic analysis. In: Proceedings of Disco 2013, Workshop on Human Computation and Machine Learning in Games, Palm Springs, CA, USA (2013)
60. Chen, W., Nottveit, T.: Digital map application for historical photos. In: Chowdhury, G., Koo, C., Hunter, J. (eds.) ICADL 2010. LNCS, vol. 6102, pp. 158–167. Springer, Heidelberg (2010). https://doi.org/10.1007/978-3-642-13654-2_20
61. Gall, A.: Konstruieren, kommunizieren, präsentieren. Bilder von Wissenschaft und Technik. Wallstein, Göttingen (2007)
62. Göbel, M.: Graphics Modeling and Visualization in Science and Technology. Springer, Berlin (1993). https://doi.org/10.1007/978-3-642-77811-7
63. Gallagher, R.S.: Computer Visualization. Graphics Techniques for Scientific and Engineering Analysis. CRC Press, Boca Raton (1995)
64. Dress, A.: Visualisierung in Mathematik, Technik und Kunst. Grundlagen und Anwendungen. Vieweg, Braunschweig (1999)
65. Gouveia, J., Branco, F., Rodrigues, A., Correia, N.: Travelling through space and time in Lisbon's religious buildings. Paper presented at the 2nd International Congress on Digital Heritage, Granada (2015)
66. Schindler, G., Dellaert, F.: 4D cities: analyzing, visualizing, and interacting with historical urban photo collections. J. Multimed. (2012). https://doi.org/10.4304/jmm.7.2.124-131
67. Gaillard, J., Vienne, A., Baume, R., Pedrinis, F., Peytavie, A., Gesquière, G.: Urban data visualisation in a web browser. In: Proceedings of 20th International Conference on 3D Web Technology (Web3D 2015), Heraklion, Crete, Greece, pp. 81–88. ACM (2015). https://doi.org/10.1145/2775292.2775302

68. Snavely, N., Seitz, S.M., Szeliski, R.: Photo tourism: exploring photo collections in 3D. ACM Trans. Graph. (SIGGRAPH Proc.) **25**(3), 835–846 (2006)
69. Agarwal, S., Furukawa, Y., Snavely, N., Simon, I., Curless, B., Seitz, S.M., Szeliski, R.: Buidling Rome in a day. Commun. ACM **54**(10), 105–112 (2011). https://doi.org/10.1145/2001269.2001293
70. Samuel, J., Périnaud, C., Servigne, S., Gay, G., Gesquière, G.: Representation and visualization of urban fabric through historical documents. In: Catalano, C.E., De Luca, L. (eds.) 14th Eurographics Workshop on Graphics and Cultural Heritage, Genova, Italy. The Eurographics Association (2016)
71. Maiwald, F., Vietze, T., Schneider, D., Henze, F., Münster, S., Niebling, F.: Photogrammetric analysis of historical image repositories for virtual reconstruction in the field of digital humanities. Int. Arch. Photogramm. Remote Sens. Spat. Inf. Sci. **XLII-2/W3**, 447–452 (2017). https://doi.org/10.5194/isprs-archives-xlii-2-w3-447-2017
72. Lengyel, D., Toulouse, C.: Darstellung von unscharfem Wissen in der Rekonstruktion historischer Bauten. In: Heine, K., Rheidt, K., Henze, F., Riedel, A. (eds.) Von Handaufmaß bis High Tech III, pp. 182–187. Verlag Philipp von Zabern, Darmstadt/Mainz (2011)
73. Apollonio, F.I.: Classification schemes for visualization of uncertainty in digital hypothetical reconstruction. In: Münster, S., Pfarr-Harfst, M., Kuroczyński, P., Ioannides, M. (eds.) 3D Research Challenges in Cultural Heritage II. LNCS, vol. 10025, pp. 173–197. Springer, Cham (2016). https://doi.org/10.1007/978-3-319-47647-6_9
74. Kensek, K.M., Dodd, L.S., Cipolla, N.: Fantastic reconstructions or reconstructions of the fantastic? Tracking and presenting ambiguity, alternatives, and documentation in virtual worlds. Autom. Constr. **13**, 175–186 (2004)
75. Fitzmaurice, G., Matejka, J., Mordatch, I., Khan, A., Kurtenbach, G.: Safe 3D navigation. In: Proceedings of 2008 Symposium on Interactive 3D Graphics and Games, Redwood City, California, pp. 7–15. ACM (2008). https://doi.org/10.1145/1342250.1342252
76. Chagnaud, C., Samuel, J., Servigne, S., Gesquière, G.: Visualization of documented 3D cities. In: Eurographics Workshop on Urban Data Modelling and Visualisation, Liège, Belgium. The Eurographics Association (2016)
77. Lerm, M.: Denkmale in der Stadt - die Stadt als Denkmal: Dresden als Beispiel. In: Meier, H. R. (ed.) Denkmale in der Stadt - die Stadt als Denkmal: Probleme und Chancen für den Stadtumbau, pp. 41–49. TUDpress, Dresden (2006)
78. Blaschke, K., John, U., Gross, R.: Geschichte der Stadt Dresden: Von den Anfängen bis zum Ende des Dreißigjährigen Krieges, vol. 1. Theiss, Stuttgart (2005)
79. Guckes, J.: Dresden in den 1920er und 1950er Jahren: Wandel und Kontinuität städtischer Selbstbilder. In: Lühr, H.-P. (ed.) Mythos Dresden: Faszination und Verklärung einer Stadt, pp. 65–72. Dresdner Geschichtsverein, Dresden (2005)
80. Sigel, P.: Zeitlos? Urbane Identitätskonstruktionen und die Suggestionskraft des historischen Stadt-Bildes. In: Sulzer, J. (ed.) Stadt Raum Zeit: Stadtentwicklung zwischen Kontinuität und Wande, pp. 34–43. Jovis, Berlin (2008)
81. Löffler, F.: Das alte Dresden: Geschichte seiner Bauten. Seemann (1992)
82. Lerm, M.: Abschied vom alten Dresden: Verluste historischer Bausubstanz nach 1945. Hinstorff (2000)
83. Greve, A., Lupfer, G., Plaßmeyer, P.: Der Blick auf Dresden: Die Frauenkirche und das Werden der Dresdner Stadtsilhouette. Staatliche Kunstsammlungen (2005)
84. Lühr, H.-P.: Mythos Dresden: Faszination und Verklärung einer Stadt. Dresdner Hefte no. 84 (2005)

85. Bauer, E.: Analoge Bildarchive auf dem Weg ins digitale Zeitalter: Chancen und Heraus-forderungen für die Bereitstellung und Benutzung bildhafter Materialien. In: Becker, I. (ed.) Digitalisierung im Archiv - Neue Wege der Bereitstellung des Archivguts: Beiträge zum 18. Archivwissenschaftlichen Kolloquium der Archivschule Marburg, pp. 61–74. Archivschule Marburg, Marburg (2015)

86. Huth, S., Möbius, W.: Der Fotograf Walter Möbius: 1900-1959. Kreismuseum Freital, Freital (1975)

87. Peter, R.: Eine Kamera klagt an. Desdener Verlagsgesellschaft, Dresden (1949)

88. Ziegner, S.: Der Bildband "Dresden – eine Kamera klagt an" von Richard Peter senior. Teil der Erinnerungskultur Dresdens. Philipps-Universität Marburg, Marburg (2012)

89. Agosti, M., Orio, N.: User requirements for effective access to digital archives of manuscripts. J. Multimed. **7**(2), 217–222 (2012)

The Production of 3D Digital Archives and the Methodologies for Digitally Supporting Research in Architectural and Urban Cultural Heritage

Fabrizio I. Apollonio[(✉)]

Department of Architecture, Alma Mater Studiorum – University of Bologna,
Bologna, Italy
fabrizio.apollonio@unibo.it

Abstract. The paper presents a critical analysis regarding the methodological approach useful to produce 3D digital contents of Cultural Heritage artifacts in context of Digital Archives. The structure of 3D model and the reconstruction process are analyzed in order to elaborate and formalize semantic knowledge concerning the work of art, object of study. Some experiences recently carried-out can show the development of some web-based platform able to allow the use of contents properly related to the characteristics of the case study.

Keywords: 3D digital libraries · 3D digital reconstruction · 3D modeling
Knowledge systems

1 Introduction

Over the last twenty-five years the digital revolution produced an important development of new tools and methods for 3D data acquisition, documentation and dissemination of information related to Cultural Heritage (CH). The development achieved by digital technologies, i.e., 3D data acquisition, Cognitive Information Systems (CIS), Building Information Modeling (BIM), Real-Time Rendering (RTR) of 3D models, multimedia techniques, animations and simulations, has opened new scenarios for reading, analyzing and interpreting CH, allowing all the information to be available in a visual and integrated manner [1]. The availability of new and more effective digital technologies introduces the possibility of interchangeable media able to offer multiple nodes of access to a given term or object, and enable a multidimensional approach to knowledge on several levels [2]. As demonstrated by Veltman's [3] knowledge levels, Moles's [4] iconic degrees and the Gooding's influence of visual contents in scientific work [5] digital technologies make it available to multidimensional and multilevel approach to knowledge (Fig. 1). But despite these potentials, especially in the field of visual humanities research there is a deep cultural gap as well as skills. As already widely discussed [6–8] these issues concern the broader and articulated field of access to and assessment of models, the transparency of authorship, and the connection between the reconstruction process and results as well as its sources, citation of model

S. Münster et al. (Eds.): UHDL 2017/DECH 2017, CCIS 817, pp. 139–158, 2018.
https://doi.org/10.1007/978-3-319-76992-9_9

sources/data, visualization of different degree of certainty, and modification of a certain model produced over time by different/subsequent authors.

Fig. 1. The multi-layer structure of a 3D digital architectural archive

Nowadays, the protection, managing, fruition and enhancement of CH is supported by a wide range of digital environments and platforms able to provide reliable documentation, but also able to make available the asset of knowledge developed during the study, analysis and reconstruction activities.

The idea to use Information Communication Technology (ICT) platforms/environment able to allow the managing of data concerning CH is not new anymore [8–12], but day by day it becomes more and more necessary to have a system able to provide not only the access to a huge amount of fragmented and incomplete data of different nature and coming from various sources, but especially to make retrievable the documentation process [7] behind the production of 3D models of a not more extant building, as well as that concerning the cultural asset and the preservation of the data during the whole lifecycle of an art work.

Operating on modeling CH means, usually, to collect, manage, store and use a huge and heterogeneous amount of records resulting from the historical research phase [13]. A work of art, existing or no more extant, usually dates back to several centuries [14], and documents gathered include historical notes and descriptions (texts), drawings, engravures, paintings, different kind of graphic materials, analogue/digital pictures, technical and archaeological excavation reports, construction and archaeological site records filled out during lifecycle of the artifact. All those available information helps to reconstruct the evolution in time or a state at a defined time and consequently to produce a hypothetical reconstruction of a no more extant artifact or to plan a proper restoration and maintenance project.

The digital technologies propose new meanings of architectural representation, adding an extra dimension, the temporal one (diachronic and synchronic), which allows to know artifact not only in its evolution and transformation during its life cycle, but also through the analysis of its composition and geometric-formal matrix.

The advent of virtual reconstruction [15] opened the debate, not only in the archaeological field, on the multidisciplinary approach to a huge amount of virtual reconstruction projects. Wide is the series of reconstructions works of urban sites, as early as 1990, as well as applied to architectural reconstruction of never built edifices, that used 3D digital modeling techniques. Kőller et al. [6] focused on the need to make visible the traceability of all additions, subtractions, and changes to 3D models, in order to let understandable the hypothesis and display of differences between 3D models of the object/artifact, and stated a wide list of topics that would characterize the use of 3D models, through Digital Archives (DA) or Libraries (DL).

Similarly 3D reconstruction methods – reality or source-based – have been becoming very popular with a large proliferation, application and use of 3D digital models, accessible via web or by means of installation in museums or exhibitions. 3D reconstruction of the real as well as of the no more extant artifacts widely improves the understanding studies of a large amount of CH.

Besides an accurate geometric reproduction of a work of art with all its physical details (reality-based reconstruction) we are able to produce an analytical representation of a work of art, producing a wide range of semantically enriched model even starting from documentary sources (source-data reconstruction) [8, 9].

1.1 Web-Based Platforms and Virtual Environments for CH Management

Over last decades several studies and researches have been designed with the purpose to produce web-based platforms and environments for the managing of a multitude of heterogeneous data concerning the history of monumental cultural heritage artifacts as well as to support collaborative art-historical research [16, 17].

Thanks to ICT and 3D web technologies improvement, it is currently possible to use a 3D model as an interface for localizing and querying data concerning a work of art. This way allows you to widely improve understanding studies about any work of art heritage characterized by the third dimension, using 3D model of the real artifact or reconstruction of those no more extant, in order to documenting their historical evolutions for their reconstruction or restoration or any kind of analysis.

Those kind of environments and platforms could be designed as a Cognitive Information System (CIS). An environment characterized on one hand by an exhaustive documentary base - qualified through a full transparency of analytical methods, surveying techniques and the criteria used-, covering the entire process of research and data collection, related to the creation of digital content within the reconstruction process, and on the other hand by the possibility to provide a uniform framework for scientific study, able to provide a space and a toolset that enable research teams to examine digital replicas of works of art and primary source materials, create comparisons, build a bibliography, annotate transcription and translation on texts, and exchange ideas, in a word allowing effective collaborative space for integration and presentation of web-based heterogeneous data and exploration and analysis of large volumes of data with geo-spatial, temporal and semantic characteristics.

The base of these environments is the documentation. A documentary base that has to be able to assure [7] the "preservation of knowledge" [18], to qualify the outcomes carried out (reference ontology, application ontology) [19–21], and mainly to record/document the creative process adopted behind any reconstructive process [18, 22, 23]. Such reconstructive process has to be focused/designed not only on "documenting" data sources and reality data used, but on "documenting" the process of knowledge reconstruction too.

The methodologies adopted in order to produce 3D Digital Archives for digitally supporting research in architectural and urban cultural heritage is based on the following keypoints:

- Reconstruction workflow
- 3D Model Quality/Properties
- Semantic Structure of the 3D Digital Model
- Knowledge reconstruction and formalization process.

2 Reconstruction Workflow

From a methodological point of view, therefore, the reconstruction process adopted is of fundamental importance, depending on whether the reconstruction is based on documentary data or data derived/acquired from the real. As can be seen in Fig. 2, the workflow and methodology are not related to the applied technological application, but to the whole of the data that is acquired and subsequently used to produce not only the 3D model but above all the semantic characterization/enrichment of the elements that compose it.

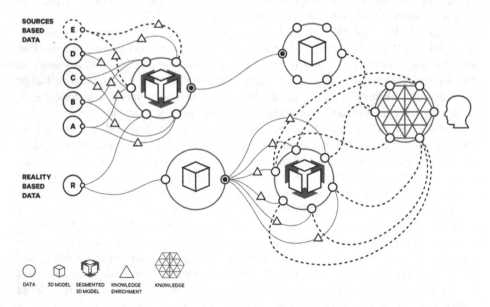

Fig. 2. The reconstruction process workflow

In both cases of a reconstruction workflow, the main purpose is the production of a virtual 3D model, characterized by the highest level of quality that the sources data allow us [8, 24] and qualified (parametric [28], numerical and/or mathematical model), as stated in [7, 25–27] in respect to 3D models produced, following different process:

- Geometrical model, produced by acquisition of all dimensions using sensing (active or passive) technologies;
- Manual model, derived from an analysis of plan/drawing and similar kind of sources in 2D to obtain 3D without direct measurements;
- Hybrid model, produced by a combination of 2D with 3D data sources through measurements by means of an instrument;
- Reconstructed model, just produced following a reconstructive process entirely based on data derived from sources, without any measurements.

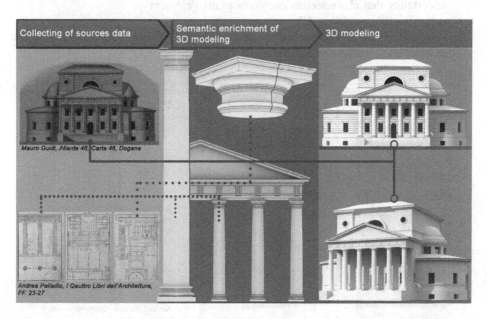

Fig. 3. Sources-based 3D reconstruction workflow

2.1 Sources-Based the Reconstruction Process

On one side (sources-based) the reconstruction process (Fig. 3) carried out produces a geometrical interpretation of each element in which the entire artifact has been semantically segmented, starting from documentary sources available. They are not able to integrate/implement the semantic interpretation of the artifact shapes and constructive characteristics. The sources-based reconstructive process is a reverse process [8, 29] which starts from the documentary sources, defines a semantic structure of case stydy, interprets its shapes (dimensional and geometric consistency), and produces a 3D digital model. This sources-based reconstruction process is developed according to two steps: the first one related to analysis and subjective interpretation of documentary sources available, characterized by a different level of uncertainty and a different level of the geometrical accuracy, and its use in order to produce a 3D digital model semantically enriched; the second one related to the production of 3D model.

This process can be developed according to the following operational pipeline:

1. collection of documentary sources-based data
2.a. semantic structuring of the artifact
2.b. analysis of documentary sources and extrapolation of information on the consistency of the artifact (geometrical shape, surface appearance, physical characteristics) through a process of analysis/interpretation (induction/deduction/analogy)/ decision assumed to extract the data based on the evidence, the relationship between information, deduction or conjecture
3.a. semantic enrichment of 3D reconstructed model
3.b. linkage between data used in the process of reconstruction and the level of uncertainty that characterizes each constitutive element
4. reconstructive modeling 3D
5. validation of the reconstructive hypothesis obtained through the data enrichment of each constitutive element and its displaying.

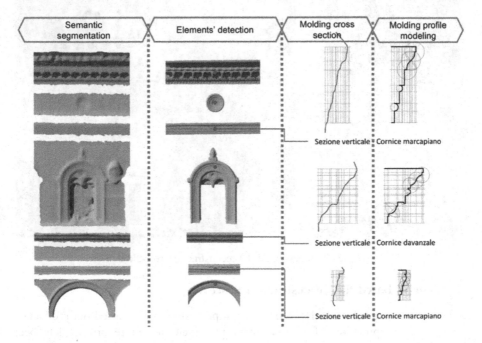

Fig. 4. Extraction and construction of the moulding ideal profiles from the numerical model

2.2 Reality-Based Reconstruction Process

On the other side (reality-based) the actual reality-based reconstruction techniques provide a high quality surface (shape and radiometric) reconstructions, but they are not able to automatically integrate/implement the semantic interpretation of the artifact shapes and constructive characteristics. The reality-based reconstructive process is a reverse process [8, 9] which starts from the real object, produces a 3D digital model and can interpret its shapes, trying to fit/match the idea which one suppose could upstream of its realization. This reality-based reconstruction process is developed according to two steps: the first one related to the coarse processing and editing of the 3D data sets; the second one related to the further processing of significant semantic information aimed (Fig. 4) at producing an enhanced 3D model of the real artifact.

This process can be developed according to the following operational pipeline:

1. acquisition of reality-based data
2. 3D modeling production
3.a. semantic structuring of the artifact
3.b. formalization of the theoretical knowledge concerning the artifact (geometrical shape, surface appearance, physical characteristics) through a process of analysis/interpretation able to identifying the genesis/rules of significant element shape
3.c semantic enrichment of 3D semantically segmented model through the definition of its measurement and its representation.

3 3D Model Quality/Properties

The construction rules do not determine the appearance; they define the assemblage of physical objects in 3D space. The adopted method refers to the hypothetical Shape (geometry, size, position), Appearance (surface features), Material (physical form, stratification of building systems) and History (temporal features) of the case study. Therefore, not only the schema but also the constructive rules can be identified, highlighted and discussed, and it addresses a wider gamma of objects that range from a simple vase or bas-relief to an entire building, or urban settlement.

The output of a digital reconstructive process acts in the definition of four areas intimately related one each other, which concurs to define the digital consistency, fidelity and quality of the produced 3D digital model:

- geometrical (shape, size, spatial position, topological relationship)
- radiometric (surface features)
- constructive (physical form, stratification of building/manufacturing systems)
- temporal (evolution/transformation over life cycle).

Each of these four aspects is characterized by a level of accuracy, coherence and certainty that may be of relevance for a classification of the digital outcome.

The geometrical fidelity (shape accuracy, geometrical detail, topological coherence, etc.) in respect to the reconstructed object is related to the question of accuracy of information that we can obtain by the data sources available as well as to the level of geometrical detail we would like to (or we can) reach/obtain. This implies a reference to a Level Of Detail (LOD), concerning outcomes of the geometrical model, as well as to Level of Definition (LoD), concerning the level of definition of characteristics of elements/objects of which the reconstructed object is made up. It means a digital reconstruction can show only the outer surface at a defined level of detail of the original or it can show more detailed geometrical or constructive information.

The radiometric fidelity (surface granularity properties, property depending accuracy, detail, coherence) in respect to the reconstructed object describes the virtual reproduction of the object's material surface properties. This concerns information about surface physical properties, such as colors, reflectance and glossiness properties of a surface.

The constructive fidelity (physical form, stratification of building/manufacturing systems) concerns inherent properties, including visible or invisible qualities, as well as behavior-related attributes, such as opacity or plasticity, which may be relevant for a numeric simulation.

The temporal fidelity (properties, property depending accuracy, detail, coherence) in respect to the reconstructed object describes the related criteria for the classification of a temporal fidelity, concerning for example a qualification/simulation of transition/transformation processes, or related context historic everyday life, or technical workflows, may be properties, accuracy, detail, and coherence.

In summary, this means that in a digital reconstruction project we must go beyond the mere reconstruction of the visual aspect that the case study could have, based on the knowledge/document sources we possess.

4 Semantic Structure of the 3D Digital Model

According with the principles established by Dudek and Blaise [30], a Cognitive Information System has to be necessarily based on identification and organization of non-ambiguous morphological elements to which different kind of information (including raw data, as well as documentation strategies, documentation results and process of documentation) can be attached.

The semantic structure applied to 3D digital modeling can be usefully used to reconstruct the hypothetical model, for identifying the characters, limitations and inconsistencies of those sources, for displaying the reconstructive conjectures adopted and not documented in the same documentation, and the reconstructive solutions more likely, giving back self-representation to the same instrument.

The semantic structure allows us:

(a) to manage 3D models in multi-resolution and divide them into subsets that are hierarchically consistent
(b) to efficiently manage the metadata related to the models themselves
(c) the ability to view and represent data relating to
    (c.1) reconstructive uncertainty
    (c.2) the level of accuracy/precision guaranteed
    (c.3) as well as control of the different versions of the models
(d) to facilitate the comparative analysis between the parties or sets of art works
(e) to evaluate different reconstructive or analytical conjectures or predict the chronological development of a building over its life [31].

The methodology used to structure the 3D models are based on the concept of a structured 3D information system using semantics that follows the 'shape grammar' for architectural elements, as introduced by Stiny and Mitchell [32] and Stiny [33], and on a structure of different level of abstraction of architectural space [34]. The base of this system of classifications is analogue to that of the architecture treaties [35, 36], which organize the 'art to build' knowledge, developing - relatively to the different styles and historical periods – a kind of 'identity coding' of architectural elements [9], in turn normally expressed through a hierarchical description, at geometrical, topological and spatial level, of all the elements which build up a group/unit.

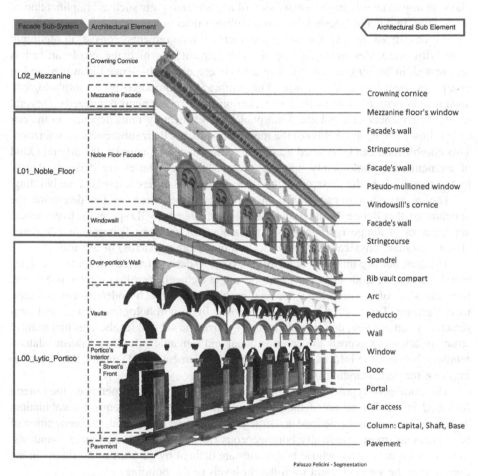

Fig. 5. Semantic segmentation of a numerical (reality-based) model: Palazzo Felicini, Bologna

According to Quintrand et al. [37], the artifact has to be seen as a system of knowledge, an association of semantics and shape, where the model is extracted from its description, while its representation is defined according to the objectives of the analysis. De Luca et al. [38] have subsequently developed an application simple and intuitive web-based interface. In this case, the multiple representations of buildings and their associated information have been organized around semantic models.

The segmentation of a model is an important step for its analysis and understanding. A wide variety of applications benefit from a process of pre-processing that uses a segmentation method efficient and reliable. The semantic 3D modeling methodology has been largely applied in different fields (archaeological [11] and architectural [39]) as well as on different types of artifacts, from a typological point of view (size, geometry, surface and textural properties, and semantics) and ranging from simple decorative apparatus to entire buildings [28]. In the field of reverse engineering of CAD models, as well as in that of computer graphics, for example, the segmentation plays an important role in the subdivision of a model into parts such as simplification of procedures in different meshes or in the collision detection.

As described in [8] the semantic method requirements consist in defining/ identifying the nodes that make up the sub-element in which the whole artifact is segmented, in building-up the relationship between each sub-element identified and in groupings them into macro-groups. The artifact is decomposed by a morphological, design and/or constructive point of view, defining several elements organized on several levels. The number of typological/morphological/elementary units depends on the criteria followed in the distinction of the minimum units and their subsequent combination. This combination can be defined according to the change of material, the different kind of elements, morphologically homogeneous, whose boundaries are defined by geometric transitions in the presence of the same element on different levels of the building.

The construction rules adopted in semantic segmentation do not determine the appearance; they define the assemblage of physical objects in 3D space: the hypothetical appearances of Shape (geometry, size), Radiometric (surface features) and Material characterization (physical form, stratification of building systems) of the artifact.

The semantic organization of an artifact (Fig. 5) derives from a vocabulary analysis which defines the nodes that make up the single element, identifies a reference space, formalizes as composition links the relationship between each node/element and their macro-groups. The artifact is then decomposed by a morphological, design and constructive point of view, defining elements organized on several levels. This hierarchical structure allows to express the compositional and semantic rules, to establish bilateral relations between the information sources and the elements of 3D model, that means to improve the understanding of the artifact.

The number of typological/morphological/elementary units depends on the criteria followed in the distinction of the minimum units and their subsequent combination. This combination can be defined according to the change of material, the recognition of type elements, morphologically homogeneous (for a building, e.g., frames, windows, moldings, capitals, etc.), whose boundaries are defined by geometric transitions in the presence of the same element on different levels of the building.

5 Knowledge Reconstruction and Formalization Process

The development of a Cognitive Information Systems in the CH field is based on the process of knowledge reconstruction, that means an interpretative study and a comparative analysis of documentary and historical sources and of different real elements, able to formalize the theoretical knowledge which is at the base of any cultural heritage artifact, which then can be used to support any further investigation stages, from analytical study to rendering and handling in a 3D real-time environment.

To reach this purpose, a system of knowledge rules, that means a collection of structured objects, identified through a precise vocabulary, have to be formalized. A Semantic-based representation of works of art, able to allow their qualitative descriptions, as well as merely quantitative. The scientific analysis of pure documentary sources supported by a proper graphical visualization and a transparent reference to the art of works' morphology allow the integration of quantitative information supported by reality-based digital data and qualitative information and knowledge extracted from documentation sources, associated to the art of works.

Both in sources-based, and in reality-based the semantic description and the semantic enrichment start from the analysis of different kind of sources of knowledge, in order to elaborate and extract semantic (geometrical, topological, spatial) rules related to each sub-element in which the work of art was semantically segmented.

The result of the semantic segmentation process is expressed in the combination of the different sub-elements, declined in their turn according to the manufacturing system used and according to the styles that characterize the different epochs. 2D geometric primitives (profiles, sections, generating lines of each architectural details), as well as dimensional values associated the parameters of the primitives instanced are extracted from the 3D elements.

The 3D model represents a digital replica/reconstruction of an artifact collected within an environment that allows the browsing through the single element hierarchically structured, retrieving the information related to the element and interactively check or manage the related knowledge information (Fig. 6).

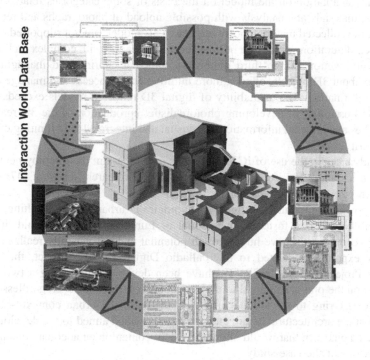

Fig. 6. 3D model as collector of information and knowledge

6 Two Open 3D Archives of Architectural and Urban Historical Systems

Within this wide field of research and investigation some experiences have been carried out concerning, albeit in a transdisciplinary manner, issues related to the systematization, technical access and proper research on architectural and urban cultural heritage [12, 40]. Urban history, in fact, concerning both architectural heritage and cultural history, is one of the key areas in digital humanities in which, regarding, in example, to the research interest, digital libraries and repositories could play an important role. Therefore, the common field of possible research is wide, as well as the need to face to different approaches, new methodologies and application of reconfigured technologies.

Some interesting examples of projects concerning the context reconstruction, at at the Max Planck Institute for the History of Science, include ECHO [41], the Virtual Laboratory (VL) [42] or the ColorConText [43].

Recently, thanks to further research in the domain of 3D model-based information systems, novel solutions are available, providing additional and reliable information on more and more complex tridimensional works of art.

Many online platforms such as Sketckfab [44] or ARIADNE [45] allow community users to upload 3D digital contents for visualization and web-based widespread dissemination, as well as specific tools for information analysis and sharing results in Cultural Heritage. CHER-Ob [46] (CULTURAL HERITAGE-Object) [17] is an open source platform developed by the Computer Graphics Group of Yale University. The system allows easy annotation on the model on the basis of some categories related to documentation, materials and analysis with possible upload of photographs and report generation of the collected material; however, heavy 3D models are not supported under the standard configuration, which can be an issue when dealing with complex architectures.

The introduction of the third dimension aimed at storing and managing documentation about 3D objects, offers a more intuitive way to access and manage different kinds of information. The availability of digital 3D rendered models exceeds, in fact, the simple possibility of developing photorealistic reproduction of the 3D real object, and it makes available all information in a visual and integrated way limiting errors due to granularity.

The advances in the use of ICT, as well as an increase in their deployment opened new scenarios and allow for further development in research, teaching [47] and dissemination programs on urban history.

The growing importance of digital technologies in urban history teaching, learning and researching, albeit fostered by national or European investment and initiatives, however, seems to still have huge growth potential and not yet fully realized.

Other experiences related to the Palladio Digital Library project, the Bologna Porticoes Project and SACHER [48] have been developed following a two-pronged approach: on the one hand aimed to the production of 3D models - regardless whether they were referring to the architectural heritage or to the urban context – has been designed at the architectural detail, and on the other hand aimed to the development of a web-based platform that would allow the use of content in an adequate manner to the characteristics of the case study.

6.1 Palladio Digital Library

The first case study - Palladio Digital Library [49] - is a complete 3D Web geo-database hosting an integrated and comprehensive Information System, in order to become the preferred interface for accessing this database, managed with ease and immediacy it gives access to the recordings relating to individual buildings by Palladio. The application has been developed in order to allow a complete representation of a wide-spread architectural heritage, whose complexity can hardly be approached and understood through textual or iconographic documents (Fig. 7).

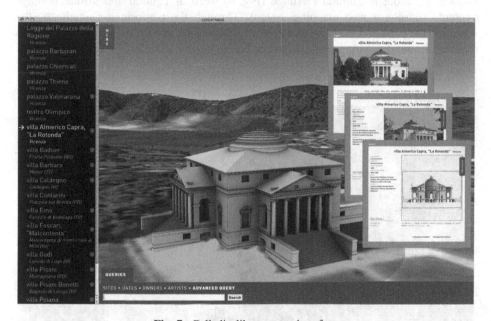

Fig. 7. Palladio library user interface

Concerning the ICT, and the usability, harvesting of data and the desirable added value, the IS, due to the inclusion of the 3D models in a DTM representing the landscape, allow to discover unknown relationships between the villas and their environment, to evaluate their architectural occupancy and to quickly access a complex system of information collected by several extensive researches developed by the CISAAP [50] over the years.

The Palladio Library 3D open archive concerns a complete 3D web geo-database grounded on GoogleEarth [51] where 3D models support a complex IS including 3D digital models, as well as 2D textual and iconographic materials.

This archive represents the core application of a PALLADIO Library [12] launched in 2012, and aimed to let accessible all the key materials for an understanding and appreciation of an architect's work: his drawings, the largest existing photo library devoted to him, thousands of survey drawings, original architect's writings, as well as a set of multimedia and 3D virtual reconstructions of his masterpieces, 54 edifices scattered over a regional area.

6.2   Bologna Porticoes Project

The second project – Portici di Bologna - concerns the development of a platform conceived for on-line accessing the wealth amount of data and resources related to a historic city center (historical, artistic, architectural, besides resources data regarding its actual state). The platform of historical porticoes in Bologna will perform the harvesting of several already existing databases, making the data available to citizens, tourists and scholars thanks to a graphic interface allowing a navigation in space and time.

The platform of Bologna Porticoes Project aimed to foresee the visualization of knowledge about it Cultural Heritage (Fig. 8), seen as cultural and virtual heritage contents through a web mapping system. Through the platform the architects, the scholars, the planners, the economists, as well as tourists and the citizens should have a representation of a wide urban context at the architectural scale.

Fig. 8. Bologna Porticoes Project: user interface retrieving of data collected mock-up

The structure of the 3D models developed for the platform dedicated to the Bologna arcades have been conceived as a prototype/model for implementations that can be made in the future.

The system of the Bologna Porticoes is the result of a centuries-long process of construction, transformation and planning of urban structure that led to the creation of the specific conditions for the realization of this exceptional and unique structure.

The approach used under the Bologna Porticoes Project, divided into three steps mutually connected to each other (modeling, segmentation and display), has been defined and implemented as general as possible, testing architectural objects characterized by different and specific characteristics and using different modeling procedures, in order to cover a sufficiently wide typological range of case studies.

6.3   SACHER Project

The third – SACHER project - consists in an active, widespread and free fruition by users, in which the platform allow an open-source and distributed cloud-computing environment.

The definition of operational protocols about cultural assets with an in-depth study on the process of the Cultural Heritage management - still an ongoing research activity - will provide a suitable data modelling in order to define data requirements needed to efficiently support activities and the information system. The analysis work done so far has involved academics, ICT experts, public bodies and final users working in this field. This useful collaboration provided suggestions and information on the ongoing project (Fig. 9).

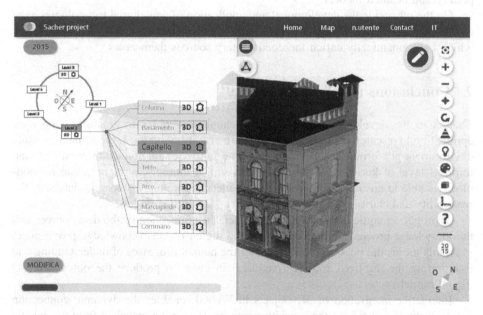

Fig. 9. SACHER Project: user interface browsing 3D model mock-up

Behind these three experiences there is a methodological approach aimed in obtaining 3D models allowing a semantic reading of the reality and the design intents throughout the interpretation of the shapes described by the model itself. The 3D modeling system adopted is based on the accepted convention of architectural analysis whereby structures are described as a series of structured objects using a specific architectural lexicon, obtaining semantic models ready-to-use as a knowledge system.

A Cognitive Information Systems offers new possibility for reading and interpreting architectural, urban as well as archaeological heritage, allowing all the information to be made available in a visual and integrated manner [1].

The development achieved by digital technologies has opened new scenarios, allowing the possibility to currently use a 3D model as an interface for localizing and querying data associated with it. 3D web-based technologies are able to provide a uniform framework for scientific display, allowing effective integration and presentation of web-based heterogeneous data and exploration and analysis of large volumes of data with geo-spatial, temporal and semantic characteristics.

On one side through this methodological approach the semantic structuring of digital models, give us the possibility to develop a process of acquiring and progressively adding knowledge that is able to note and make understandable and reusable the analysis of preliminary data and interpretation criteria used to validate the entire process. This opens the way towards a broad range of possible re-use of this knowledge, e.g. in the virtual reconstruction, from heterogeneous sources, of historical urban context [52–54], in scientific field as well as in educational or gaming one, utilizing an appropriate procedural and parametric modeling techniques to create visually compelling and detailed models.

On the other side the development and application of new digital technologies even in the examination of sources provide the ability to add new interpretive possibilities, which can semantically enrich the documentary sources themselves.

7 Conclusions and Further Works

Thanks to the development of the ICT technologies and infrastructures, and their application to research on architectural and urban cultural heritage, the semantic virtual environment platforms can become the engine for dissemination of different and customized level of knowledge. Besides a powerful technology an appropriate methodology is able to ensure, through descriptive metadata jointly a semantic database, the readability and clarity of digital data related to 3D digital models.

A proper semantic database allows, in fact, the connection of the data-sources and the knowledge processes involved in creating digital objects (knowledge provenance) [55], this means the possibility to modeling the human processes of understanding and interpreting the digitized sources (paradata) in order to produce the outcoming 3D digital models.

Interactive integration of 3D objects in WebGL enables the dynamic connection between the 3D data from the repository and its descriptive metadata from a semantic database. Web-based ICT systems can offer increasingly updated tools for the Cultural Heritage management, mainly for querying and storing historical/life cycle documentation, but also for integrating public and private archives, connecting professionals to public bodies in a quicker and easier way and, if available, providing a smart 3D navigation system, always accessible to the users via internet.

One of the key points is the appropriate methodological approach that future research will take in order to combine and make the documentation and knowledge related to any 3D modeling (source or reality-based) reconstruction fully accessible in its three different declinations" [7]: (a) documentation strategies addressing the "preservation of knowledge", (b) documentation of results through appropriate metadata, and (c) documentation process of any knowledge production related to Cultural Heritage artifacts.

A standardized methodology of source or reality-based 3D reconstruction of tangible Cultural Heritage, based on (i) a transparent reconstruction workflow, (ii) 3D model qualified by readable quality/properties, (iii) a proper semantic structure of the 3D digital model, and (iv) a retrievable knowledge reconstruction and formalization process, would ensure the interoperability of data sets by referring to recognized standard reference ontologies. It would be able to ensure mapping the data sets through 3D-objectoriented records with an integrated inline description of geometry, appearance and materials.

The described method of digital reconstruction and the semantic enrichment of 3D data sets allow the possibilities, for different kind of artifact, to render its analytical representation, alongside their semantic metadata, and valuable information concerning transparency, consistency, certainty and long-time preservation access.

Even though some of these issues still need to be largely investigated, as well as others connected to the full fruition of 3D contents, the experiences here presented represent the outcome of a multidisciplinary cooperation between architects, urban historians and information scientist that have been able to develop applicable working techniques, to define valid strategies, and to apply classifications useful to supporting scientific work besides the conveyance of knowledge.

Acknowledgement. Author would like to thank Giorgio Dall'Osso and Riccardo Foschi for their valuable contribution to drawing-up the diagrams, the research group of Palladio Library, coordinated by Marco Gaiani, and Bologna Porticoes Project, coordinated by Municipality of Bologna, and Sacher Project, coordinated by Rebecca Montanari.

References

1. Kuroczyński, P., Hauck, O.B., Dworak, D.: Digital reconstruction of cultural heritage – questions of documentation and visualisation standards for 3D content. In: Ioannides, M., Mageanat-Thalmann, N., Fink, E., Zarnic, R., Yen, A., Quak, E. (eds.) Digital Heritage. Progress in Cultural Heritage: Documentation, Preservation and Protection. 5th International Conference, EuroMed 2014, Limassol, Cyprus, 3–8 November 2014, Proceedings. Springer, Heidelberg (2014). https://doi.org/10.1007/978-3-319-13695-0
2. Stefani, C., Busayarat, C., Lombardo, J., De Luca, L.: A web platform for the consultation of spatialized and semantically enriched iconographic sources on cultural heritage buildings. Int. J. Comput. Cult. Herit. **6**(3), 13:1–13:17 (2013). https://doi.org/10.1145/2499931. 2499934. ACM
3. Veltman, K.: Electronic media and visual knowledge. Knowl. Organ. **20**(1), 47–54 (1993)
4. Moles, A.: Vers une théorie écologique de l'image. In: Thibault-Lalan, A.-M. (ed.) Image et Communication. Editions Universitaires, Paris (1979)
5. Gooding, D.C.: Visualizing scientific inference. Top. Cogn. Sci. **2**(1), 15–35 (2010). https://doi.org/10.1111/j.1756-8765.2009.01048.x
6. Kőller, D., Frischer, B., Humphreys, G.: Research challenges for digital archives of 3D cultural heritage models. ACM J. Comput. Cult. Herit., **2**(3), Article no. 7 (2009). https://doi.org/10.1145/1658346.1658347

7. Münster, S., Hegel, W., Kröber, C.: A model classification for digital 3D reconstruction in the context of humanities research. In: Münster, S., Pfarr-Harfst, M., Kuroczyński, P., Ioannides, M. (eds.) 3D Research Challenges in Cultural Heritage II. LNCS, vol. 10025, pp. 3–31. Springer, Cham (2016). https://doi.org/10.1007/978-3-319-47647-6_1

8. Apollonio, F.I.: Classification schemes for visualization of uncertainty in digital hypothetical reconstruction. In: Münster, S., Pfarr-Harfst, M., Kuroczyński, P., Ioannides, M. (eds.) 3D Research Challenges in Cultural Heritage II. LNCS, vol. 10025, pp. 173–197. Springer, Cham (2016). https://doi.org/10.1007/978-3-319-47647-6_9

9. De Luca, L., Véron, P., Florenzano, M.: Semantic-based modelling and representation of patrimony buildings. In: SVE Workshop Towards Semantic Virtual Environments, Mar 2005, Villars, Switzerland, pp. 1–11 (2005)

10. Apollonio, F.I., Corsi, C., Gaiani, M., Baldissini, S.: An integrated 3D geodatabase for Palladio's work. Int. J. Archit. Comput. 8(2), 111–133 (2010)

11. Apollonio, F.I., Gaiani, M., Benedetti, B.: 3D reality-based artefact models for the management of archaeological sites using 3D Gis: a framework starting from the case study of the Pompeii Archaeological area. J. Archaeol. Sci. 39(5), 1271–1287 (2012). https://doi.org/10.1016/j.jas.2011.12.034

12. Apollonio, F.I., Baldissini, S., Beltramini, G., Borgherini, M.M., Clini, P., Gaiani, M., Palestini, C., Sacchi, L., et al.: I geo-modelli per la PALLADIO Library: un archivio condiviso e in divenire. Disegnare Idee Immagini 47, 46–59 (2013)

13. Meyer, E., Grussenmeyer, P., Perrin, J.P., Durand, A., Drap, P.: A virtual research environment for archaeological data management, visualization and documentation. In: 35e Conférence du CAA "Layers of Perception. Advanced Technological Means to Illuminate our Past", pp. 1–6 (2007)

14. De Luca, L., Busarayat, C., Stefani, C., Renaudin, N., Florenzano, M., Vèron, P.: An iconography-based modeling approach for the spatio-temporal analysis of architectural heritage. In: SMI Conference 2010, pp. 78–89. IEEE (2010). https://doi.org/10.1109/SMI.2010.28

15. Reilly, P.: Towards a virtual archaeology. In: Proceedings of Computer Applications in Archaeology, pp. 133–139 (1990)

16. Fernàndez-Palacios, B.J., Remondino, F., Stefani, C., Lombardo, J., De Luca, L.: Web visualization of complex reality-based 3D models with NUBES. In: Digital Heritage International Congress (Digital Heritage), 2013, vol. 1, pp. 701–704. IEEE (2013). https://doi.org/10.1109/DigitalHeritage.2013.6743821

17. Shi, W., Kotoula, E., Akoglu, K., Yang, Y., Rushmeier, H.: CHER-Ob: a tool for shared analysis in cultural heritage. In: Catalano, C.E., De Luca, L. (eds.) EUROGRAPHICS Workshop on Graphics and Cultural Heritage (2016). https://doi.org/10.2312/gch.20161404

18. Pfarr-Harfst, M.: Documentation system for digital reconstructions. Reference to the Mausoleum of the Tang-Dynastie at Zhaoling, in Shaanxi Province, China. In: 16th International Conference on "Cultural Heritage and New Technologies", Vienna, pp. 648–658 (2011)

19. Ronzino, P., Amico, N., Niccolucci, F.: Assessment and comparison of metadata schemas for architectural heritage. In: XXIII CIPA Symposium – Proceedings (2011)

20. Doerr, M.: The CIDOC CRM – an ontological approach to semantic interoperability of metadata. AI Mag. 24(3), 75–92 (2003)

21. Felicetti, A., Lorenzini, M.: Metadata and tools for integration and preservation of cultural heritage 3D information. In: XXIII CIPA Symposium – Proceedings (2011)

22. Münster, S., Prechtel, N.: Beyond software. Design implications for virtual libraries and platforms for cultural heritage from practical findings. In: Ioannides, M., Magnenat-Thalmann, N., Fink, E., Žarnić, R., Yen, A.-Y., Quak, E. (eds.) EuroMed 2014. LNCS, vol. 8740, pp. 131–145. Springer, Cham (2014). https://doi.org/10.1007/978-3-319-13695-0_13

23. Hermon, S., Nikodem, J., Perlingieri, C.: Deconstructing the VR - data transparency, quantified uncertainty and reliability of 3D models. In: Arnold, D., Ioannides, M., Niccolucci, F., Mania, K. (eds.) 7th International Symposium on Virtual Reality, Archaeology and Cultural Heritage (VAST 2006), pp. 123–129. Eurographics Association, Nicosia (2006). https://doi.org/10.2312/VAST/VAST06/123-129

24. Apollonio, F.I., Gaiani M., Sun, Z.: 3D modeling and data enrichment in digital reconstruction of Architectural Heritage. In: XXIV International CIPA Symposium 2013, Strasbourg, France, pp. 43–48 (2013). https://doi.org/10.5194/isprsarchives-XL-5-W2-43-2013

25. De Francesco, G., D'Andrea, A.: Standards and guidelines for quality digital cultural three-dimensional content creation. In: Ioannides, M., Addison, A., Georgopoulos, A., Kalisperis, L. (eds.) Digital Heritage: Proceedings of the 14th International Conference on Virtual Systems and Multimedia. Project Papers, pp. 229–233. Archaeolingua, Budapest (2008)

26. Apollonio, F.I., Fallavollita, F.: Elementi per una morfologia dei portici bolognesi. In: Gaiani, M. (ed.) I Portici di Bologna Architettura, Modelli 3D e ricerche tecnologiche, pp. 117–142. BUP, Bologna (2015)

27. Fallavollita, F., Ballabeni, M., Foschi, R., Perugini, G.: Semantic description of three-dimensional models of Bologna porches. SCIRES-IT 5(1), 31–40 (2015). https://doi.org/10.2423/i22394303v5n1p31

28. Apollonio, F.I.: Architettura in 3D. Modelli digitali per i sistemi cognitivi. Bruno Mondadori, Milano (2012)

29. Pfarr-Harfst, M.: Typical workflows, documentation approaches and principles of 3D digital reconstruction of cultural heritage. In: Münster, S., Pfarr-Harfst, M., Kuroczyński, P., Ioannides, M. (eds.) 3D Research Challenges in Cultural Heritage II. LNCS, vol. 10025, pp. 32–46. Springer, Cham (2016). https://doi.org/10.1007/978-3-319-47647-6_2

30. Dudek, I., Blaise, J.-Y.: New experimentation of a generic framework for architectural heritage data visualisation. In: Proceeding WSCG 2003, pp. 109–117 (2003)

31. Stefani, C., De Luca, L., Véron, P., Florenzano, M.: Modeling building historical evolutions. In: Proceedings of Focus K3D Conference on Semantic 3D Media and Content. INRIA, Sophia Antipolis (2010)

32. Stiny, G., Mitchell, W.J.: The Palladian grammar. Environ. Plann. B 5, 5–18 (1978)

33. Stiny, G.: Introduction to shape and shape grammars. Environ. Plann. B 7, 343–351 (1980)

34. Tzonis, A., Lefaivre, L.: Classical Architecture: The Poetics of Order. MIT Press, Cambridge (1986)

35. Palladio, A.: I Quattro Libri dell'Architettura. De Franceschi, Venezia (1570)

36. Vignola, J.B.: Regola delli cinque ordini d'architettura. Remondini, Bassano (1787)

37. Quintrand, P., Autran, J., Florenzano, M., Fregier, M., Zoller, J.: La CAO en Architecture. Hermes, Paris (1985)

38. De Luca, L., Florenzano, M., Veron, P.: A generic formalism for the semantic modeling and representation of architectural elements. Vis. Comput. 23, 181–205 (2007). https://doi.org/10.1007/s00371-006-0092-5

39. Apollonio, F.I., Gaiani, M., Corsi, C.: A semantic and parametric method for 3D models used in 3D cognitive-information system. In: Schmitt, G., Hoverstadt, L., Van Gool, L., Bosché, F., Burkhard, R., Coleman, S., Halatsch, J., Hansmeyer, M., Konsorski-Lang, S., Kunze, A., Sehmi-Luck, M. (eds.) Future Cities, 28th eCAADe 2010 Conference, pp. 717–726. ECAADE – ETH Zurich, Zurich (2010)

40. Apollonio, F.I., Gaiani, M., Felicori, M., Guidazzoli, A., Virgolin, L., Liguori, M.C., Fallavollita, F., Ballabeni, M., Sun, Z., Baglivo, A.: Bologna porticoes project: a 3D repository for WHL UNESCO nomination. In: Addison, A.C., Guidi, G., De Luca, L., Pescarin, S. (eds.) 2013 Digital Heritage International Congress, Marseille, France, 28 Oct – 1 Nov 2013, pp. 563–570. IEEE, Piscataway (2013). https://doi.org/10.1109/DigitalHeritage.2013.6743617

41. http://echo.mpiwg-berlin.mpg.de/home

42. http://vlp.mpiwg-berlin.mpg.de/index_html

43. https://arb.mpiwg-berlin.mpg.de/

44. https://sketchfab.com/

45. http://visual.ariadne-infrastructure.eu/

46. http://graphics.cs.yale.edu/site/cher-ob-open-source-platform-shared-analysis-cultural-heritage-research

47. Hillis, P., Munro, B.: ICT in history education, Scotland and Europe. Soc. Sci. Comput. Rev. 23(2), 190–205 (2005). https://doi.org/10.1177/0894439304273268

48. SACHER project is a project, coordinated by CIRI-ICT, University of Bologna, granted by Regione Emilia Romagna (POR FESR 2014-2020) within the European Regional Development Fund. http://www.sacherproject.com

49. Apollonio, F.I., Baldissini, S., Clini, P., Gaiani, M., Palestini, C., Trevisan, C.: The PALLADIOlibrary geo-models: an open 3D archive to manage and visualize information-communication resources about Palladio. In: XXIV International CIPA Symposium. ISPRS Archives, XL-5-W2-49-2013, pp. 49–54 (2013). https://doi.org/10.5194/isprsarchives-XL-5-W2-49-2013

50. PALLADIO Library is a Geo-Database outcome of a research project, coordinated by Guido Beltramini and Marco Gaiani, and made possible thanks to the grant of Arcus spa. https://www.palladiomuseum.org/exhibitions/museum/about?lang=en

51. Jones, M.T.: Google's geospatial organizing principle. Comput. Graph. and Appl. 27(4), 8–13 (2007). https://doi.org/10.1109/MCG.2007.82

52. Rome Reborn Projects. http://romereborn.frischerconsulting.com/

53. Apollonio, F.I., Giovannini, E.C.: A paradata documentation methodology for the Uncertainty Visualization in digital reconstruction of CH artifacts. SCIRES-IT 5, 1–24 (2015). https://doi.org/10.2423/i22394303v5n1p1

54. Webster, A.: Building a better Paris in 'Assassin's Creed Unity'. Historical accuracy meets game design. The Verge (2014). http://www.theverge.com/2014//10/31/7132587/assassins-creed-unity-paris

55. Bruseker, G., Guillem, A., Carboni, N.: Semantically documenting virtual reconstruction: building a path to knowledge provenance. In: XXV International CIPA Symposium. ISPRS Annals, II-5/W3-33-2015, pp. 33–40 (2015). https://doi.org/10.5194/isprsannals-II-5-W3-33-2015

Practice – Research Challenges – Standards!
A Reflection of Digital 3D Reconstructed
Models for Urban Structures

Mieke Pfarr-Harfst(✉)

Digital Design Unit, Technische Universität Darmstadt,
El-Lissitzky-Str. 1, 64287 Darmstadt, Germany
pfarr@dg.tu-darmstadt.de

Abstract. This paper includes a work report of two reconstruction projects realized at the research department "digital reconstruction" at TU Darmstadt. A special focus is on the importance of the urban context and its digital 3D reconstruction for the particular research project and its challenges related to the working process and model structures. Furthermore, current research questions like e.g. documentation, standards, methodology and archiving are interlinked with this.

Keywords: Digital cultural heritage · Model structures · LOD

1 Introduction

For more than 25 years, digital 3D reconstructed models [1] of historic buildings or urban structures in the field of the Cultural Heritage have been found. These 3D models are established as medium in exhibitions as well as in TV documentation. Hereby it is important to differentiate between a visualization and digital 3D reconstruction of a historical building or urban structure. A visualization is only an illustration of the past without a scientific basis; a digital 3D reconstruction is in contrast a detailed digital replica of such a Cultural Heritage site based on the respective scientific state of knowledge. The level of detail as well as the model structures of such digital 3D reconstruction ranges from an urban level as a general overview up to a detailed digital replica of a building or a building element.

In the last decade, these digital 3D reconstructed models are also used as a research tool, which are extending the methodology of traditional scholarship [2]. However, this has also expanded the discussion about these models with topics such as usability, methodology and standards. A partial aspect is certainly also the meaningful structuring of the models according to their level of detail in such a research process and the linking of the data and information. Particularly large-scale structures, such as urban areas, are a great challenge in terms of project structures, organization of workflows, data management as well as documentation. These aspects have a direct impact on the quality of the scientific work and thus on the recognition of digital 3D reconstruction as a scientific methodology.

© Springer International Publishing AG, part of Springer Nature 2018
S. Münster et al. (Eds.): UHDL 2017/DECH 2017, CCIS 817, pp. 159–176, 2018.
https://doi.org/10.1007/978-3-319-76992-9_10

This paper includes a work report of two reconstruction projects realized at the research department "Digital Reconstruction" at Digital Design Unit, Technische Universität Darmstadt. A special focus is on the importance of the urban context and its digital 3D reconstruction for the particular research project and its challenges related to the working process. Furthermore, current research questions like e.g. documentation, standards, methodology and archiving are interlinked with this.

2   Practice! - Research Projects

2.1   General Basics and Principles

Digital 3D reconstructed models are the main focus of the research department "Digital Reconstructions" at Digital Design Unit, Technische Universität Darmstadt, for more than 25 years. A lot of important World Cultural Heritage sites such as Moscow Kremlin, Cathedral of Florence (Fig. 1), St. Peter in Rome, Templo Mayor in Mexico, Crystal Palace London (Fig. 2) as well as destroyed German Synagogues (Fig. 3) have been reconstructed and presented to a broad public during this time period.

These reconstruction projects and the research was done in interdisciplinary and international cooperation with different project partners, project intentions and results.

Hereby the main interest was not on creation of a digital 3D reconstructed model of a single historical building, but rather on the digital replica of the complete building structure as well as its urban context.

Against this background of practical experiences a further focus of the department is on critical reflection of these digital 3D reconstructed models and their use in dissemination and research. Some of the topics are documentation of digital 3D reconstructions, defining of general terms and basic principles as well as guidelines for scientifically based working processes.

Fig. 1. Digital 3D reconstruction of Cathedral of Florence (© DDU, TU Darmstadt)

Fig. 2. Digital 3D reconstruction of Crystal Palace (© DDU, TU Darmstadt)

Fig. 3. Virtual Synagogues (© DDU, TU Darmstadt)

In order to establish such guidelines in the long term, basic research in the field of working and creation processes as well as methodology is needed.

Therefore, as first step a study at different international institutes (e.g. University College London, King's College London, University Sarajevo, Technische Universität Darmstadt) was carried out to determine the status quo related to differences or similarities of processes and methods.

In this study working processes and methodology of more than 25 research projects in the field of digital 3D reconstructions were investigated and evaluated based on same parameters [1]. As a result, a schema of a typical working process within four main phases – preparation, data acquisition, data processing and finishing – were defined. The process achieves the highest degree of complexity during the phase "data processing". Within this phase four steps are interlinked in a circulating procedure. Between the four main phases and the single steps in the phase "data processing" an input-output principle has been found.

Parameters such as project partner, financial and personal resources, intention, timeline as well as historical resources as basis for a digital reconstruction are building the framework, the background of the complete process. This framework as well as some milestones between the single working phases have to be defined at the very beginning of each project as contribution of quality assurance [1, 2].

Therefore, the following guidelines are a binding basis for working processes of each project carried out at Digital Design Unit [3]:

1. Definition of model structures (macro- and micro-structures) and level of detail
2. Creation of reference models within the defined model structures
3. Classification and structuring of sources
4. Definition of a nomenclature for 3D models and sources
5. Archiving of important stages of the 3D models
6. Defining of milestones between the working phases and within the phase data processing
7. Documentation of the reconstruction process with R-A-M (Reconstruction-Argumentation-Method) [4]

But, generally valid principles for digital 3D reconstructed models and their creation processes at an international level do not exist at the moment. Binding rules, best practice examples or standards for structuring a digital 3D reconstructed models are not available.

The definition of the model structures at the beginning of the project as well as the creation of reference models are crucial in order to organize workflows and data management.

Today different kinds of definition of such model structures exist. The most famous one is the definition of LODs of CityGML for 3D models within geographic information systems [5] or the LOD as Level of Development within BIM [6].

But, these currently usual classification of LOD according to the CityGML or BIM specification is not sufficient for a scientifically based digital 3D reconstruction with regard to urban structures as well as architectural and construction elements of a building (inside and outside).

The city GML classification has only five model structure levels (LOD 0–LOD 4), which are to be used for the archiving and exchange of 3D city models. The most important aspect is the representation of an overall urban situation with building structures, topography and infrastructure [5]. These five model structures are defined as follows:

- LOD 0 – regional, landscape
- LOD 1 – city, region
- LOD 2 – city districts, projects
- LOD 3 – architectural models (outside), landmarks
- LOD 4 – architectural models (interior)

Last year, this division was extended to sixteen LODs, for which the five levels were subdivided into more detailed levels [7]. Here "a refined set of 16 LODs focused on the grade of the exterior geometry of buildings" is presented.

As mentioned above there is another type of definition of model structures, their level of detail and information: the so-called level of development from BIM. This is an architecture related specification and correlates with the work phases of Fee Structure of Architects and Engineers in Germany (HOAI). Within this specification five LOD (LOD 100 – LOD 500) are defined [6].

- LOD 100: Conceptual Model (with parameters like area, volume, orientation)
- LOD 200: General Model (elements with approximate quantities, size, shape, location and orientation)
- LOD 300: Accurate Model (elements with specific assemblies, precise quantity, size, shape, location and orientation)
- LOD 400: Detailed Model
- LOD 500: As-built-Model

The definition of these model structures is strongly geared to the needs of building industry and its processes.

Both definition of model structures do not really fit to the needs of a digital 3D reconstruction of single buildings within its urban context. An unique assignment of both LOD-concepts to model structures of reconstruction project is most often not possible.

To understand an urban pattern with all its variety it is often not enough to visualize it as a flat textured 3D model. Here, again, it has to differentiate between a visualization, such for TV documentation or the game industry, and digital 3D reconstruction as a method for answering research questions, e.g. of urban development.

This is similar to the digital 3D reconstruction of a single building. Here, too, it is not sufficient for the intention of research to visualize e.g. the facade with a simple texture, often it is necessary to reconstruct all architectural and designing elements more detailed.

Against this background, the idea of macro- and microstructures as a concept structuring digital 3D reconstructed models arises (Fig. 4). Furthermore, from the practical point of view this system of macro- and microstructures is a flexible, extensible and adaptable kind of classification and depends on the project, its content, intention and aims. Thus, it is quite useful to define the macro- and microstructure individually for each research project and carry out several levels of these structures within a project.

As a generally valid concept the macrostructures could be defined as structures of whole areas, landscapes, city structures as well as building environments. The level of microstructures includes more detailed 3D models of urban districts, streets, single buildings or objects within these buildings.

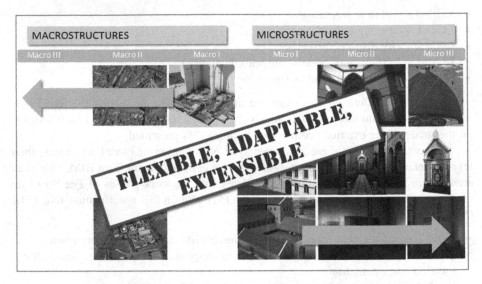

Fig. 4. Concept of micro- and microstructures

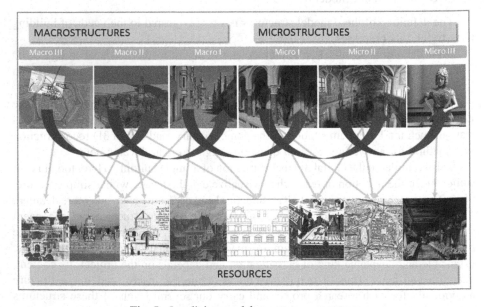

Fig. 5. Interlining model structures – resources

Furthermore, all these different model-structures are interlinked to each other as well as to the resources of the project (Fig. 5). This underlines the high complexity of the creation process of such digital 3D reconstructions.

The challenges of the above-mentioned model structures (macro- and micro-structures) and LOD will be deepened in the following by means of two examples of digital 3D reconstruction projects and later related to current challenges.

2.2   Project "The Imperial Tombs of Xi'an"

This project consisted of the reconstruction of the tomb of the first emperor Qin Shihuangdi and the tomb of the emperor Taizong at Zhaoling. It was produced for the exhibition "Xi´an - Kaiserliche Macht im Jenseits" at Bundeskunsthalle in Bonn (2006), in which the results of fifteen years of German-Chinese co-operation in the field of Cultural Heritage were presented to the public [8]. Intention of the project was to illustrate the spatial dimension of the area around Xi´an and the archaeological findings contained therein. Furthermore, the newest archaeological research results about the imperial tombs should be visualized by means of digital 3D reconstructed models. By use of digital 3D reconstructed models the exhibits were placed in their overall context. Following international project partners from Germany and China were involved: Römisch-Germanisches Zentralmuseum Mainz (RGZM), Germany; Archaeological Institute of Xi´an, China; Museum of the First Emperor Qin, Lintong, China; Bayerisches Amt für Denkmalpflege München, Germany; i3mainz, Germany.

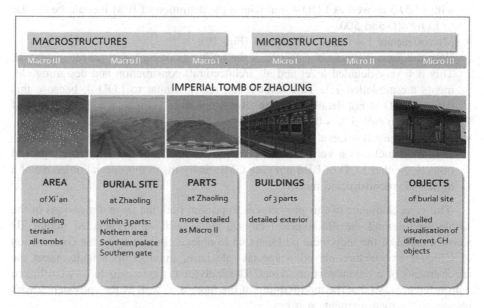

Fig. 6. Project Xi án: Schema of macro- and microstructures

Beside this, students of nine nations were involved in the creation of the digital 3D reconstruction models. The close cooperation with Chinese and German scientists characterized the reconstruction process. The entire complex of burial site at Zhaoling consists of 187 ancillary graves, four main parts and a total of 29 individual buildings therein. Within the research project the four main parts and all of the individual buildings were digitally reconstructed. Within the project part "Burial Side at Zhaoling" three macro- and three microstructures were defined (Fig. 6). In the following the content of these structures is describes as well as interlinked to the LOD-Definition of City GML and BIM.

- Macrostructure III – Level of area around the city Xi´an (Fig. 7).
  Within this level a structural 3D model, in which all ancillary graves and the capital cities of the emperors of three Dynasties were placed, is represented. Neither the definition of City GML with LOD 0 nor LOD 100 of BIM and their definition really fit for this. For example, the digital 3D reconstructed model is a real 3D model and not a 2,5D model such as LOD 0.
- Macrostructure II – Level of burial site at Zhaoling (Fig. 8).
  The burial site of Zhaoling with four parts is included here and the 3D models is up to LOD 2 and LOD 3 of City GML or related to the definition of BIM similar to LOD 400.
- Macrostructure I – Level of single parts (Fig. 9).
  This is the reconstruction of the four parts of Zhaoling (Northern and Southern part, Southern Gate, Tomb within the mountain) including details such as architectural and construction elements. Therefore, the level of detail does not quite correspond with LOD 3 as well as LOD 4, but within the definition of BIM it could be similar to LOD 400 and 500.
- Microstructure I – Level of buildings (Fig. 10).
  Here the interior spaces and façade of the buildings of each part are reconstructed. This is a very detailed level and all architectural, construction and designing elements are modelled 1:1. This level is not really similar to LOD 4, because this defined LOD is not detailed enough. But it could be compared with LOD 500 of BIM as a so called "As-built-Modell".
- Microstructure II – Level of objects (Fig. 11).
  This level includes a very detailed reconstruction of archaeological findings and objects. Neither LOD of BIM nor City GML really fits to this special objective of a digital 3D reconstructed model.

The great challenge of this project was to present both the large dimensions of the whole area around the old imperial city Xi'an as well as the detailed digital 3D reconstruction of the individual buildings up to objects. In particular, the construction of Chinese architecture played a special role here, in order to actually meet the requirements of a reconstruction model. The individual model structures were linked with references, so that the modifiability of the models as well as the consistency with respect to the measurements was ensured.

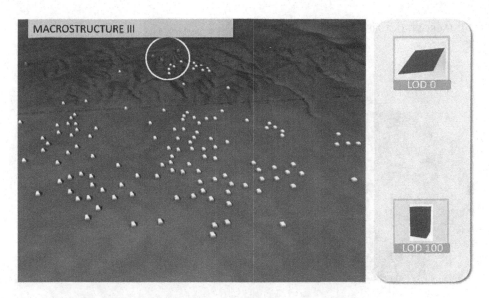

Fig. 7. Macrostructure III – Area around Xi´an (© DDU, TU Darmstadt)

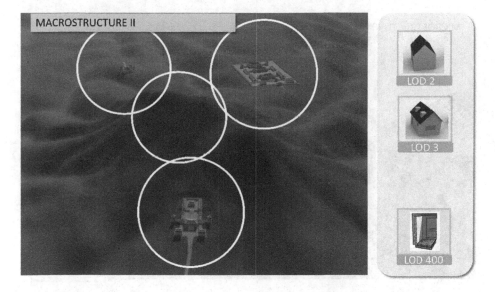

Fig. 8. Macrostructure II – Burial Site at Zhaoling (© DDU, TU Darmstadt)

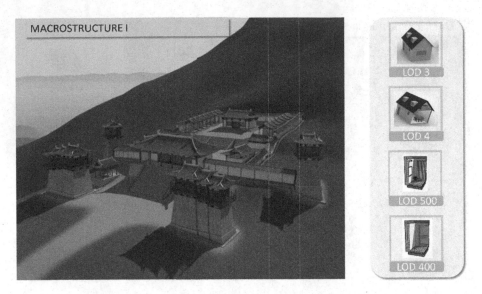

Fig. 9. Macrostructure I – Northern part of the burial site (© DDU, TU Darmstadt)

Fig. 10. Microstructure I – Single buildings (© DDU, TU Darmstadt)

Fig. 11. Microstructure II – Archaeological findings (© DDU, TU Darmstadt)

2.3   Project "Ephesus During the Byzantine Period"

The main goals of this project were to reconstruct the historical city structure of the ancient city of Ephesos in three time periods (Hellenistic, Roman and Byzantine) and ten selected buildings during the Byzantine Period. Intention for this project was the exhibition "Pracht und Alltag in Byzanz" at Bundeskunsthalle in Bonn in 2009 [9]. Similar to project Xi´an the context of archaeological findings and objects should be visualized by means of digital 3D reconstruction. For this purpose, it was necessary to create digital 3D reconstructions of the city structure, street spaces as well as individual buildings and objects.

Beside the intention of dissemination, the digital reconstruction was used as a research tool to answer questions about construction or building structures.

Partners in this project were Römisch-Germanische Zentralmuseum Mainz, Germany; Österreichisches Archäologisches Institut (ÖAI), Austria; Austrian Academy of Science (ÖAW), Austria; i3mainz, Germany. The project was funded by Federal Ministry of Building and Education (BMBF), Germany.

Depending on the intention and purpose of the project model structures from macro II to micro III were defined (Fig. 12). The level macrostructure III doesn´t really exist in this project, because it was not necessary to show the entire area around Ephesos.

The content of these levels as well as their link to LOD of CityGML and BIM could be described as follows:

- Macrostructure II – Level of city of Ephesos (Fig. 13).
  This level includes models of urban structures of the three time periods and their infrastructure and organisation. The 3D reconstructed model is similar to LOD 0, 1, and 2, but according to the focus on urban structure the definition of model structures of BIM does not really fit.

- Macrostructure I – Level of streets (Fig. 14).
  Here two important streets as urban pattern are reconstructed with all surrounding houses. This level is a mixture between LOD 2 and 3 of CityGML, because two level of details are combined: The city structure in the background, which is not so detailed as the area of the street. Here all important architectural elements are reconstructed. It was necessary here to find the right balance between detailed reconstruction of single elements and data volume. Therefore, it is not really a reconstruction 1:1. Related to the classification of BIM this level could be classified as a mixture of LOD 400 and 500.
- Microstructure I – Level of single buildings (Fig. 15).
  Selected historical buildings with all their details (inside and outside) were digitally reconstructed in this level. Here again the level is similar to LOD 3 and 4, but both are not detailed enough. It is possible to classify it as a so called "As built model" in LOD 500 of BIM
- Microstructure II – Level of single objects and details of buildings (Fig. 16).
  Within this level the interior of the different buildings were modelled. Intention of these detailed digital 3D reconstructed models was to contextualize the objects shown in the exhibition.
  Similar to the project "Xi´an" this level includes a very detailed reconstruction of archaeological findings and objects. There is no definition of usual model structures (BIM or City GML), which fits to this.

The focus of this project was more on the representation of the archaeological findings and objects as well as their context. Therefore, a detailed description of the interior spaces as well as the urban structure was necessary. The digital 3D reconstruction of the streets and squares required a combination of different models of a structural level.

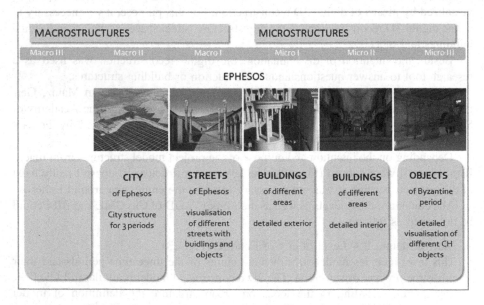

Fig. 12. Project Ephesos: Schema of macro- and microstructures

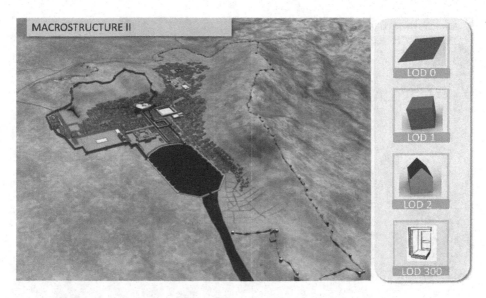

Fig. 13. Macrostructure II – City of Ephesos (Byzantine Period) (© DDU, TU Darmstadt)

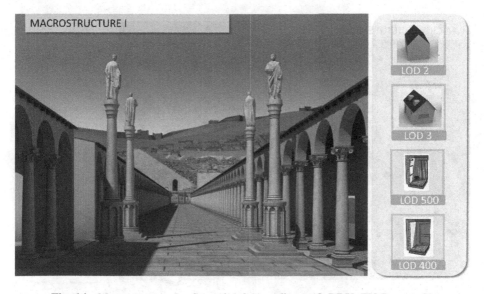

Fig. 14. Macrostructure I – Street level (Arcadiane) (© DDU, TU Darmstadt)

Fig. 15. Microstructure I – Interior design of buildings (Basilica of St. Johan) (© DDU, TU Darmstadt)

Fig. 16. Microstructure III – Archaeological findings and objects (Stone Saw) (© DDU, TU Darmstadt)

3 Discussion

In both projects these model structures and individual defined level of details were the binding basis during the whole reconstruction project. With this it was possible to interlink the different 3D models and manage the data behind. Beside this, the differentiation between the different level of detail avoided too large amount of data (Fig. 17).

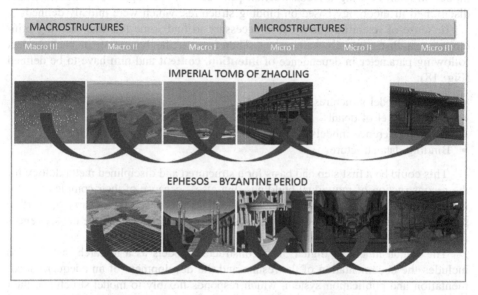

Fig. 17. Reference models – interlinking modelstructures

But, the transfer of usual classification of LOD (BIM or CityGML) to practice research projects has shown, that the current solutions about structuring of a 3D model and its level of detail does not meet the requirement of a digital replica of a building or an urban structure. However, it should be noted, that the classification of LOD of BIM as well as City GML have been created for a particular application area; BIM for building construction and CityGML for topographic applications at urban scale. The creation of digital 3D reconstructions, on the other hand, is closely linked to factors such as goals, intention, technics, partners as well as resources and their granularity, which are individual for each project. This makes finding uniform model structures very complex. Some current research projects have tried a first step to solve this problem [10], but the offered solution is often project-related and not in a general manner. But, understanding digital 3D reconstructions as an innovative future-oriented research tool, it is necessary to create digital replica and not only visualization of historical buildings and urban structures.

Model structures and LOD always depend on intention and content and have to be defined individually. Such an individual definition of model structures and level of details makes the challenges of scientifically-based digital 3D reconstructed models of individual buildings and complex urban structures visible. The proposed concept of individual defined macro- and microstructures as an adaptable, flexible and extensible system could be a generally valid solution (Fig. 4). But, this has to be solved in further studies and research.

Furthermore, it is a great challenge to handle such amounts of data and interlinked model structures during a reconstruction process. This presupposes a structured and disciplined methodology based on binding structures, which were initially defined.

In sense of scientific quality, it is necessary to find some minimal working principles as a first generally valid basis. Therefore, at the beginning of each project following parameter in dependence of **intention**, **content** and **aim** have to be defined (Fig. 18):

- Binding model structures
- Binding level of details
- Binding reference models
- Binding data structure

This could be a first step and basis for a structured and disciplined methodology for the reconstruction of individual buildings, but also - because of their complexity - for urban structures. But, to implement such guidelines it is necessary to carry out further studies, e.g. with a special focus on the granularity of resources and the consequences for meaningful model structures.

The establishment of digital 3D reconstructed models as a research method also includes the documentation of the results and the development of an adequate documentation and publication system, which responds flexibly to model structures, their level of detail and data behind. A first step could be the open-access documentation tool called "Reconstructions-Argumentation-Method" developed at Digital Design Unit, in which an image of the digital 3D reconstructed model is directly interlinked to its resources and the process represented by the argumentation [4].

All these above-mentioned aspects and challenges have to be solved before high complex virtual research environments will be created.

The practice of research projects in this field as well as the study about adequate model structures has shown all these challenges. The described guidelines of research department "Digital Reconstruction" as well as the presented suggestion of first basic principles are certainly only a beginning to solve these. However, practice has also shown that a neglect of these open questions leads to a loss of data and knowledge, and ultimately to a loss of the digital cultural heritage.

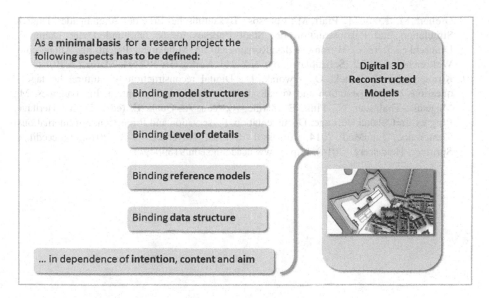

Fig. 18. First principles

References

1. Pfarr-Harfst, M., Wefers, S.: Digital 3D reconstructed models – structuring visualisation project workflows. In: Ioannides, M., Fink, E., Moropoulou, A., Hagedorn-Saupe, M., Fresa, A., Liestøl, G., Rajcic, V., Grussenmeyer, P. (eds.) EuroMed 2016. LNCS, vol. 10058, pp. 544–555. Springer, Cham (2016). https://doi.org/10.1007/978-3-319-48496-9_43
2. Hermon, S.: Scientific Method, Chaîne Opératoire and Visualization - 3D Modeling as a Research Tool in Archaeology, 10 January 2017. https://www.academia.edu/1227042/Scientific_Method_Chaine_Operatoire_and_Visualization_-_3D_Modelling_as_a_Research_Tool_in_Archaeology
3. Pfarr-Harfst, M.: 25 years of experience in virtual reconstructions - research projects, status quo of current research and visions for the future. In: Verhagen, P. (ed.) Across Space and Time. Proceedings of the 42nd International Conference on Computer Applications and Quantitative Methods in Archaeology (CAA), Paris, France (2014)
4. Pfarr-Harfst, M., Grellert, M.: The reconstruction – argumentation method. In: Ioannides, M., Fink, E., Moropoulou, A., Hagedorn-Saupe, M., Fresa, A., Liestøl, G., Rajcic, V., Grussenmeyer, P. (eds.) EuroMed 2016. LNCS, vol. 10058, pp. 39–49. Springer, Cham (2016). https://doi.org/10.1007/978-3-319-48496-9_4
5. City GML. https://de.wikipedia.org/wiki/City_Geography_Markup_Language
6. BIM. http://gesamtleitung.vdf-online.ch/post/4-fertigstellungsgrad-lod
7. City GML. https://3d.bk.tudelft.nl/news/2016/05/16/CEUS-improved-CityGML-LODs.html
8. Grellert, M., Koob, M., Pfarr, M.: Dreidimensionale Computerrekonstruktion und Simulation der Kaisergräber von Xi'an. In: Kunst- und Ausstellungshalle der Bundesrepublik Deutschland GmbH (eds.) Unter der Gelben Erde. Die deutsch-chinesische Zusammenarbeit im Kulturgüterschutz – Kongressbeiträge, pp. 113–121. Verlag des RGZM, Mainz (2010)

9. Grellert, M., Koob, M., Pfarr, M.: Ephesos - Byzantinisches Erbe des Abendlandes. Digitale Simulation und Rekonstruktion der Stadt Ephesos im 6. Jahrhundert. In: Daim, F., Drauschke, J. (eds.) Byzanz - das Römerreich im Mittelalter: Pracht im Alltag eines Weltreiches. Teil 2,2, Schauplätze, pp. 731–744. Verlag des RGZM, Mainz (2010)
10. Kuroczyński, P., Hauck, O., Dworak, D.: Digital reconstruction of cultural heritage – questions of documentation and visualisation standards for 3D content. In: Ioannides, M., Mageanat-Thalmann, N., Fink, E., Zarnic, R., Yen, A., Quak, E. (eds.) Digital Heritage. Progress in Cultural Heritage: Documentation, Preservation and Protection. 5th International Conference, EuroMed 2014, Limassol, Cyprus, November 3–8, 2014, Proceedings. Springer, Heidelberg (2014). http://www.academia.edu/9189049/

Education in Urban History

Grenzgang

When Promenadology Meets Library

Tabea Lurk[1], Markus Schwander[2(✉)], Daniel Brefin[2],
and Beate Florenz[2]

[1] Media Library, Academy of Art and Design FHNW, Basel, Switzerland
tabea.lurk@fhnw.ch
[2] ILGK, Academy of Art and Design FHNW, Basel, Switzerland
{markus.schwander, daniel.brefin, beate.florenz}@fhnw.ch

Abstract. The text describes specific aspects of the documentation of the research project *Grenzgang* in the *integrated catalogue* of the media library of the Academy of Art and Design (FHNW HGK). *Grenzgang – Artistic Investigations on Perception and Communication of Space in a Trinational Border Area* – is anchored geographically in Basel and the surrounding region, while its method can be located between artistic research and promenadology. References to research results from various project phases are documented with diverse analogue and digital media in the media library's *integrated catalogue*. This catalogue attempts to display such artistic works in their heterogeneity and variety and to make them accessible for research alongside other more classic library resources. The contribution submitted here elucidates typical challenges which can occur on the threshold of the catalogue/archive in the aftermath of complex artistic research projects. Specifically, the question arises of what happens when an active investigation like "walking" encounters an apparently static collection facility like the media library.

Keywords: Artistic research · Promenadology · Art education
Documentation · Catalogue

1 Introduction

With support from the Swiss National Science Foundation (SNF),[1] the research project *Grenzgang – Artistic Investigations on Perception and Communication of Space in a Trinational Border Area* combined the method of promenadology, following Burckhardt [6], with divergent artistic methods – applied in a mode of research. Particularly worth mentioning here are performance, installation, improvisation, audio, drawing and

---

[1] The project *Grenzgang – Artistic Investigations on Perception and Communication of Space in a Trinational Border Area* was conceived as a team research project between the Institut Lehrberufe für Gestaltung und Kunst (Institute for Art and Design Education) and the Hochschule für Musik (School of Music) at the University of Applied Sciences and Arts Northwestern Switzerland and was financed by the Swiss National Science Foundation (SNF) [24]. Duration: Jan. 1, 2014–Dec. 31, 2015. Research team: Daniel Brefin, Amadis Brugnoni, Corinne Hasler, Simone Etter, Beate Florenz (co-direction), Markus Schwander (co-direction).

S. Münster et al. (Eds.): UHDL 2017/DECH 2017, CCIS 817, pp. 179–195, 2018.
https://doi.org/10.1007/978-3-319-76992-9_11

video. In a first project phase, team members experimented with their own artistic approaches in order to develop valid research modi for their approaches respectively. Differing concepts resulted, which in turn determined and structured these approaches in space. Assuming that our perception is inalienably individual and bound to our physical experience, Burckhardt's promenadology offered a methodic approach with which to place the body in (urban) space as a starting-point.

1.1   Promenadology in Artistic Research and Art Education

Walking was of high relevance to the entire project. Artistically, *Grenzgang* thereby took up a tradition since the 1960's (e.g. Long [8]), while at the same time invoking contemporary positions which also apply walking as a method (Alÿs [1]; Lerjen [14]). Walking – as the common denominator of heterogenous artistic approaches – occurred both individually and in the group. In each case, walks were taken based on rules defined by the team members beforehand.

In contrast to historically motivated, documentary-photographic, architectonic or archaeological documentations, the (research) results generated by *Grenzgang* can be understood as individual, artistic protocols of space, perception and/or intervention; sketches and interpretive snapshots of the border situation. They possess a partly performative character and reflect or test both historically developed as well as inno-vative methods of notation and communication. These are to be conceived of not only in the context of urbanistic studies of space, but also with the professions of the participants in mind and in the context of artistic research and mediation. As the following examples showcase, the project is anchored in different fields ranging from music (notation, audio recording) to the visual arts (performance, drawing, video documentation) and from artistic research to the praxis of art education (artistic intervention, interactive/participative workshops).

In a later project phase, each team member assigned tasks to the entire team, based on his/her respective individual research modus. This yielded a correlation between individual research modi as well as a – temporarily desired – shift of perception for the team members. Walking together and the mutual completion of various praxes were the preconditions of a phenomenologically oriented, intersubjective production of knowledge. During the course of the project, this approach proved to be a crucial moment for the artistic research of the perception of space; in light of which the databank for the project *Grenzgang* can be seen as a digital extension of the inter-subjective production of knowledge.

Workshops with external experts (e.g. Markus Ritter, Fred Frith, Christine Heil, Elke Bippus, Francesco Careri, Bernadett Settele) accompanied the project and opened the team's internal discussion. The provisional conclusion of the project took on form with the *Research Platform Grenzgang* in the Salon Mondial on the Campus of the Arts, which presented the project *Grenzgang* for public discussion (Fig. 1).

The *Research Platform Grenzgang* in the Salon Mondial [2] brought notations and permutations from the research team together spatially, created superpositions of diverse approaches and enabled public events to take place in connection with the project. These included the *Table Conversations* as thematic forums as well as the *IRMAT Concert*, a *Walk* through the urban site Dreispitz (Basel/Münchenstein) and

Fig. 1. Public *Table Conversations (Tischgespräche)* with experts of praxis and theory were part of the *Research Platform Grenzgang*. Photo: Damaris Meury

work with school classes. The students undertook different walks around Dreispitz during which they completed actions according to the posts they selected. The resulting materials were played back at the *Research Platform*, thus continuing the team's notations. On this basis, the work with students was carried beyond the framework of the *Research Platform*, resulting in the conception of educational resources which can be used by teachers (Figs. 2 and 3).

With the Multitouch-Interface InfraRedMultiActionTracker *IRMAT* [19], visitors at the Research Platform could retrace selected walks from the project and, thanks to audio and visual material made available through *IRMAT*, locate it (Fig. 4).

1.2   Research Layout of the Project Grenzgang

Grenzgang pursued goals on multiple levels: questions about the specifications of the trinational border region around Basel were united with fundamental question of how we perceive space. The region is, thanks to its dense population and notably diverse utilization, particularly illuminating: "Production and traffic zones, nature sanctuaries, residential areas, and recreational, industrial and harbor facilities" intermingle with one another [12]. On an interdisciplinary level, the project was intended to demonstrate the genesis of knowledge in artistic research [5, 16] and to achieve a transfer of knowledge from artistic research to art education, as understood as an epistemic practice [11, 17]. The investigation of the trinational border region around Basel through the lenses of cultural history, sociology or urban planning imparts *Grenzgang* with a possibility for artistic access.

Fig. 2. Working with students was an important component of the *Research Platform*. On their own walks they were able to establish individual connections to the research questions posed in *Grenzgang*. Photo: Damaris Meury

Fig. 3. School classes experimented with the perception and presentation of space with artistic and participative approaches. Photo: Damaris Meury

Fig. 4. The Multitouch-Interface *IRMAT* as an interactive educational tool in the framework of the *Research Platform*. Photo: Damaris Meury

The question of how knowledge is generated and established as such occupies a prominent position in the discussion surrounding artistic research, which has intensified since the 1990's [4]. Bound to this question is another, regarding the power of deciding what should be declared knowledge: who determines the criteria for what should be considered knowledge? Whereby this last question was sparked against the background of scientific-theoretical thoughts on hierarchies of knowledge going back to Rheinberger [23]. However, to be able to show how knowledge is generated in a project which handles explicitly in the mode of artistic research, a detailed documentation of the procedures and resulting notations and applications was essential [25]. That applies equally for the application to art education: for an epistemic praxis of art education, the approaches used, the steps taken, the open questions and speculations emerging from notations and applications and the breaks and irritations which arise in the modus of artistic research are all relevant.

1.3 Artistic Approaches

Due to the heterogenous artistic approaches of the team members, the data available for the documentation of the project is decidedly divergent. Furthermore, said data can take on the status of notations as well as evaluations. The divergence of the artistic approaches – and therefore also of the resulting material – accounts for a central source of momentum for the project: it was precisely the intention to be able to correlate the individual modi of artistic work, relating as they do to the same space. Thus, the divergence of the material is not only founded in the layout of the project. It is constitutive for the attainment of project goals, without reducing the perception of space to single sensory experiences, personal memories, culturally determined observations or the momentary states of the team members. Although, exactly such individual and momentary conditions were incorporated in notations, rather than being supressed.

Considering the heterogeneity of the artistic approaches, walking, as it relates to promenadology and as a form of movement which is tied to the body and which occurs in space, provides a methodical access to space which was valid for all team members. The following references to the artistic approaches and forms carried out in the *Grenzgang* project grant a brief insight into the modus of artistic research and illustrate the rich variety of the resulting material (Fig. 5).

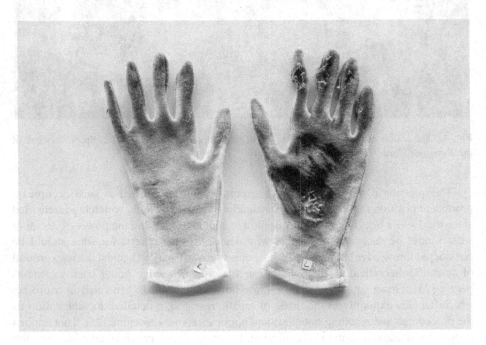

Fig. 5. The accumulated traces of a path rubbed over for multiple kilometers turn the gloves into an artistic condensation of a walk by Simone Etter. Photo: Simon Mader

The dirt- and scuff-covered white cloth gloves are the drawn notation of a walk which Simone Etter completed in the frame of her performative examination of the space in the trinational border region. The walk began at her home in Basel's (CH) inner city and ended at the Hotel Ibis in St Louis, France. Her path was guided by the cues of an audio route planner in Google Maps, which she listened to on headphones. The headphones had two functions: they were the pilot that determined the direction of her walk; and they shielded her acoustically from her environment. Her gloved hands remained in direct contact with her immediate surroundings during the entire walk: with walls, railings, stairs and thresholds, traffic signal posts, pedestrian crosswalks, etc. The gloves become a continuous notation of walking, while the body experiences space continuously anew: from walking upright to a stooped position and vice versa. Instead of the upright hominid's eyes, the hands' sense of touch becomes central for the forward propulsion of walking.

The bag in which the gloves were stored is labeled with a tag on which the topographical coordinates of the starting and ending points of the walk are noted. The gloves, with their traces and in combination with these specifications, chronicle a completed action without needing to define it in more detail. They take on the status of a notation of a performative act, the pertinence of which for our perception of the trinational space only becomes apparent upon completion. Even if in regards to the gloves we can deduce that the urban environment on this or that side of the border leaves the same traces. The reactions of passersby are as invisible in the gloves as the experience of the body, which completes the walk (Fig. 6).

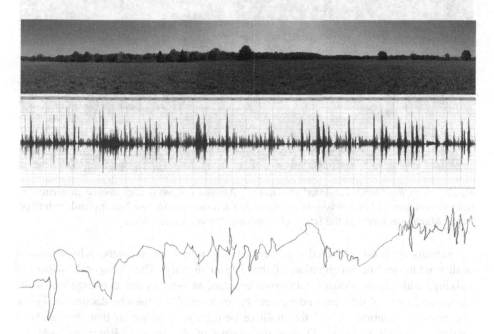

Fig. 6. Daniel Brefin's *rauf-runter (up-down)* is a performative translation of a real horizon (above) on the border of the media *seeing > speaking* (middle: wave-form representation of the audio data) and *hearing > drawing* (below). Photo: Daniel Brefin

At first glance, the drawn translations of Daniel Brefin's acoustic landscape portraits *rauf-runter (up-down)* appear to be abstract lines drawn on paper. In the portraits, at a particular point in the landscape Brefin's speech traces the horizon line verbally, in the medium of an audio recording. To this end he uses the verbal descriptions "rauf" (up) und "runter" (down). The alternation of the words and their articulation in the speech recording are the directions for the visitors in the *Research Platform Grenzgang* to translate the horizon onto a sheet of paper with a drawn line. Having never seen the horizon itself, which can only be viewed from a single point, the acting person traces graphically what has been noted acoustically. The artistic notation in the medium audio overlays itself thus with the drawn gesture of the later action (drawing) of project-external individuals (Fig. 7).

Fig. 7. With the Multitouch-Interface *IRMAT*, Amadis Brugnoni implements an archive of auditive notations and improvises with the guitarist and media artist José Navarro and the trumpet player Marco von Orelli in the frame of a concert. Photo: Damaris Meury

Amadis Brugnoni collected specific tones and sounds on his walks whose musical quality addresses the imagination of the listener directly. The "temporal dilation of walking, with all its acoustic inconspicuousness, as well as the convergence of the sounds and tones of the surroundings and his own steps" are thereby documented [12]. The acoustic notations reveal the auditive perception of space in that they make it available through isolation. During the course of the project, Brugnoni used the resulting archive of sound material and tone tracks both for conceptional considerations in regards to the *Research Platform Grenzgang* and for a concert during which Brugnoni improvised with the audio tracks on the Multitouch-Interface *IRMAT*. The performance, accompanied by the guitarist and media artist José Navarro and the trumpet player Marco von Orelli, could also be understood as a (sound-)spatial walk, allowing for associations with tangible space. The soundscapes that emerged during the concert included the audience in an auditive knowledge of the trinational region Basel. This is connected through hearing to a personal, acoustic, experimental knowledge. In this respect, the concert expands the auditive knowledge of space generated by Brugnoni through the presence of the concert's attendees (Fig. 8).

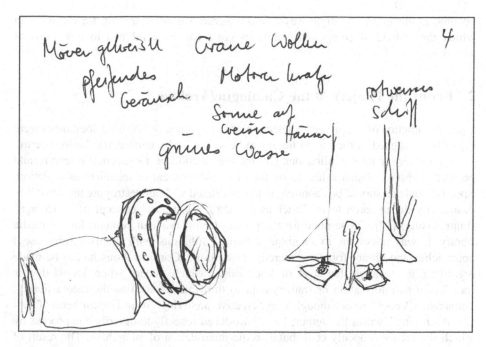

Fig. 8. Markus Schwander used ballpoint pen sketches and written notations like "cries of seagulls", "grey clouds" etc., to examine the imaginary border between the landscape and that which lies between the drawer and the landscape. Drawing: Markus Schwander

During his walks, small-format DIN-A6 cards enabled Markus Schwander to contend, through drawings and descriptions, with Lucius Burckhardt's *Nullmeter*; with the question, by extension, of where landscape begins. In *Grenzgang*, Schwander meets the question of the perception of space with an artistic reflection on that western tradition which perceives/conceives of an expansive exterior space as landscape. Schwander sketched objects from his immediate surroundings on his small-format cards and supplemented the sketches with spatial terms which either applied to the (abstract) distance, as in, for example, "white sky", "knolls", "forest edges", or named distant acoustic impressions and tones which characterized both the actual environment for the drawer and the imaginable landscape. Thus landscape became a space which could not be packed into a picture, the human in the midst of its surroundings is being evoked as a central theme instead. In the final abundance of cards, words and sketches create a sort of conglomerate occurs which explores our perception of space through the interplay of seeing and designating.

The different artistic notations and realizations developed by participating researchers in *Grenzgang* can become incitements to further action in a continuing epistemic praxis. If different perspectives are accessible and connections are drawn, for example, between texts from the project and images and sounds, the projects knowledge can further evolve. Same with performances or drawings which are combined with literary texts on spatial experience while walking (e.g. [18, 22, 29]). All that can become applicable in multiple ways. In this sense, we are searching for the ways in which the individual components of *Grenzgang* can be combined to new units of meaning.

2 From the Project to the Catalogue/Archive

Upon completion of the project, a selection of approximately 120 filed documents were digitally consigned to the media library to be stored and mediated for the long-term.

As a filter for later publications and for the creation of a structured research (and project) archive, a balance had to be found in the moment of technical assimilation. Specific contexts should be capture/documented/fixed without destroying the flexibility desired by the research team. Whereas Claude Lévi-Strauss' concept of "bricolage" (improvising) [15] was seminal for the project members about content, for the media library it was important to combine technical solutions with archival (file-based) approaches and library (object-centered) conventions. Considerations had to be made regarding the unavoidable loss of knowledge, which occurs when knowledge is transferred as information or (rather) data to third parties such as the media library. Athanasios Velios' recent thoughts on "creative archiving" were helpful here: "Creative Archiving", writes the author, "was introduced recently to describe the process by which the archivist openly contributes to the interrelation of an archive. The result of creative archiving is an additional layer of interpretation, typically through an online interface, which illustrates the archivist's ideas about the core concepts kept within the archive material. This delivers a result which is unique to the specific archive rather than a standardized view of the collection as presented by popular library or archiving software. The proposal of creative archiving comes as a result of recent discussions in the archiving profession" [27]. This additional layer described can, in technical regards, be compared to the Curation-Layer from Choudhury, Palmer et al., which distinguishes itself by "adding value throughout life-cycle" [7].

Thus, in the conception phase, the core areas of the *Grenzgang* project were modelled in a Wiki, in which CiDOC-CRM [13] is stored as a structural schema [9]. The units "Walk" and "Testwalk" emerge as logical core elements, specified through the orientation in space (path), time (when) and the constellation of participants. A distinction was made between "Authors" und "Participants", since the walks were realized either alone or collectively in the group: generating the collected material in terms of artistic research, as previously mentioned. Then, the data was clustered according to the "Walks" and ingested into the *integrated catalogue*.

2.1 From File to Display

Because of the project's self-containedness, the collection was sorted by search terms, following the (archival) principle of provenance. Selecting, sorting out and parts of the classification were adduced by the research team. The fragmentary inventory was developed with the goal, "to identify its parts, bring them into an adequate arrangement and register them" [30]. Beyond the specific core attributes, like people involved (artists/authors), main genre (work, notation, event, documentation, GPS raw data, etc.)

title, media type, material type and extent (number of respective documents, access rights), each object could be seen as a constituent part of a temporal, spatial and local continuum. The multi-dimensional approach was in part reminiscent of archaeological documentations. To obtain the most precise survey possible, such documentations combine photographic methods of documentation (which document e.g. the excavation progress and findings) with drawn views (incl. technical, e.g. schematic measurements) and sedimentological descriptions (including geological and anthropological material descriptions), in order to identify the connections between the documents and their possible meanings during the course of the archaeological description.

- Space (and spatial reference) means here aspects of the perception of surroundings. In addition to actual environmental occurrences, the (phenomenological) description of the (internal) state of the acting/recording person can play an important role.
- The location (of the actual scene) is usually localized in the form of GPS coordinates.
- In regards to time, a distinction is made between the temporality (date, time) and the duration (period of time/start-end) of the event.

The category of the "Walk" served as a further harmonizing trait. As a base method, it either aided the collection of data (Brefin, Brugnoni, Florenz) or appeared as a performative event with *in situ* character (Etter, Schwander). Thus the category of the work was devised as an abstract entity (compare FRBR: work or CIDOC: E70 Thing) and could, by means of an entity of itemization, contain a multi-part object (file/Dossier). Local (GPS coordinates) and temporal (date/time) coordinates "located" the work's formation history and ca now be supplemented through semantic description(s).

2.2   Ingest Process

The *integrated catalogue* makes it possible to integrate these types of research data into the regular catalogue of the media library. Research data becomes thereby equally accessible as the rest of the library's media [10]. The *integrated catalogue* consists of a data warehouse with SOLR-Index, data server, web server with different web front ends and a transcoding system, in which entire collections as well as somewhat weakly structured material bundles can be registered.

Within the ingest process, completely new integrated material is analyzed, structurally filtered and enriched with semantic information through a half-automated analyzing cascade. The following tools, among others, are used to this end:

- **Apache Tika** for extracting the MIME type and encodings, as well as full texts in the case of texts
- **ffmpeg** for transcoding and extracting technical metadata from data which is identified (from Tika) as time-based media (MIME type "video/*" or "audio/*")
- **GPSBabel** for transcoding GPX-data
- **gvfs-info** for identifying the MIME type. This has similar capabilities as Libmagic but can deliver different results

- **imageMagick** for analyzing image- & PDF-data. imageMagick creates furthermore thumbnails and preview images
- **Libmagic** for creating the initial list of files. It tries to identify also the MIME type and encoding
- **OpenLayers** is a JavaScript library which detects/transcodes well-known waypoint formats (GPX data)
- **(OpenOffice Server)** for transcoding for office documents [not jet implemented]
- **SAC** (Spatial Audio Coding) for transcoding audio
- **Sonogram**(s) are generated by a C++ software which was developed by Jürgen Enge
- **External services**: Bing Maps (for GPX-display), info-age GmbH (design/3D-modelling/data management), Zencoder (for large stocks of video data or specific formats).

Since the search operation is technically based on the SOLR-(full text-)Index, content and metadata do not have to be harmonized to according to a standardized metadata scheme. Data is rather mapped implicitly according to the common displaying principles, which are embedded within the template. A unified appearance of heterogeneous search results makes them readable/comparable with other catalogue content, despite formal differences. Nevertheless, the original data set is stored unchanged in the index and used for the display. Keeping the original data set is not only helpful regarding complex metadata set such as MARC21 for library media, but it is especially interesting for other data, since these resources often come from historically evolved sources (Filemaker, SQL, etc. or even from simple Excel tables, directory structures and others), where the design contains non-factual knowledge.

It is planned to embed the *integrated catalogue* in further university infrastructures such as for example the recently developed website (search routine), which makes the system an active element of the creative data cycle. The creative data cycle is a model, which describes how results, generated at the HGK, are made accessible as resources and how they can be recurrently (re-)used. This is important for multiple reasons: data remains relevant in regards to the active accumulation of knowledge and, especially at art academies, data generally gains in value as it ages. In addition, interfaces for the active reuse of the data can be created which keep track of the (re-)use. This form of updating and reuse is especially exciting regarding the *Grenzgang* project, because it was from the very beginning about the perception and communication/transfer of space experiences. These experiences can only be shared/anticipated/incorporated by actively using (and realizing) the existing resources or their concepts: when e.g. a particular practice, which led to a specific resource within a walk, is imitated/imagined/updated. Thus later users can make their own personal space experience and (intangible) knowledge is passed as.

2.3 Data Curation and Communication

The web interface of the *integrated catalogue* provides access to data on three levels: list view, list preview, detail page. These views process the search results as situated in particular contexts. Thus different ways of browsing or searching are enabled, which we all know: from the non-targeted search, which leads us in the real spaces of a library through different shelves according to thematic topics, to specific search via author, subject, date etc. These routines are transposed into a virtual environment which contextualizes the data on the catalogue level. While the list preview offers a first impression of the found results/objects (Fig. 9), the detail pages contextualize the resources. In that, for example, the background of their creation or semantic framing are displayed (Fig. 10).

Fig. 9. List view (screenshot) of the web interface of the *integrated databank*. Screenshot: Tabea Lurk

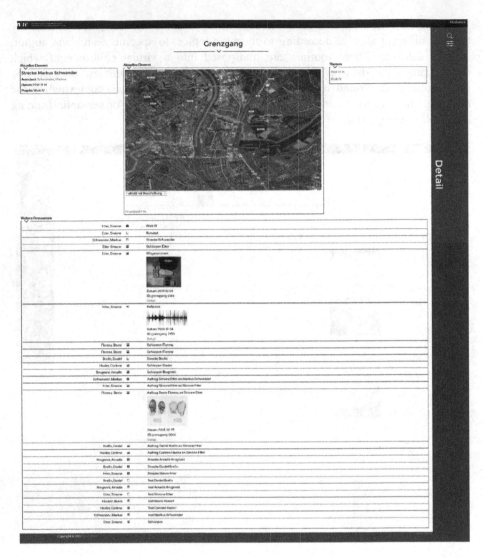

Fig. 10. Detail Page (screenshot) of Walk IV with selected resources open. Screenshot: Tabea Lurk

If applicable, supplemental information on further resources is provided.

In *Grenzgang's* case, the detail pages display the "Walks": each folder outlines information respective to one "Walk" and contextualizes the actual data (texts, images, audio and video files, GPX-data) by referencing information about author/participants, space, time, type of resource and additional information regarding meaning and semantics.

One part of curating the *Grenzgang* project consisted, therefore, in contextualizing the resources, which meant to visualize the aforementioned heterogeneity of research modi and forms of experience in all their plurality. The benefit in regards to the catalogue occur most evidently in inter-collection connections. If one searches finds additional resources, texts or objects etc. from the same person, from the same time/time-frame, from the same place etc. but e.g. from other research projects, etc. by research all collections. In the data set itself, the source of the information is recognizable. Furthermore, the media library can instigate their own indexing or mapping based on standardized classification systems, thesauri or ontology-based models, without disturbing the original language of the project. Thus, not only the various sources of the indexing become visible (accountability), but also shifts in meaning (semantic drift) which occur over the course of time. Regarding *Grenzgang*, the sensory data of space could later be loaded on mobile phones or navigation devices for users who might observe transformations in an urban context. Since not only pure GPX-data is entailed but also the descriptions/instructions of the "Walks", the method becomes applicable to different contexts. Also the notation forms, developed by the artists, contribute to the sensory experience of the trinational border region for later users, and serve to keep the principles of promenadology present.

3   Conclusion and Outlook

The availability of digital cartographies may seem to provide some relief from (supposedly) objective documentary and classical constraints on representation. Yet subjectively accumulated perceptual, artistic and/or communicative forms of experiencing space can add specific knowledge and dedicated value to the current state of research. *Grenzgang* offers a plausible example for this development. Simultaneously, parallels to the (new) discourse on materiality [20, 21, 28] can be identified. In this context the focus shifts from "things in and of themselves" in a direction, which take society and the (broader cultural) scene into consideration: "what psychoanalytic theory calls 'object relations' in the explanation of identity formation, what sociology invokes as the physical manifestation of culture, and anthropology refers to as the objectification of social relations" [3].

From the perspective of *Grenzgang*, the digital processing of the project data induces a sort of a flexible correlation of the present material [26]. Within the scope of the databank, relationships, consequences and continuing routines, which were not visible during the course of the project, can be newly constituted; thus revealing the process of artistic research can be continued. The data gathered should therefore be understood as discursive material, which generates knowledge continuously anew, rather than established knowledge, which functions statically in accumulation.

In regards to the documentational and communicative (/educational) situation, which includes the formats and raster of the description, the systematics of metadata and their forms of usage need to become more and more flexible. Alternative forms of description and organization are required, just as there are different views of reality. Alternative search filters, which take the needs of the searcher into account, will allow for a plurality of descriptive forms. Project-internal/artistic/creative terminologies can then be offered in parallel to formalized descriptive forms. This coexistence will, in return, facilitate accidental (browsing) encounters with the unknown or the unexpected.

Renewed creativity can be yielded and the scientific reuse of data can be supported. It becomes evident that automatic recommending systems, which make large amounts of data available based on algorithmic patterns, have their justifications in this regard. That doesn't relativize the assessment abilities of users (regarding information competence), but on the contrary, it promotes diversity.

References

1. Alÿs, F. (2017). http://francisalys.com
2. Atelier Mondial, Christoph Merian Stiftung (ed.): Salon Mondial (2015). http://www.ateliermondial.com/de/ateliers/salon-mondial.html
3. Attfield, J.: Wild Things: The Material Culture of Everyday Life. Berg, Oxford (2000)
4. Badura, J., Dubach, S., Haarmann, A.: Vorweg. Warum ein Handbuch zur künstlerischen Forschung. In: Badura, J., Dubach, S., Haarmann, A., Mersch, D., Rey, A., Schenker, C., Toro, G. (eds.) Künstlerische Forschung. Ein Handbuch, pp. 9–16. Diaphanes, Zurich (2015)
5. Bippus, E.: Modelle ästhetischer Wissensproduktion in experimentellen Konstellationen der Kunst. In: Caviezel, F., Florenz, B., Franke, M., Wiesel, J. (eds.) Forschungsskizzen. Einblicke in Forschungspraktiken der Hochschule für Gestaltung und Kunst FHNW, pp. 47–57. Scheidegger & Spiess, Zürich (2013)
6. Burckhardt, L., Ritter, M., Schmitz, M. (eds.): Warum ist Landschaft schön? Die Spaziergangswissenschaft. Berlin, Schmitz (2006). http://www.gbv.de/dms/faz-rez/FD120070129953404.pdf
7. Choudhury, G.S., Palmer, C.L., Baker, K.S., DiLauro, T.: Levels of services and curation for high functioning data. CIRSS Center for Informatics Research in Science and Scholarship (ed). University of Illinois (2013). http://cirss.ischool.illinois.edu/Documents/Publications_docs/Choudhury_2013a.pdf
8. Long, R. (ed.): Design and Artist's Copyright Society. http://www.richardlong.org
9. Enge, J.: CIDOC CRM - Digitales Objekt (2013). http://doc.objectspace.org/cidoc/D1_Digital_Object.html
10. Enge, J., Lurk, T.: Integrierter Katalog. Mediathek der Künste. Mediathek HGK FHNW (2015). https://mediathek.hgk.fhnw.ch
11. Florenz, B.: Kunstvermittlung. Eine epistemische Praxis. In: Caviezel, F., Florenz, B., Franke, M., Wiesel, J. (eds.) Forschungsskizzen. Einblicke in Forschungspraktiken der Hochschule für Gestaltung und Kunst FHNW, pp. 41–46. Scheidegger & Spiess, Zürich (2013)
12. Florenz, B., Schwander, M.: ‹Grenzgang›. Vom Dreispitz in den trinationalen Raum. In: Langkilde, K. (ed.) Ortszeit. Aufzeichnungen der Hochschule für Gestaltung und Kunst FHNW 2014, pp. 281–292. Christoph Merian Verlag, Basel (2014)
13. FORTH Institute of Computer Science (ed.): CRMdig: a model for provenance metadata (2010). http://www.cidoc-crm.org/
14. Lerjen, M.A.: Warum gehen? Was geht? Wer geht mit? (ed.): lerjentours. Agentur für Gehkultur (2011). http://www.lerjentours.ch
15. Lévi-Strauss, C.: Das wilde Denken. Suhrkamp, Frankfurt am Main (1989)
16. Mersch, D.: Epistemologies of aesthetics. Diaphanes, Zurich (2015)
17. Mörsch, C.: Undisziplinierte Forschung. In: Badura, J., Dubach, S., Haarmann, A., Mersch, D., Rey, A., Schenker, C., Toro, G. (eds.) Künstlerische Forschung. Ein Handbuch, pp. 77–80. Diaphanes, Zurich (2015)

18. Murakami, H., Gräfe, U.: Wovon ich rede, wenn ich vom Laufen rede. 2. Aufl. Köln, DuMont (2008). http://www.gbv.de/dms/faz-rez/FD1200808011854378.pdf
19. Musik Akademie Basel (ed.): Willkommen auf IRMAT.ch. Fachhochschule Nordwest Schweiz (2008/2012). http://www.irmat.ch
20. Parikka, J.: New materialism as media theory: medianatures and dirty matter. Commun. Crit. Cult. Stud. 9(1), 95–100 (2012). https://doi.org/10.1080/14791420.2011.626252
21. Parikka, J.: A Geology of Media. University of Minnesota Press, Minneapolis (2015)
22. Perec, G.: Versuch, einen Platz in Paris zu erfassen. Unter Mitarbeit von Tobias Scheffel. Konstanz, Libelle (2010)
23. Rheinberger, H.J.: Objekt und Repräsentation. In: Heintz, B. (ed.): Mit dem Auge denken. Strategien der Sichtbarmachung in wissenschaftlichen und virtuellen Welten, pp. 55–64. Edition Voldemeer, Zurich (2001)
24. Schweizer Nationalfonds (ed.): Grenzgang. Künstlerische Untersuchungen zur Wahrnehmung und Vermittlung von Raum im trinationalen Grenzgebiet. Institut Lehrberufe für Gestaltung und Kunst Hochschule für Gestaltung und Kunst FHNW (SNF Nr. 149339) (2014). http://p3.snf.ch/Project-149339
25. Tröndle, M.: Kunstforschung als ästhetische Wissenschaft: Beiträge zur transdisziplinären Hybridisierung von Wissenschaft und Kunst. Transcript, Bielefeld (2012)
26. Vaknin, J., Stuckey, K., Lane, V. (eds.): All This Stuff: Archiving the Artist. Libri Publishing, Chicago (2013)
27. Velios, A.: Archive as event. Creative archiving for John Latham. In: Vaknin, J., Stuckey, K., Lane, V. (eds.): All This Stuff. Archiving the Artist, pp. 109–121. Libri Publishing, Chicago (2013)
28. Volkart, Y.: Müll zu Gold. Über die schmutzige Materialität unserer Hightechkultur. In: Springerin (2016). https://www.springerin.at/2016/1/mull-zu-gold/
29. Walser, R.: Der Spaziergang. Ausgewählte Geschichten und Aufsätze. Diogenes, Zürich (1973). Taschenbuch-Neuausg
30. Weber, J., Kaukoreit, V.: RNA - Regeln zur Erschließung von Nachlässen und Autographen. Ed. Staatsbibliothek zu Berlin – Preußischer Kulturbesitz (2010). http://kalliope-verbund. info/_Resources/Persistent/5bf5cd96ea4448bfec20caf2e3d3063344d76b58/rna-berlin-wien-mastercopy-08-02-2010.pdf

4D Augmented City Models, Photogrammetric Creation and Dissemination

Florian Niebling[1(✉)], Ferdinand Maiwald[2], Kristina Barthel[3], and Marc Erich Latoschik[1]

[1] Informatik IX, Universität Würzburg, Am Hubland, 97074 Würzburg, Germany
{florian.niebling,marc.latoschik}@uni-wuerzburg.de
[2] Institut für Photogrammetrie und Fernerkundung, Technische Universität Dresden, 01062 Dresden, Germany
ferdinand.maiwald@tu-dresden.de
[3] Technische Universität Dresden, Medienzentrum, 01062 Dresden, Germany
kristina.barthel@tu-dresden.de

Abstract. The availability of digital image repositories of historical photographs offers new possibilities to historians in their research. In addition to representing a large collection of data records themselves, image archives allow for new methods of research, from large-scale statistical analysis, to algorithmic generation of knowledge, such as historical 3D models, directly from these sources. In this paper, we explore methods to work with digital image libraries, from the creation of 3D or in extension time-annotated 4D models, to the eventual dissemination of research findings in teaching/learning scenarios. We review pedagogical approaches to reach different learning objectives, as well as methods that allow for the inclusion of historic city models employing Augmented Reality in mobile learning environments.

Keywords: Image repositories · 4D city models
Photogrammetric reconstruction · Augmented reality

1 Introduction

1.1 Image Repositories of Historical Photographs

Photographs are an essential source for historical research and key objects in eHumanities. Numerous digital image archives, containing vast numbers of photographs, have been set up in the context of digitization projects. Information and image retrieval with these extensive repositories is still challenging.

Digital image repositories meet a wide range of needs, from research in humanities and information technologies, through museum contexts and library studies to tourist applications. Architectural historians have developed various methods of analyzing both preserved and never-built or destroyed structures [9]

© Springer International Publishing AG, part of Springer Nature 2018
S. Münster et al. (Eds.): UHDL 2017/DECH 2017, CCIS 817, pp. 196–212, 2018.
https://doi.org/10.1007/978-3-319-76992-9_12

in chronology and context. Style analysis, iconographic approaches and art sociological methods all address art historical questions. The tendency in recent research widens the focus towards a comprehensive view of art which can be supported by image repositories: The advantage of the new digitality consists in a large collection of pictures, but those repositories need to be equipped with special techniques that support art and architectural history research [6] as well as dissemination of its results. While working on urban history, issues with handling image repositories become apparent: First, the spatial frame of analyzed objects typically consists of large areas. Here, challenges while gathering, cataloguing and geo-locating the source photographies arise. Second, each source forms part of a specific time horizon, which means that often the scholarly examination will extend to several stages of urban development. The sources thus do not only need a spatial but also a temporal sorting. Computer based 3D and 4D models are helpful at this stage, as they allow to combine both components with the help of digital tools [32].

1.2   3D Models and Their Temporal Expansion

Large image repositories are often used to generate three-dimensional models using photogrammetric methods [2, 25]. The most commonly used technique is Structure-from-Motion (SfM) [35]. Here, a set of images which show one object is relatively oriented by automatically finding homologue feature points in two or more images. An algorithm to find these feature points is for example SURF [7]. After that, different filters are applied to get the most robust feature points, which are then represented by a descriptor. Using the relative orientation, 3D points of the photographed objects can be reconstructed.

In this paper, we present methods to adapt the SfM workflow on historical images. The images are taken from a large historical image archive and will be used to generate accurate *historical* point clouds. The topic of this research is also called historical photogrammetry [21]. To extend the spatial components of reconstructed point clouds with a temporal component, complex workflows are needed. First, a filtering of historical image repositories is required to include only photographs containing building information. The extracted dataset is subject to restrictions considering image quality, camera parameters, camera calibration and camera positions. E.g. the images are not taken at the same time by the same photographer or with the same camera. So the relative orientation of the dataset will be more difficult than in an usual workflow. If SfM cannot be applied to the images, different approaches may be tested like texture mapping or using additional current data [36, 50]. So after this second step of generating 3D models the last step will concern temporal information. If models of different epochs exist, a deformation analysis can be applied. Furthermore, this relates to questions how many images of one epoch should be available for a successful reconstruction and whether it will be possible to generate models of completely destroyed or changed buildings.

A four-dimensional city model can be used for different applications. Scenarios include applications that allow researchers to browse through the images and get an extended visualization in a three-dimensional environment. This can be helpful to contextualize individual photographs and even uncover historical details [41]. Other end-user scenarios contain augmented reality applications in the field of tourism, allowing historical details and different epochs to be visualized right where the actual building has been in the past.

1.3   Knowledge Transfer in Cultural Heritage Scenarios

Knowledge transfer is an important issue related to cultural heritage tourism. Some common used traditional sources of information related to cultural heritage sites are paper-based guidebooks, real-life guided tours, brochures, location-based information panels or screens and audio-guides. The increasing use of mobile devices has created new ways for stakeholders in tourism to connect with travellers and mediate information about a cultural heritage site. There are a lot of mobile services for tourists to search for information on their target regions, destinations, restaurants, hotels, transportation and entertainment (e.g. *GeoTourist, Yelp, tripwolf*). In addition, digital libraries and archives (e.g. Europeana, Deutsche Fotothek) provide ubiquitous access to a large number of repositories (text, images, audio files) wich are interesting for visitors of a certain destination. Mobile technology has the potential to give access to the huge amount of information stored in digital archives and open new dimensions for knowledge transfer about cultural heritage sites. In particular, augmented reality applications can create digital overlays to the real-world environment and encourage users to explore and gain knowledge from a new perspective [47]. They provide access to travel-related information and relevant services anytime and anywhere [54].

In recent years, a lot of augmented mobile applications and toolkits were developed to enhance the tourist experience [33]. In the same time, there has been an increasing interest in applying AR to create unique educational settings [4] and especially cultural heritage sites became a field of interest for merging both issues.

Nowadays, facilities related to cultural heritage and tourism are increasingly looking for ways to enhance their visitors' learning experience [20]. Mobile augmented tourism applications are a promising approach to support knowledge transfer for educational purposes, while enhancing visitors' experience in cultural heritage settings [19,52].

2   State of the Art

2.1   Historical Image Sources

There are challenges for working with sources from urban history, as they always represent the view on the city, mostly an internal and thereby biased view. This leads to the essential responsibility of scientific research to take this fact into account for the evaluation and interpretation of findings, by contextualizing them in order to reach objectivity.

As a result, studies often consider only delimited time spans or narrow places. Through digital tools, an easier access to the sources and wider research focuses as well as improved opportunities of utilization are given, making a multi-focus analysis of the urban development possible. This leads to new research questions: How do buildings and cities change over time? In which contexts, such as political or formal developments, does a historical cityscape evolve? What similarities can be found between objects in terms of construction standards and requirements, building codes, regional, temporal or personal tastes and styles? Furthermore, what connotation did the buildings possess? Does the number of pictures taken of one specific building change over the documented time? Are there relations to other buildings or urban spaces given? Which interactions of architecture with other artistic genres, inscriptions or infrastructural facilities can be found? Which buildings are likely to form the architectonic background for social events such as demonstrations or celebrations? Against this background, digital libraries and computer based analysis tools are a great chance to overcome existing methodic boundaries both in urban history research and dissemination of research results.

2.2 Historical Photogrammetry and Fourdimensional City Models

Support through digital tools can be provided to answer the previously outlined research questions. The computation of historical 3D — or in extension time-annotated 4D — models forms a central part.

When considering the creation of a four-dimensional model with temporal and spatial components, three-dimensional models have to be created out of historical images. Falkingham et al. entitle this problem as "historical photogrammetry" [21]. A lot of different studies have been done using historical data to receive three-dimensional models. A simple approach is using historical images just for a modeling purpose [13,45]. So the geometric information is generalized and underlies assumptions. An extended modeling approach uses edge detection and afterwards monoscopic modeling to receive structure and color just from one image [38,48]. Methods commonly used here are e.g. Single-View Perspective Imagery (SVR) or Texture Mapping [50].

For a complete reconstruction solely using the image information, SfM is usually applied. But in most cases, a completely automatic reconstruction fails and the point cloud does not represent the building very well. Hence, different recent studies use additional data (LIDAR, recent images, façade plans) of objects which are still visible today to support the SfM workflow [8,36]. Even touristic photographs can be helpful for a reconstruction [23].

The generation of a four-dimensional model requires the localization of the generated historical three-dimensional models. Researches have already been done on the reconstruction of a complete city using touristic images from online platforms such as flickr [1,25,34,44]. These models can be completed by the help of non-professional users through e.g. gamification approaches [49].

Extending these approaches with a temporal component requires data or models from varying moments in time. Kersten et al. use a wooden model and maps to reconstruct Hamburg in four epochs [30]. This technique is also used for other cities [26]. The project "4D Cities" coincides the most with our research question [41]. It organizes historical photographs, provides context and a semi-automatic 4D city construction tool for users.

These different research topics show the feasibility of our studies and the constructive steps towards a four-dimensional city model.

2.3 Mobile Augmented Reality

Stationary AR experiences (e.g. spatial AR, or stationary HMD-based AR) in museums and other installations, have enabled a first-person exploration of local and remote cultural heritage (CH) sites and contents. They also allow for an active inspection of and interaction with digitized artifacts, annotations of objects with rich multimedia elements conforming to interactive pedagogical approaches, and providing enhanced user experiences to visitors as well as advanced working paradigms to researchers. In these contexts, AR systems can be used to improve learning and interaction by providing self-guiding context aware media for presentation and interpretation of CH resources. With the emergence of affordable mobile computing systems, handheld AR has made its way into CH (see Fig. 1). Even early AR applications in CH such as ARCHEOGU-IDE [17,46,51] aim at a multitude of disciplines and research outcomes: Archaeological Research, Education, Multimedia Publishing, and Cultural Tourism, employing mobile AR for on-site visualization of reconstructed 3-dimensional virtual models of artifacts and buildings. In addition to the various benefits of

Fig. 1. Augmented reality view of the Dresden Frauenkirche

stationary AR installations in museums or at archaeological sites, mobile computing devices, i.e. handhelds or wearables, enable personalization of content and experiences to the users, and facilitate collaboration amongst the participants.

2.4 Mobile Tourism Applications

In the recent decade, many cultural heritage tourism attractions like museums and art galleries enhance visitor's experience through augmented reality applications by using wearable devices [27,37,52]. Cities like London, Montreal and Chicago started to create location-based augmented reality city tours by providing special mobile tourist applications to explore and gain knowledge about the location and especially about urban history. *London Street museum* is one of the most impressing examples of the usage of augmented reality in urban environments. The visitor has access to the vast collection of historical pictures of the London Museum by using the application on their mobile phones in their current geospatial surroundings. Historical pictures and information available through the London Museums can be explored by pointing the camera to the present street view [39].

The development of this kind of application was driven and is still driven by the latest technological interventions in the field of Virtual and Augmented Reality, as well as by findings of related research fields such as Media Pedagogy, Learning Psychology, Technology Acceptance Research, Media Research, Information and Communication Technology, and Experience Design. On the one hand, these mobile augmented tourism applications as well as a variety of frameworks and toolkits (DroidAR, Layar, PanicAR) are based on research in these disciplines. On the other hand, they became an interesting field of research itself. The following findings of an initial literature review describe the current research in the fields of Taxonomies, User acceptance, Gamification and Learning Experience related to mobile tourism applications.

Taxonomy. There are a few frameworks which classify mobile tourism applications in certain taxonomies by using different categories [28,29,54].

Kennedy-Eden and Gretzel [29] worked out a taxonomy of mobile applications in tourism to provide insights into application development trends as well as gaps in the mobile application landscape. They laid down seven categories for tourism applications: Navigation, Social, Mobile Marketing, Security/Emergency, Transactional, Entertainment, and Information. In addition, they investigated user interactivity. These taxonomies help to get an overview of different mobile tourism applications and to determine necessary services for future interventions.

User acceptance. There has been done a lot of research in the field of user acceptance of mobile applications in general and several scientists specialized on tourism applications. Tom Dieck & Jung developed a theoretical model of mobile augmented reality acceptance in urban heritage tourism [19]. Others extended the Technology Acceptance Model (TAM) originally presented by Davis [18] through new aspects, i.e. perceived enjoyment (PE) and perceived mobility value

(PMV), to enhance the explanatory power of the model for the acceptance of mobile learning [24]. To illuminate the acceptance of mobile tourism applications, these general findings can be transferred to tourists who access information about the destination (learning material) with their mobile device.

Another recent research work pointed out the factors that encourage tourists to actively use AR applications by doing a field study with 145 people in Deoksugung Palace, South Korea [14]. Goh et al. [22] investigated tourists' desires and needs.

Gamification. Despite the increasing adoption of gamification and its huge potential in tourism, research in gamification is still limited [43]. Gamification is assumed to motivate users to become more active, and is commonly implemented in commercial products [56]. It is a promising method to enhance tourist experience and learning and a current research interest related to mobile tourism applications. Recent research work by Xu et al. aim to explore the gamification trend and its potential for experience development and tourism marketing. Using a focus group, their paper discusses gaming and tourism, and explores what motivates tourists to play games [53]. Another publication describes how gamification can be used for attracting visitors' attention, arousing interest and generating the desired behaviour - visiting a particular destination [31].

Learning experience. Research on learning experience and outcomes through mobile tourism applications is limited. Recent findings present a study on visitors learning experience in an art gallery using wearable devices [20]. Furthermore, results of a study investigating the increase of learning and sense of place for heritage places by using an AR mobile guidance system, indicates significant effects on learning and sense of place through the AR application [12].

3   Combination of Large Image Archives and Historical Data

As already shown, different approaches use recent large image archives for a three-dimensional reconstruction of cities or buildings. Other studies use solely selected historical images for a specific reconstruction purpose. In our work, we want to combine these two attempts to generate time-annotated three-dimensional models out of a large historical image repository. Within the studies, we make use of the photo library of the Saxon State and University Library Dresden (SLUB), aiming to use the generated models in both research tools as well as in Augmented Reality applications for dissemination of research results.

3.1   Filtering of Data

The photo library consists of 1.8 billion images from 87 institutions (6/2017). It is possible to search through the images by keywords or use given filters such as name of the photographer, date of recording, topic of the reproduction, people visible or time and place of creation. For a photogrammetric reconstruction, several different images need to show one (or more) buildings of interest from varying angles. Considering this purpose, an initial investigation into the material provided by the chosen library shows several challenges to the process of automatic reconstruction:

- Images are sometimes labeled incorrectly or the labels are missing.
- Keyword searches do not show images of buildings (Fig. 2) exclusively.
- Some images are not yet digitized with a high enough quality needed for the algorithms employed in digital reconstruction.
- Images have different illuminations or image errors.
- Images contain no color information.
- Images are not taken by the same photographer with the same camera at the same time, which entails the need for an external post-hoc camera calibration.
- All the available images of a building of interest often show the building just from a single position and angle.

Fig. 2. Variety of hits for the keyword *Kronentor* (Crown Gate)

By now, the best method to get specific images is to look manually through different keyword searches and pick valid images for a three-dimensional reconstruction. E.g. for the Kronentor (*Crown Gate*) of the Dresden Zwinger the keyword search shows 875 hits and this image set was reduced to 44 images manually and subjectively [36]. This approach may be valid for one building/dataset but not for a reconstruction of a complete part of a city. It is also possible that some images were neglected due to missing labels or incomplete keyword search. Consequently, an automatic image search and validation would be helpful in terms of a photogrammetric reconstruction.

Considering the different problems that were already shown, the filtering should be divided into different steps. At first images with a low resolution or poor image quality should be eliminated by certain thresholds. For the remaining images, a photographic processing in terms of illumination, contrast, and sharpness, would be imaginable. All these prefiltered images should then be divided in separate groups. One approach would be the splitting into the two groups *buildings* and *no buildings*. A possible method we will focus on is content-based image retrieval (CBIR) using a Bag-of-Features approach, and afterwards an image classification employing support vector machines (SVM) [16]. Classified images in the category *buildings* will then be used for a three-dimensional reconstruction. Wrongly classified images will be eliminated in the next steps.

3.2 Orientation of Historical Images

The next step towards a three-dimensional model, and a valuable tool for e.g. art historians, is the orientation of images related to a visible model. In photogrammetry, this is called the exterior orientation of the camera (position and rotation in space). Inner orientation describes the focal length and the coordinates of the principal point. Getting all these values is accomplished by using different photogrammetric methods.

The first approach we employed was a manual orientation of the images in the web application DokuVis [11] via Drag and Drop. This can be done for a few images but becomes time consuming for a large amount of data. So a direct linear transformation (DLT) was implemented into the system [10]. This photogrammetric method calculates the inner and exterior orientation of the camera in relation to given coordinates of a three-dimensional object and their homologue image coordinates. For the calculation, no approximation values are needed, but a minimum of six point pairs (which lie not in the same plane) have to be determined. So this method orients the images one by one semi-automatically, but is quite time consuming as well. In addition, a space resection could be applied with approximation values of camera parameters and just three point pairs.

In a next step we want to implement a photogrammetric bundle adjustment. This method calculates the inner and exterior orientation of a variable number of images of the same object. For this approach object coordinates of control points, their image coordinates and approximation values of unknowns must be given. Therefore, one or more historical images must show objects that are still present and can be measured at this moment in time. It will be also difficult to approximate camera parameters, because in most cases, the camera is unknown and the historical pictures were digitized so the resolution varies from the original size. For a fully automatic approach, homologue features in all of the images have to be found.

3.3 Three-Dimensional Modeling

Different studies have already been done on getting three-dimensional models out of historical images. If there exist different views of one building it is possible to use modeling software to get 3D models of individual buildings. Historical maps, drawings and plans can easily improve the manual modeling. Nevertheless in the most approaches details get lost and structures are generalized [45]. Several studies even use current data to improve the modeling process [30]. Another solution can be applied for buildings, which are still visible today. The requirement is that the building didn't change too much. Even surrounding objects, that can be seen on historical photos are enough to support a reconstruction [8].

We want to get away from a manual modeling to an automatic reconstruction approach, so the geometric information comes directly from the images used. Methods allowing the reconstruction of three-dimensional models out of images are for example stereophotogrammetry or SfM. SfM is usually used to reconstruct objects out of one homogeneous dataset. For historical images, the algorithm has to be manipulated in order to achieve results. Possible manipulations are e.g. SfM with little overlap [40] or SfM using line geometry [5, 42]. Further researches have to be done to improve the existing results.

3.4 Handheld Augmented Reality in Cultural Heritage

We have identified different types of data that are utilized in CH applications. These include data describing buildings and landscapes, various types of CH artifacts, images, labels, semantically annotated (rich-) text, audio, video and even animated creatures and human avatars representing historical population or other visitors. The datasets include 2D and 3D polygonal geometry that is either modelled manually, or reconstructed from acquired data such as pointclouds or images, automatically processed using methods such as close-range photogrammetry. 3D volumetric data generated by CT or MRT scans can also be included into the AR experience. Handheld AR techniques are utilized to strengthen the user experience in cultural heritage sites and installations by supporting spatial awareness, personalization, as well as to enable physical exploration of historic space.

AR applications treat data in two major different modalities, information that is registered and integrated into the environment on the one hand, and data that is presented entirely outside of the AR context on the other hand. The mode of presenting data does not exclusively depend on the type of data, instead, both methods are often used for the same type of data concurrently. For instance, photos and videos describing CH artifacts are often displayed alongside the augmented view. In some applications, spatially located photos, and even video, might also be presented as augmentation to the displayed reality. Similar observations can be made for the display of text as labels as well as complex annotations in augmented views, and as additional informational presentations external to the AR context.

Interacting with data in handheld AR applications has been studied not only in practical CH use cases, but also from design, human factors, and usability engineering perspectives. User centered design methods have been employed to guide design requirements from the user's perspectives. Various studies have been performed that evaluate touch- and gesture-based interactions both on the screen as well as observed by a mobile device's camera. While there are many applications that allow interaction based on spatial proximity to a given Point Of Interest, spatial interaction, i.e. interaction that is performed by spatially moving or rotating the mobile device, is not yet used in CH contexts.

4 Approaches to Enhance Visitors' Experience and Knowledge Transfer

4.1 Tasks of Tour Guides Relevant for AR Application Development

Tour guides are one of the key front-line players in the tourism industry. Through their knowledge and interpretation of a destination's attractions and culture, and their communication and service skills, they have the ability to transform the tourists' visit from a tour into an experience [3]. The success of the tourism industry depends on the performance of tour guides in each destination [55]. A tour guide provides assistance, information and cultural, historical and contemporary heritage interpretation to people on organized tours and individual clients at educational establishments, religious and historical sites, museums, and at venues of other significant interest. These traditional tasks should be implemented in mobile augmented tourism applications, which present location-based information about a cultural heritage site. Current AR applications provide a variety of different functionalities to meet these tasks. They give access to multimedia-rich environment through the use of various multimedia formats. Such formats range from sound and image to video clips, 3D models and hyperlinks that may direct the user outside the application [33]. They assist the tourist through navigation functionalities, offer different services like tickets, reservations and shopping and a few implement a creating, sharing, collaboration, communication or social component [29]. According to their functionalities, mobile AR applications in tourism can focus on service-oriented or knowledge-mediating issues. For providing a user-friendly and sustainable mobile tourism application a mixture of both is recommended to strengthen user acceptance. Providing assistance and information are well implemented tasks. One of the main problems within mobile AR applications is the missing interpretation of cultural, historical and contemporary heritage to people and missing pedagogical approaches to connect different disciplines like geography, architecture, art, history as well as cultural, economic, social facts related to a destination.

4.2 Pedagogical Approaches to Enhance Visitors' Experience and Knowledge Transfer

There are different approaches to give visitors a unique experience in real-life city tours. A few of them are implemented in AR tourism applications, but there is still a huge potential in using pedagogical approaches to enrich AR applications for mediating knowledge about urban history or cultural heritage. Themed tours are one of the most common approaches, which are already adopted to AR tourism applications (e.g. *Chicago00*, *Timetraveler-App*). These applications give access to guided or self-guided tours under the aspect of a certain themes *The St. Valentine's Day Massacre* or *The History of the Berlin Wall*.

Another approach used in real-life scenarios are *scenic walks* or *theatre walks*, which are combined with drama. The guide slips into a role and leads the visitors to special places where other actors may live the events of earlier times to let. This kind is very similar to so-called *Ghost-Walks*, with ghost stories and legends in the foreground. These elaborately staged scenarios could be a model to implement in AR tourism applications. The development of mobile technology makes it possible to create digital scenarios, which make history become alive at certain locations. *Living History at Union Station* in Kansas City is a tourist application, which uses the principle of a theatre walk. This is a mobile augmented reality application using story telling. It takes users on a journey back through time as they take self-guided history tours that play out on their phones, as they explore the Union Station their own way. The application provides in-depth story telling within an augmented reality experience, before users can go deeper through written stories, images and artefacts [15].

To explore pedagogical and motivational approaches to enhance tourism experience and foster learning about a destination is one important issue for upcoming research. Investigate tourist responses to different pedagogical strategies within AR tourism applications and to illuminate motivational aspects and learning effects are an important part of this research. To unfold the potential of AR technology for the communication of urban history or cultural heritage it is indispensable to translate real-life approaches into digital scenarios, which can be implemented in mobile augmented tourism applications.

5   Implications

We have described the neccessary steps in a workflow toward automatic reconstruction of 3D models from historic image sources and the possibilities for their integration into mobile AR applications. The implications of our studies concerning the applicability of historical photographs in image repositories with respect to algorithmic reconstructions are manifold. We have touched upon the challenges of the usability of existing digitalized images in Sect. 3.1. Several of the introduced shortcomings, such as the image quality of scans, as well as incorrect labeling, have to be addressed manually. Other imperfections in the source material, illumination or missing camera calibrations, require algorithmic advancements with a special attention towards historic photography.

Hard problems still are the missing density of records in the source material, as well as very few dominant views even for well-documented buildings, which can make an automatic reconstruction impractical. Here, the addition of contemporary image sources can be a way to amend some of the problems in the documented record.

5.1   Four-Dimensional Modeling

Time as a fourth dimension is an important factor in our work that ist not yet addressed in depth in previous approaches. Serveral different questions can be addressed in this matter. How many images are needed for one epoch? Is it possible to generate more than one historical model? Can a change in the building's appearance be visualized properly? Is it possible to reconstruct completely destroyed buildings?

5.2   Augmented Reality in Cultural Heritage Applications

The studies outlined in Sect. 2.4 confirm that there is an increasing research interest on the development, acceptance and evaluation of tourism applications, on generalized tourist needs and behaviour as well as on tourists' desire. All mentioned research supports the design of mobile tourism applications, but there are no general guidelines for future developments yet. Compared with the general research on mobile applications, the investigation of mobile tourism applications is limited. They are often based on case studies with small sample sizes. Few investigations have been done on investigating pedagogical approaches, which affect tourism experience and learning.

The usage of mobile tourism applications for exploring and gaining knowledge is not common yet. Due to this fact, the crucial motivational variables that will affect their adoption by users still need to be explored. This includes finding strategies to gain the visitors attention in urban space and adapting educational and motivational approaches from real-life city tours into the mobile augmented tourism application. Reviewing recent research works and existing applications will help to understand tourist desires and the complex concept of tourism applications, which have to combine educational purposes and entertainment in the future.

6   Further Research

These implications lead to further questions and their realization in the future. Our research aims to generate a prototype of an augmented four-dimensional city model implementing additional user interaction. In this respect, several challenges need to be addressed. From a technical perspective, the quality of automatically generated historical models is still not sufficient for an Augmented Reality application. Though the localization of historical images works semi-automatically in our prototype, we want to generate a fully automatic tool in the future, incorporating the findings presented in this paper. Following, a generation of models with higher quality should be possible. With these building models and additional images and metadata, we want to test different Augmented Reality scenarios concerning interaction and usability of such tools. Also, suitable presentations of the data and the observation of several data types will be part of future research.

We also want to do research on how to get the attention of potential users in urban space and how mobile AR applications can benefit from gamification approaches. Additionally, the enhancement of the user's experience with varying pedagogical approaches will play an important role. Thus, we want to combine an educational purpose with entertainment, leading to studies on feasibility, utility, practicability of applications concerning demands of different user groups.

References

1. Agarwal, S., Furukawa, Y., Snavely, N., Curless, B., Seitz, S.M., Szeliski, R.: Reconstructing Rome. Computer **43**(6), 40–47 (2010)
2. Agarwal, S., Furukawa, Y., Snavely, N., Simon, I., Curless, B., Seitz, S.M., Szeliski, R.: Building Rome in a day. Commun. ACM **54**(10), 105 (2011)
3. Ap, J., Wong, K.K.F.: Case study on tour guiding: professionalism, issues and problems. Tour. Manag. **22**(5), 551–563 (2001)
4. Bacca, J., Baldiris, S., Fabregat, R., Graf, S.: Augmented reality trends in education: a systematic review of research and applications. Educ. Technol. Soc. **17**(4), 133–149 (2014)
5. Bartoli, A., Sturm, P.: Structure-from-motion using lines: representation, triangulation, and bundle adjustment. Comput. Vis. Image Underst. **100**(3), 416–441 (2005)
6. Bauer, E.: Analoge Fotografie im digitalen Zeitalter. Eine Herausforderung für Bildarchive und Geschichtswissenschaft. Zeithistorische Forschungen/Studies in Contemporary History (2015)
7. Bay, H., Tuytelaars, T., Van Gool, L.: SURF: speeded up robust features. In: Leonardis, A., Bischof, H., Pinz, A. (eds.) ECCV 2006. LNCS, vol. 3951, pp. 404–417. Springer, Heidelberg (2006). https://doi.org/10.1007/11744023_32
8. Bitelli, G., Dellapasqua, M., Girelli, V.A., Sbaraglia, S., Tinia, M.A.: Historical photogrammetry and terrestrial laser scanning for the 3D virtual reconstruction of destroyed structures: a case study in Italy. In: ISPRS - International Archives of the Photogrammetry, Remote Sensing and Spatial Information Sciences XLII-5/W1, pp. 113–119, May 2017
9. Brassat, W., Kohle, H.: Methoden-Reader Kunstgeschichte. Deubner Verlag für Kunst, Theorie & Praxis, Cologne (2003)
10. Bruschke, J., Niebling, F., Maiwald, F., Friedrichs, K., Wacker, M., Latoschik, M.E.: Towards browsing repositories of spatially oriented historic photographic images in 3D web environments. In: Proceedings of the 22nd International Conference on 3D Web Technology, Web3D 2017, pp. 18:1–18:6. ACM, New York (2017). https://doi.org/10.1145/3055624.3075947
11. Bruschke, J., Wacker, M.: Simplifying documentation of digital reconstruction processes. In: Münster, S., Pfarr-Harfst, M., Kuroczyński, P., Ioannides, M. (eds.) 3D Research Challenges in Cultural Heritage II. LNCS, vol. 10025, pp. 256–271. Springer, Cham (2016). https://doi.org/10.1007/978-3-319-47647-6_12
12. Chang, Y.L., Hou, H.T., Pan, C.Y., Sung, Y.T., Chang, K.E.: Apply an augmented reality in a mobile guidance to increase sense of place for heritage places. J. Educ. Technol. Soc. 18(2), 166–178 (2015). http://dml:regis:edu/login?url=http://search:ebscohost:com/login:aspx?direct=true&db=aph&AN=102557867&site=ehost-live&scope=site
13. Chevrier, C., Maillard, Y., Perrin, J.P.: A method for the 3D modelling of historic monuments: the case of a gothic abbey. In: International Archives of Photogrammetry, Remote Sensing and Spatial Information Science, vol. 38, no. 5 (2009)
14. Chung, N., Han, H., Joun, Y.: Tourists' intention to visit a destination: the role of augmented reality (AR) application for a heritage site. Comput. Hum. Behav. **50**, 588–599 (2015). http://dx.doi.org/10.1016/j.chb.2015.02.068
15. Collins, L.: Union station, VML join to launch augmented reality app. Kansas City Bus. J. (2014)

16. Csurka, G., Dance, C., Fan, L., Willamowski, J., Bray, C.: Visual categorization with bags of keypoints. In: Workshop on Statistical Learning in Computer Vision, ECCV, Prague, vol. 1, pp. 1–2 (2004)
17. Dähne, P., Karigiannis, J.N.: Archeoguide: system architecture of a mobile outdoor augmented reality system. In: Proceedings of International Symposium on Mixed and Augmented Reality, ISMAR 2002, Darmstadt, Germany, pp. 208–209, September 2002
18. Davis, F.D.: Perceived usefulness, perceived ease of use, and user acceptance of information technology. MIS Q. **13**(3), 319–340 (1989). http://www.jstor.org/stable/249008
19. tom Dieck, M.C., Jung, T.: A theoretical model of mobile augmented reality acceptance in urban heritage tourism. Curr. Issues Tour. 1–21 (2015). http://www:tandfonline:com/doi/full/10:1080/13683500:2015:1070801
20. tom Dieck, M.C., Jung, T.H., tom Dieck, D.: Enhancing art gallery visitors' learning experience using wearable augmented reality: generic learning outcomes perspective. Curr. Issues Tour. 1–21 (2016). https://doi.org/10.1080/13683500.2016.1224818
21. Falkingham, P.L., Bates, K.T., Farlow, J.O.: Historical photogrammetry: Bird's Paluxy River dinosaur chase sequence digitally reconstructed as it was prior to excavation 70 years ago. PLoS ONE **9**(4), e93247 (2014)
22. Goh, D.H., Ang, R.P., Lee, C.K.: Determining services for the mobile tourist. J. Comput. Inf. Syst. **51**(1), 31 (2010)
23. Grun, A., Remondino, F., Zhang, L.: Photogrammetric reconstruction of the great Buddha of Bamiyan, Afghanistan. Photogramm. Rec. **19**(107), 177–199 (2004)
24. Huang, J., Lin, Y., Chuang, S.: Elucidating user behavior of mobile learning. Electron. Libr. **25**(5), 585–598 (2007). https://doi.org/10.1108/02640470710829569
25. Ioannides, M., Hadjiprocopi, A., Doulamis, N., Doulamis, A., Protopapadakis, E., Makantasis, K., Santos, P., Fellner, D., Stork, A., Balet, O., Julien, M., Weinlinger, G., Johnson, P.S., Klein, M., Fritsch, D.: Online 4D Reconstruction Using Multi-images Available Under Open Access. ISPRS Ann. Photogramm. Remote Sens. Spat. Inf. Sci. II-5/W1, 169–174 (2013)
26. Jedrzejas, T., Przybilla, H.J.: Generating historical urban 3D-scenarios for use in Google Earth representing the medieval city of Duisburg. Photogramm. Fernerkund. Geoinf. **2009**(3), 199–207 (2009)
27. Kang, J.: AR teleport: digital reconstruction of historical and cultural-heritage sites for mobile phones via movement-based interactions. Wirel. Pers. Commun. **70**(4), 1443–1462 (2013)
28. Karanasios, S., Burgess, S., Sellitto, C.: A Classification of mobile tourism applications. In: Global Hospitality and Tourism Management Technologies, pp. 165–177 (2011). http://services.igi-global.com/resolvedoi/resolve.aspx?doi=10.4018/978-1-61350-041-5.ch011, http://www.igi-global.com/chapter/classification-mobile-tourism-applications/56440
29. Kennedy-Eden, H., Gretzel, U.: A taxonomy of mobile applications in tourism. e-Rev. Tour. Res. **10**(2), 47–50 (2012). http://ro.uow.edu.au/commpapers/2510
30. Kersten, T.P., Keller, F., Saenger, J., Schiewe, J.: Automated generation of an historic 4D city model of Hamburg and its visualisation with the GE engine. In: Ioannides, M., Fritsch, D., Leissner, J., Davies, R., Remondino, F., Caffo, R. (eds.) EuroMed 2012. LNCS, vol. 7616, pp. 55–65. Springer, Heidelberg (2012). https://doi.org/10.1007/978-3-642-34234-9_6

31. Királová, A.: The place of gamification in tourism destinations' marketing. In: IDIMT 2015: Information Technology and Society - Interaction and Interdependence - 23rd Interdisciplinary Information Management Talks, pp. 201–206 (2015). http://www.scopus.com/inward/record.url?eid=2-s2.0-84947054125&partnerID=tZOtx3y1

32. Kohle, H.: Digitale Bildwissenschaft. Glückstadt, Hülsbusch (2013)

33. Kounavis, C.D., Kasimati, A.E., Zamani, E.D.: Enhancing the tourism experience through mobile augmented reality: challenges and prospects. Int. J. Eng. Bus. Manag. **4**(1), 1–6 (2012)

34. Li, Y., Snavely, N., Huttenlocher, D.P.: Location recognition using prioritized feature matching. In: Daniilidis, K., Maragos, P., Paragios, N. (eds.) ECCV 2010. LNCS, vol. 6312, pp. 791–804. Springer, Heidelberg (2010). https://doi.org/10.1007/978-3-642-15552-9_57

35. Lowe, D.G.: Distinctive image features from scale-invariant keypoints. Int. J. Comput. Vis. **60**(2), 91–110 (2004)

36. Maiwald, F., Vietze, T., Schneider, D., Henze, F., Münster, S., Niebling, F.: Photogrammetric analysis of historical image repositories for virtual reconstruction in the field of digital humanities. In: ISPRS - International Archives of the Photogrammetry, Remote Sensing and Spatial Information Sciences XLII-2/W3, pp. 447–452 (2017)

37. McNamara, A.M.: Enhancing art history education through mobile augmented reality. In: Proceedings of the 10th International Conference on Virtual Reality Continuum and Its Applications in Industry - VRCAI 2011, vol. 1, no. 212, p. 507 (2011). http://dl.acm.org/citation.cfm?doid=2087756.2087853

38. Miranda, A.R., Melón Valle, M.J.: Recovering old stereoscopic negatives and producing digital 3D models of former appearances of historic buildings. In: The International Archives of Photogrammetry, Remote Sensing and Spatial Information Sciences (2017)

39. Morais, A.R.: Streetmuseum in Screenspace: Exploring Urban Museums and Cultural Archives Through Augmented Reality Applications. http://www.interdisciplinary.net/critical-issues/wp-content/uploads/2015/08/AR-Morais-sp6-dpaper.pdf

40. Salaun, Y., Marlet, R., Monasse, P.: Robust SfM with little image overlap (2017)

41. Schindler, G., Dellaert, F.: 4D cities: analyzing, visualizing, and interacting with historical urban photo collections. J. Multimed. (2011)

42. Schindler, G., Krishnamurthy, P., Dellaert, F.: Line-based structure from motion for urban environments. In: Third International Symposium on 3D Data Processing, Visualization, and Transmission, pp. 846–853. IEEE (2006)

43. Sigala, M.: Applying gamification and assessing its effectiveness in a tourism context: behavioural and psychological outcomes of the TripAdvisor's gamification users. Asia Pac. J. Inf. Syst. **25**(1), 179–210 (2015). http://www.earticle.net.lib.jejunu.ac.kr:8010/article.aspx?sn=240813

44. Snavely, N., Seitz, S.M., Szeliski, R.: Photo tourism. In: ACM SIGGRAPH 2006 Papers on - SIGGRAPH 2006. Association for Computing Machinery (ACM) (2006)

45. Stojakovic, V., Tepavcevica, B.: Optimal methods for 3D modeling of devastated architectural objects. In: Proceedings of the 3rd ISPRS International Workshop 3D-ARCH, vol. 38 (2009)

46. Stricker, D., Karigiannis, J., Christou, I.T., Gleue, T., Ioannidis, N.: Augmented reality for visitors of cultural heritage sites. In: Conference on Artistic, Cultural and Scientific Aspects of Experimental Media Spaces (CAST), pp. 89–93 (2001)

47. Sungkur, R.K., Panchoo, A., Bhoyroo, N.K.: Augmented reality, the future of contextual mobile learning. Interact. Technol. Smart Educ. **13**(2), 123–146 (2016)
48. Tsai, F., Chang, H.: Evaluations of three-dimensional building model reconstruction from LiDAR point clouds and single-view perspective imagery. Int. Arch. Photogramm. Remote Sens. Spat. Inf. Sci. **40**(5), 597 (2014)
49. Tuite, K., Snavely, N., Hsiao, D.Y., Tabing, N., Popovic, Z.: Photocity: training experts at large-scale image acquisition through a competitive game. In: Proceedings of the SIGCHI Conference on Human Factors in Computing Systems, pp. 1383–1392. ACM (2011)
50. Tzur, Y., Tal, A.: FlexiStickers. ACM Trans. Gr. **28**(3), 1 (2009)
51. Vlahakis, V., Karigiannis, J., Tsotros, M., Gounaris, M., Almeida, L., Stricker, D., Gleue, T., Christou, I.T., Carlucci, R., Ioannidis, N.: Archeoguide: first results of an augmented reality, mobile computing system in cultural heritage sites. In: Proceedings of the 2001 Conference on Virtual Reality, Archeology, and Cultural Heritage, pp. 131–140. ACM, New York (2001). https://doi.org/10.1145/584993.585015
52. Waruwu, A.F.: Augmented Reality Mobile Application of Balinese Hindu Temples: DewataAR. pp. 59–66, January 2015
53. Xu, F., Tian, F., Buhalis, D., Weber, J., Zhang, H.: Tourists as mobile gamers: gamification for tourism marketing. J. Travel Tour. Mark. **33**(8), 1124–1142 (2016). http://www.tandfonline.com/doi/full/10.1080/10548408.2015.1093999
54. Yovcheva, Z., Buhalis, D., Gatzidis, C.: Smartphone augmented reality applications for tourism. e-Rev. Tour. Res. (eRTR) **10**(2), 63–66 (2012)
55. Zhang, H.Q., Chow, I.: Application of importance-performance model in tour guides' performance: evidence from mainland Chinese outbound visitors in Hong Kong. Tour. Manag. **25**(1), 81–91 (2004)
56. Zuckerman, O., Gal-Oz, A.: Deconstructing gamification: evaluating the effectiveness of continuous measurement, virtual rewards, and social comparison for promoting physical activity. Pers. Ubiquitous Comput. **18**(7), 1705–1719 (2014)

Organizational Perspectives

CIPA's Perspectives on Cultural Heritage

Andreas Georgopoulos[✉]

Laboratory of Photogrammetry, NTUA, Athens, Greece
drag@central.ntua.gr

Abstract. Taking care of mankind's cultural heritage is a well-established obligation to us and to our future generations. To that end numerous experts are contributing. Contemporary technological advances, i.e. digital achievements, have helped a lot to this end. In this paper these technological advances are briefly presented and explained. It is attempted to show how these advances may help Cultural heritage if applied correctly and wisely. The argument is not how they will replace traditional documentation or conservation methods, but how they will support, enhance and supplement them for achieving the desired result with sensitivity and knowledge. The available digital documentation techniques are described along with the contemporary non-destructive techniques for cultural heritage pathology diagnosis and conservation. Their advantages are investigated along with their implementation actions. These techniques include image based methodologies for producing three dimensional models of which traditional two-dimensional products may be extracted, laser scanning techniques to acquire directly three-dimensional information from the object, Nondestructive techniques in order to diagnose pathology problems etc. In order to highlight these techniques, several examples are presented. The alternative uses of the contemporary digital techniques are highlighted through these examples. Among others the following applications will be presented: The virtual restoration of a collapsed stone bridge, the virtual restoration of a monument exposed to the weather conditions and the development of a virtual museum are presented. Finally, a future outlook is attempted, in order to envisage the path that the implementation of these technological advances will lead the worldwide effort to document and preserve our cultural heritage.

Keywords: Cultural heritage · Geometric documentation · Digitization

1 Introduction

Cultural Heritage, tangible or intangible is recognized by all civilized countries of the world as the most important carrier of historic memory for mankind. However, it is not respected and protected as it should be in all cases. Hence, Cultural heritage is in great danger as it may be destroyed, lost, altered, forgotten for a number of reasons. The main sources of danger are natural hazards, violent actions, such as wars, terrorism etc., looting, illicit trafficking, vandalism, modern construction activities, globalization, modern way of life and indifference, urban population growth and many more. In Fig. 1 some examples of such destructions are depicted.

© Springer International Publishing AG, part of Springer Nature 2018
S. Münster et al. (Eds.): UHDL 2017/DECH 2017, CCIS 817, pp. 215–245, 2018.
https://doi.org/10.1007/978-3-319-76992-9_13

Fig. 1. Destruction of Cultural Heritage (Natural Hazards, looting and violent actions) (Image copyrights: http://www.topontiki.gr (top left), Author (top right), UNITAR-CNES (bottom left), http://www.independent.co.uk (bottom right)

The ideal way to protect Cultural Heritage is to constantly take care of it through certain protective actions. Such actions, as dictated by the numerous International Conventions adopted by UNESCO, ICOMOS (International Council of Monuments and Sites) and other bodies are:

- **Documentation** (Geometric, Architectural, Historic etc.), involving 2D and/or 3D for archiving, for studies, for planning protective interventions etc.
- **Accurate measurements,** suitable for restoration actions, reconstructions, structural studies, protection etc.
- **Monitoring** of its state, involving recording deformations, state of materials, assessing pathology etc.
- Proper **Management** of its data for sustainability, risk management etc.
- **Preservation** possibilities specially suitd for fragile objects (e.g. libraries etc.)
- **Public Outreach**, which involves visualization, dissemination, raising awareness of the public and many more

Consequently, their thorough study, preservation and protection is an obligation of our era to mankind's past and future. Respect towards cultural heritage has its roots already in the era of the Renaissance. During the 19th century archaeological excavations became common practice, while they matured in the 20th century. Over the recent decades, international bodies and agencies have passed resolutions concerning the obligation for protection, conservation and restoration of monuments. The Athens Convention (1931), The Hague Agreement (1954), the Chart of Venice (1964) and the

Granada Agreement (1985) are some of these resolutions in which the need for the full documentation of the monuments is also stressed, as part of their protection, study and conservation. Nowadays, all countries of the civilized world are using all their scientific and technological efforts towards protecting and conserving the monuments within or even outside their borders assisting other countries. These general tasks include geometric recording, risk assessment, monitoring, restoring, reconstructing and managing Cultural Heritage. Indeed, it was in the Venice Charter (1964) that the necessity of the Geometric Documentation of Cultural Heritage was firstly set as a prerequisite. In Article 16 it is stated "... *In all works of preservation, restoration or excavation, there should always be precise documentation in the form of analytical and critical reports, illustrated with drawings and photographs...* ".

1.1 Interdisciplinary Cooperation

The geometric documentation has been the responsibility of experts concerned with the care of the Cultural Heritage. Traditionally these mainly belonged to the field of archaeology and architecture. However, over the past thirty or forty years more and different specialists developed an interest for the monuments, as they were definitely able to contribute to their study, maintenance and care. Among them are surveyors, photogrammetrists and geomatics engineers in general, as the technological advances have enabled them to produce interesting, alternative and accurate geometric documentation products. Until the end of the 19th century, architectural heritage had been a matter of national concern only and most of the laws regarding the protection of historic buildings, in Europe at least, date back to that period. Countless associations existed in each country, but their scope never went beyond national borders. Cultural internationalism, as we know it today, was an outcome of the First World War, with the creation of the League of Nations, and most of all of the Second World War, with the creation of the United Nations Organisation and the establishment of the UNESCO. The Athens Conference (1931) on restoration of historic buildings was organised by the International Museums Office, and the Athens Charter, drafted by Le Corbusier at the fourth Assembly of the International congresses on Modern Architecture (1933) was published anonymously in Paris in 1941 both represent a major step in the evolution of ideas because they reflect a growing consciousness among specialists all over the world, introducing for the first time in history the concept of international heritage.

Today the mentality is gradually changing and traditionally involved experts, like Archaeologists and architects, tend to accept and recognize the contribution of other disciplines to the agenda of Cultural Heritage. Hence it is rapidly becoming an interdisciplinary and intercultural issue (Fig. 2).

UNESCO (1946) and the Council of Europe have formed specialized organizations for taking care of mankind's cultural heritage. ICOMOS (International Council for Monuments and Sites) is the most important one, but also CIPA-Heritage Documentation (International Committee for Architectural Photogrammetry, initially: Comité International de Photogrammétrie Architecturale), ISPRS (International Society for Photogrammetry & Remote Sensing), ICOM (International Council for Museums),

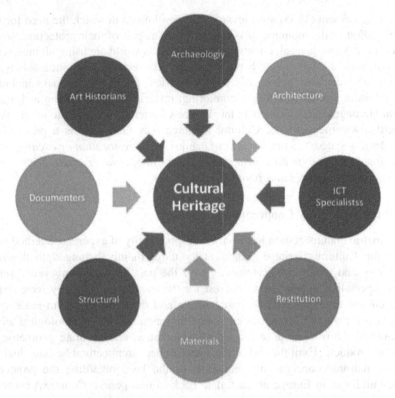

Fig. 2. The interdisciplinary contribution to Cultural Heritage (© Author)

ICCROM (International Centre for the Conservation and Restoration of Monuments) and UIA (International Union of Architects) are all involved in this task (Fig. 3). The Venice Charter was born from the need to create an association of specialists of conservation and restoration independent of the already existing associations of museologists, ICOM. In 1957, in Paris, the First Congress of Architects and Specialists of Historic Buildings recommended that the countries which still lack a central organization for the protection of historic buildings provide for the establishment of such an authority and, in the name of UNESCO, that all member states of UNESCO join the International Centre for the Study of the Preservation and Restoration of Cultural Property (ICCROM) based in Rome.

ICCROM is an intergovernmental organization dedicated to the conservation of cultural heritage. Its members are individual states which have declared their adhesion to it. It exists to serve the international community as represented by its Member States, which currently number 133. It is the only institution of its kind with a worldwide mandate to promote the conservation of all types of cultural heritage, both movable and immovable. The decision to establish the International Centre for the Study of the Preservation and Restoration of Cultural Property was made at the 9th UNESCO

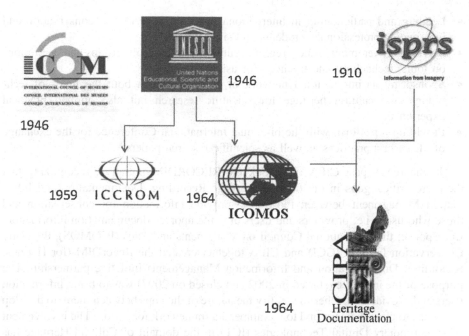

1946

1910

1946

1959 ICCROM   1964

ICOMOS

1964   Heritage
Documentation

Fig. 3. International organizations involved in Cultural Heritage (© Author)

General Conference in New Delhi in 1956, at a time of mounting interest in the protection and preservation of cultural heritage. It was subsequently established in Rome in 1959 at the invitation of the Government of Italy. ICCROM aims at improving the quality of conservation practice as well as raising awareness about the importance of preserving cultural heritage. The Second Congress of Architects and Specialists of Historic Buildings, in Venice in 1964, adopted 13 resolutions, the first one being the International Restoration Charter, better known as Venice Charter, and the second one, put forward by UNESCO, provided for the creation of the International Council on Monuments and Sites (ICOMOS).

1.2 CIPA Heritage Documentation

CIPA Heritage Documentation was founded in 1964 as an International Scientific Committee (ISC) of ICOMOS and ISPRS (International Society for Photogrammetry and Remote Sensing) and hence is a dynamic international organization that has twin responsibilities: keeping up with technology and ensuring its usefulness for cultural heritage conservation, education and dissemination. These two sometimes conflicting goals are accomplished in a variety of ways, through (cipa.icomos.org):

- Encouraging and promoting the development of principles and good practices for recording, documentation and information management of cultural heritage;

- Leading and participating in international training programs for conservation and informatics professionals, students and site personnel;
- Advising government bodies, regional authorities, non-profit groups and institutions on tools, technology and methods for using technology;
- Sponsoring an international network of professionals in both the fields of technology and cultural heritage for scientific research but also applied practical experience;
- Providing a platform with the bi-annual International Conference for the exchange of ideas, best practices as well as scientific research papers.

In the recent past CIPA undertook the RECORDIM initiative, recognizing that there are critical gaps in the fields of heritage Recording, Documentation and Information Management between those who provide information for conservation and those who use it, i.e. providers and users of contemporary documentation information. In response, the International Council on Monuments and Sites (ICOMOS), the Getty Conservation Institute (GCI) and CIPA together created the RecorDIM (for Heritage Recording, Documentation and Information Management) Initiative partnership. The purpose of the initiative (started in 2002 and closed on 2007) was to bring information users and providers together to identify the nature of the gaps between them, to develop strategies to close the gaps and to recommend a framework for action. The involvement of contemporary Digital Technologies (ICT) in the domain of Cultural Heritage has increased the gap between Providers, i.e. those who master these techniques and are able to apply them and the Users, i.e. those scholars traditionally concerned with the Cultural Heritage. This gap was caused mainly due to the mistrust of the latter towards contemporary technologies and lately ICT. However systematic efforts have been applied, like CIPA's RecorDIM (http://cipa.icomos.org/index.php?id=43) which have managed to narrow if not bridge this gap.

This current effort concerned with the 3D virtual reconstruction of monuments is motivated exactly by this endeavour to bridge this gap. This will only be done through deep understanding of each other's needs and through proper exploitation of ICT with the benefit of Cultural Heritage always in mind. In addition, the notion of virtual reconstruction is introduced and its use for bringing the reconstructed monuments into a museum environment is investigated. This interdisciplinary approach to the issue of Cultural heritage has opened vast new possibilities and led to new alternative products for the benefit of monuments. These new possibilities include, among others, the production of 3D models, virtual reconstructions, virtual restorations, monitoring of constructions and the applications of serious games for educational and dissemination purposes.

Digital surveying and geometric documentation of cultural heritage requires the cooperation of several disciplines and expertise in order to produce results that sufficiently satisfy the high demanding environment of conservation, restoration, research and dissemination. It should not escape our attention that resources are frequently inadequate while the infrastructure used (equipment, hardware and software) is expected achieve the maximum possible benefit.

2 Digitization of Cultural Heritage

Nowadays, the rapid advances of Digital Technology (DT) also referred to as Information Communication Technologies (ICT), have provided scientists with new powerful tools. We are now able to acquire, store, process, manage and present any kind of information in digital form. This may be done faster, more completely and it may ensure that this information may be easily available for a larger base of interested individuals. Those digital tools include instrumentation for data acquisition, such as scanners, digital cameras, digital total stations etc., software for processing and managing the collected data and -of course- computer hardware, for running the software, storing the data and presenting them in various forms.

The introduction of digital technologies has already altered the way we perceive fundamental notions like *indigenous, artifact, heritage, 3D space, ecology* etc. At the same time, they tend to transform the traditional work of archaeologists and museums as they are so far known. In other words, DT redefines the relationship to CH, as they enable universal access to it and they also connect cultural institutions to new "audiences". Finally, they appeal to new generations, as the latter are, by default, computer literate. In this way we experience a "democratization" of cultural information across geographic, religious, cultural and scientific borders. Cultural Heritage is nowadays, an international, interdisciplinary and intercultural responsibility.

The introduction of Digital Technologies may contribute to all traditional steps of Archaeological practice. It goes without saying that the degree of contribution of Information and Communication Technologies (ICT) is different in the various stages and in the various cases. Modern technologies of remote sensing and archaeological prospection assist the touch less and rapid detection of objects of interest. Spectroradiometers or ground penetrating radars or even the simple processing of multispectral satellite images may easily lead to the rapid location of underground or submerged objects of interest. Contemporary non-contact survey technologies, such as photogrammetry, terrestrial laser scanning and digital imaging, may be used to produce accurate base maps for further study, or 3D virtual renderings and visualizations. The collected data may be stored in interactive databases, georeferenced or not, and be managed according to the needs of the experts. Finally, ICT may assist in the presentation stage, by producing virtual models, which may be displayed in museums or be included in an educational gamification, or serve purposes of enabling handicapped persons to admire the treasures of the World's cultural heritage.

The use of Digital technologies in preservation and curation in general of cultural heritage is also mandated by UNESCO. With the *Charter on the Preservation of the Digital Cultural Heritage* [32] this global organization proclaims the basic principles of Digital Cultural Heritage for all civilized countries of the world. At the same time numerous international efforts are underway with the scope to digitize all aspects of Cultural heritage, be it large monuments, or tangible artifacts or even intangible articles of the world's legacy.

The impact of digital technologies to the domain of Cultural Heritage has increased speed and automation of the procedures which involve processing of the digital data and presentation of the results. At the same time accuracy and reliability has been substantially enhanced. However, most important is the ability to provide to the users new and alternative products, which include two dimensional and three-dimensional products, such as orthophotos and 3D models. 3D modelling, on the other hand, is the process of virtually constructing the three-dimensional representation of an object. The use of 3D models is highly increased nowadays in many aspects of everyday life (cinema, advertisements, games, museums, medicine etc.). All in all, the digitization of the world's Cultural Heritage whether it is tangible or intangible is now possible.

3 ICT at the Service of Cultural Heritage

The integrated documentation of monuments includes the acquisition of all possible data concerning the monument and which may contribute to its safeguarding in the future. Such data may include historic, archaeological, architectural information, but also administrative data, past drawings, sketches, photos etc. Moreover, these data also include metric information which defines the size, the form and the location of the monument in 3D space and which document the monument geometrically. The geometric documentation of a monument, which should be considered as an integral part of the greater action, the integrated documentation of Cultural Heritage may be defined as [31]:

- The action of acquiring, processing, presenting and recording the necessary data for the determination of the position and the actual existing form, shape and size of a monument in the three-dimensional space at a particular given moment in time.
- The geometric documentation records the present of the monuments, as this has been shaped in the course of time and is the necessary background for the studies of their past, as well as the care of their future.

The geometric documentation of monuments actually is the orthogonal projection of a carefully selected set of points on -usually- horizontal or vertical planes (Fig. 4), in order to record all geometric properties of the monument in the best possible way. The action of selecting those points implies deep knowledge of the monument and its structure, as well as mastering of the traditional and contemporary techniques for determining the position of these points in 3D space. This implies that all determined points lie in a common reference system in 3D space, which is a great advantage for further studies. In this process notions as scale of the final documentation product and accuracy of positioning the points are of utmost importance and are directly related to the data collection method.

For the geometric recording, several recording methods may be applied, ranging from the conventional simple topometric methods, for partially or totally uncontrolled surveys, to the elaborated contemporary surveying and photogrammetric ones, for completely controlled surveys. The simple topometric methods are applied only when the small dimensions and simplicity of the monument may allow it, when an uncontrolled survey is adequate, or in cases when a small completion of the fully controlled methods is required. Surveying and photogrammetric methods are based on direct measurements of lengths and angles, either on the monument or on images thereof.

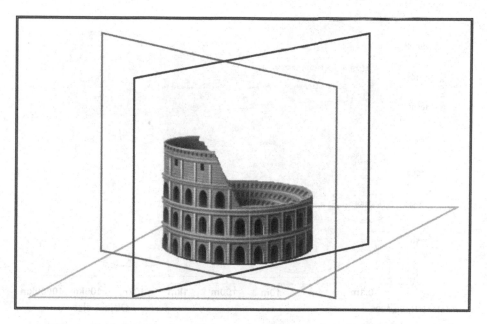

Fig. 4. Vertical and horizontal planes of geometric documentation (© author)

They indirectly determine three-dimensional point coordinates in a common reference system and ensure uniform and specified accuracy. Morcover, they provide adaptability, flexibility, speed, security and efficiency. All in all, they present undisputed financial merits, in the sense that they are the only methods, which may surely meet any requirements with the least possible total cost and the biggest total profit. To this measurement group belong complicated surveying methods with total stations, 3D image based photogrammetric surveys and terrestrial laser scanners (TLS). All these methods manage to collect a huge number of points in 3D space, usually called point cloud, in a very limited time frame [28].

All these techniques can be categorized in different ways. The experience shows that the most efficient method is to characterize them by the scale at which they can be used as well as by the number of measurements they can be used during data acquisition. Practically, this means that they are related to the object size as well as to the complexity of the object. Boehler and Heinz proposed and developed a system to summarize all existing techniques in terms of scale and object complexity. This is adapted to include modern technologies and is shown in Fig. 5 [4].

According to this figure, the metric surveying techniques are organized considering the scale of the outcome which is a function of the object size and the representation based on the required details. The complexity of the survey can be conveyed by the number of recorded points. In practice, this ranges from one single point describing the geographic location of a single cultural heritage object, to some thousands of points

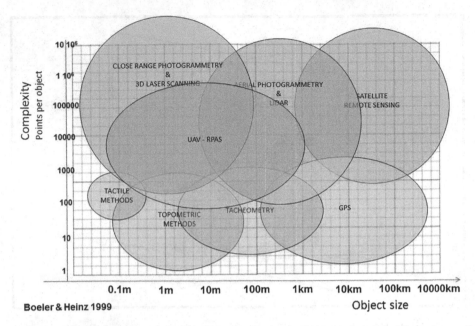

Fig. 5. Three-dimensional survey techniques characterized by scale and object size and complexity (adapted from [4]) (Color figure online)

(e.g. a single CAD drawing of a simple monument) or to a few millions of points (e.g. a point cloud) for the detailed representation of a cultural heritage site. In Fig. 5 the methods depicted in blue use images, while the yellow ones do not.

Recording techniques are based on devices and sensors which perform the necessary measurements either directly on the object, or indirectly by recording energy reflected from the object. In the latter category one may broadly distinguish between active and passive sensors. Active sensors send their own radiation to the object and record the reflectance, while passive ones rely on the radiation sent to the object from some other source. Usually, the latter are image-based sensors, which record the visible light reflected from the objects of interest.

Terrestrial image-based survey comprises all those methods, techniques and technologies that are using images in order to extract metric and thematic information from the object imaged. Within this section the most important image-based digital technologies supporting the digital surveying and documentation of cultural heritage will be discussed and presented. The main concern will be given to digital cameras and sensors, especially the new entries, the contribution of the Unmanned Air Vehicle (UAV) or Remotely Piloted Aircraft Systems (RPAS) or Unmanned Aerial Systems (UAS), but also the useful role that Image Assisted Total Station (IATS) technologies are playing in the recording, monitoring and documentation of cultural heritage.

Nowadays, contemporary technologies have integrated traditional and modern measuring and data acquisition techniques with advanced management and georeference software. This software is also known as Geographic Information Systems and enables the storing, managing and correlation of information collected, always referring it to its geographic location. This combination has led to what today is known as Geoinformatics or Geomatics (Fig. 6).

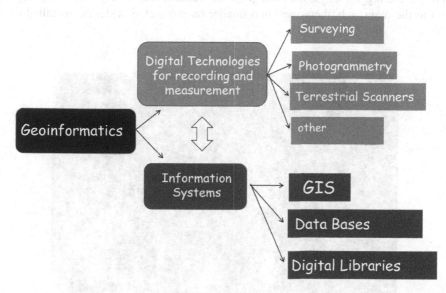

Fig. 6. Geoinformatics as a link between data acquisition and cultural heritage management (© author)

4   Selected Examples

In order to illustrate the above, some representative examples of Cultural Heritage Digitization will be presented. They include (1) the successful attempt to digitize a collapsed traditional stone bridge for assisting the restoration study, (2) the complete geometric documentation of a prominent Athens monument based entirely on image based techniques and (3) the implementation of an HBIM (Historic Building Information Modelling) system for cultural Heritage.

4.1   The Restoration of a Collapsed Bridge[1]

A variety of arched stone bridges exist in the Balkan area, built mainly in the 18th and 19th centuries or even earlier. Just in the Epirus region in north western Greece there are more than 250 magnificent examples of such historic structures spanning over the

_____

[1] Adapted from [27].

rivers and streams and bridging them with one to four arches. Such structures were built for pedestrian and animal passage, as the rivers did not allow easy crossing, especially during winter [18].

The stone bridge of Plaka over river Arachthos (Fig. 7) was a representative example of the aforementioned monuments. It was built in 1866 by local Greek stonemasons in order to facilitate transportation and trade needs (http://www. petrinagefiria.uoi.gr/). It was the widest stone bridge in the area of Epirus with 40 m span and the biggest single-arch bridge in the Balkans with a height of 20 m (Fig. 7). Next to the main arch, there were two smaller ones 6 meters wide, the so-called relief arches.

Fig. 7. The Plaka stone bridge Image copyrights: Google Earth (above) and ntua.gr (below)

Apart from its significant size and age, the stone bridge of Plaka was a renowned stone bridge in Greece because of its emblematic historic meaning. Firstly, it was the border between free Greece and the occupied part of Greece by the Ottoman Empire between 1881 and 1912. During World War II the bridge was bombed by the German army with partial damages. At the same period, representatives of the various armed groups of Greek Resistance signed the Treaty of Plaka on this very bridge. Unfortunately, in February 2015 the emblematic stone bridge collapsed after severe flooding and fierce water volumes coming from the mountains (Fig. 8).

Before the implementation of any actions, a thorough geometric documentation is necessary, as clearly dictated by the Venice Charter (1964). For that purpose, the Laboratory of Photogrammetry undertook two tasks (a) to produce digital three-dimensional drawings from a documentation study conducted in 1984 using traditional surveying techniques [14] and (b) to produce a textured three dimensional model of the Plaka Stone Bridge in order to geometrically document its shape and size before the collapse. This 3D model would be produced from existing images taken by visitors of the bridge over the years. These documentation products will form the basis for any eventual reconstruction study.

Fig. 8. The remains of the bridge after destruction (http://epirusgate.blogspot.gr/2015/02/blog-post_32.html)

Common image-based 3D modelling of the current state of a monument requires data acquisition in the field. Surveying, photogrammetry and laser scanning techniques can be combined to produce a full and accurate 3D model of the object. Such approaches cannot be applied in cases of sudden loss of cultural heritage objects due to a number of reasons such as fire, earthquakes, floods, looting, armed conflict, terrorism, attacks etc.

Modern photogrammetry and computer vision techniques manage to create useful and accurate 3D models of objects of almost any size and shape, by combining robust algorithms and powerful computers. Multiple images depicting the object from different viewpoints are needed and the so-called SfM and MVS procedures are implemented. These images do not necessarily need to have been captured by calibrated cameras, though. Compact or even mobile phone cameras can also be used. Moreover, capturing geometry is nowadays flexible, in contrast with the traditional strict stereo-normal case of the past. A variety of recent studies are examining the creation of 3D models of cultural heritage objects and sites with the use of SfM algorithms [2, 15, 24, 25]. The lack of images or other surveying data in lost cultural heritage objects has led to the use of random, unordered images acquired from the web. However, few projects, many of them EU funded, make use of data available in the web for such a purpose. Some recent studies are dealing with the 4D (space-time) virtual reconstruction of Cultural Heritage objects using web-retrieved images [16, 20, 26]. An approach for diachronic virtual reconstruction of lost heritage based on historical information integrated with real metric data of the remains was proposed by Guidi and Russo [12].

For image-based virtual reconstruction many images from different points of view are required. As already implemented in similar cases in the past, the contribution of people that have visited the area for tourism or other reasons and have taken pictures was sought. Crowdsourcing has already been used for applications in the cultural heritage domain [23]. However, none of the similar actions produced a metric product like the present one.

The key aspects of a project like the present one, concerning crowdsourcing information can be summarized as follows:

- The project has a time limit.
- The contribution of the users is of one type of content, i.e. images or video sequences.
- Special information (metadata) about the viewpoint of the images, the equipment used or the time taken could be useful.

To provide a suitable framework for the above, a website has been developed using the Drupal CMS (Fig. 9). Drupal is a Content Management System (CMS) with proper functions for community websites and has been used for educational and research crowdsourcing purposes [13, 22]. More specifically, the website developed includes five sections: (a) a news and announcements page, (b) a general info page, (c) a submit content (images) page, (d) a submit page for volunteers and (e) a blog page. To collect the images, the "submit images" page is the only section utilized, since it also provides the required information to the contributors.

Within the first month of its operation the website has been visited around 2800 times. More than 470 images were uploaded to the platform during these sessions by more than 130 contributors. Apart from the uploaded content, approximately 200 images and 15 videos were collected through other means, mainly by ordinary mail delivery, by contacting the contributors.

The majority of the collected images were of high resolution, correctly focused and without significant perspective or optical distortions. However, we had to cope with some special challenges in order to exploit as much as possible the rest of the images, which had many different problems. In addition, the majority of the collected photos were taken facing upstream and mainly from the east riverside due to landscape inaccessibility. This causes gaps and difficulties for the algorithm to converge to a stable geometry. After a thorough and careful sorting, it was established that less than 60 images fulfil the needs of the project in terms of viewpoint, image resolution, lighting conditions, occlusions etc., which corresponds to 10% of the total contributions.

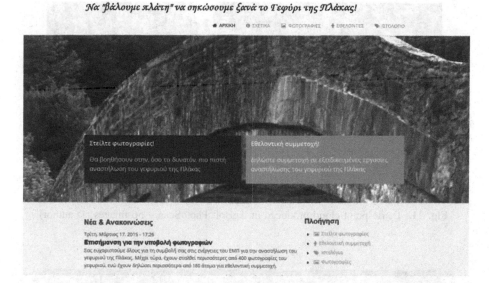

Fig. 9. Home page of the crowdsourcing webpage (© author)

The selected data have been processed using commercial as well as free software. VisualSfM is a free GUI application for 3D reconstruction that implements SfM and PMVS along with other tools [6, 7, 33–35]. In this case study, a dense point cloud was produced by 51 images (Fig. 10).

Fig. 10. Dense point cloud after PMVS software (VisualSfM) – 51 images (© author)

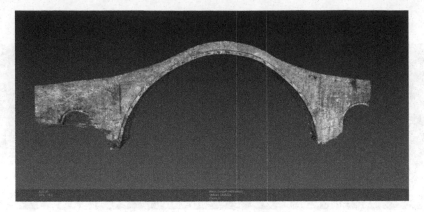

Fig. 11. Dense point cloud produced in Agisoft PhotoScan – 56 images (© author)

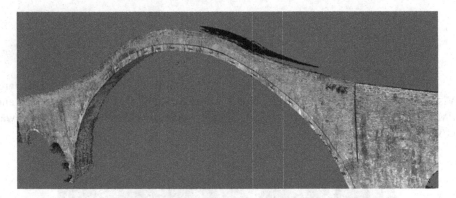

Fig. 12. A view of the textured mesh created in Agisoft PhotoScan (© author)

In order to improve the results, a masking procedure was applied on the images while processed in Agisoft PhotoScan. Therefore, background elements that are subjected to temporal changes and obstacles (people, trees, mountains etc.) have been excluded during photo alignment. This results to less noisy dense point clouds (Fig. 11). A mesh has also been created, followed by the texturing procedure (Fig. 12).

The experts working for the restoration proposal needed also the documentation of the current situation. Hence during a campaign some months ago, data was collected for the creation of the 3D models of the remaining pedestals. They were imaged with a high resolution DSLR and some Ground Control Points (GCP) were measured. Using again SfM/MVS software the three-dimensional models were produced (Fig. 13) and served as a detailed geometric basis for the restoration proposal.

Fig. 13. 3D models of the remaining parts of the bridge (© author)

It should be stressed that the wide promotion of the 3 × 3 Rules proposed by CIPA [32] and revised in 2013, available at the relevant webpage (www.cipa.icomos.org) would ensure the existence of more useful images and related metadata for the Plaka Stone Bridge, as the public would be more aware of the eventual future significance of their souvenir images. This may be useful in the future for other monuments in similar situations.

4.2   Geometric Documentation of the Holy Aedicule[2]

The Church of the Anastassis (Resurrection) or of the Holy Sepulchre, as it is mostly known to western visitors, lies majestically in the heart of the Old City of Jerusalem, and has a very long history spanning over seventeen centuries (Fig. 14). The first church in this site was erected by Saint Helen, the mother of Emperor Constantine the Great, when she discovered the Holy Cross at the beginning of the fourth century A.D. Since then, a lot of constructions, modifications, additions, renovations and alterations took place, the major one being that imposed by the crusaders in the 12th century A.D. when they conquered the Holy Land. The Church of the Holy Sepulchre in Jerusalem comprises within its walls, among others, the main large Greek Orthodox church, the Catholicon, the Holy Rock of Golgotha, the Tomb of Christ and the place where the Holy Cross was discovered. Adjacent to these main places of worship and pilgrimage are numerous little chapels, monk cells, store rooms, corridors and staircases, extending to approximately 8000 m² in plan area and to about 35 m of height difference. The main building complex has common borders with the Greek Orthodox Patriarchate, the Syrian Patriarchate, the Roman Catholic Monastery, the Ethiopian Monastery and a series of little souvenir stores.

---

[2] Adapted from [10].

Fig. 14. The Church of the Holy Sepulchre (© author)

Fig. 15. The south façade of the Holy Aedicule in 2015 (© author)

Today the Church complex is a living monument and it is visited every year by thousands of pilgrims. All different Christian Communities are represented and active within its walls. Greek Orthodox, Roman Catholic Franciscan, Armenian and Coptic priests and monks and others are coexisting in harmony worshipping the same God.

The monument is divided into sections each one "belonging" to a Community. There are, of course, sections of it common to everybody. All Christian Communities respect this unique state of ownerships while it is hardly sensed by the visitors. It constitutes the Status Quo of the Church of the Holy Sepulchre, which has its origins in historical tradition.

The Tomb of Christ is in the Church of the Holy Sepulchre in Jerusalem. The original Holy Rock is covered by the Holy Aedicule, a majestic little structure situated within the large complex of the Church of the Holy Sepulchre in the centre of the Rotunda, a 25 m tall cylindrical building. The Holy Aedicule is the latest in a series of constructions and additions to the initial Crusader Aedicule which had occupied the same site for centuries [3]. Responsible for the design and reconstruction of this latter one was the architect Komnenos in the early 19th century. The present form of the Holy Aedicule, which exists without significant alterations since 1810, is a result of repair and restoration of the earlier building after the catastrophic fire of 1808. It has approximately a length of 8.3 m, a width of 5.5 m, and a height of 6.7 m plus a dome of 6.0 m on its roof.

In 1927, this construction was badly damaged by an earthquake which also weakened the dome over the Rotunda and other parts of the complex. Marble slabs cover the outside surface of the Aedicule, while it is also surrounded by a metallic construction (Fig. 15) erected by the British in 1947 which provides support and stops the collapse of the Holy Aedicule. Timber wedges were inserted between the steel girders and the load-bearing stone walls of the Holy Aedicule. It appears that this steel girdle is no longer functional, as lately deformations were observed especially as far as the Komnenos' marble slabs are concerned. The inside the Holy Aedicule is a complex structure with two very confined, highly ornamented rooms.

However, the state of preservation of the Holy Aedicule continued to deteriorate due to the water and humidity transfer phenomena within, around and below the Aedicule structure, due to incompatible past interventions and due to the successive earthquake activity, to the extent that proper conservation, reinforcement and repair interventions were needed to rehabilitate the Holy Aedicule. The first task of the interdisciplinary team of NTUA was to perform the geometric documentation of the Holy Aedicule, as foreseen in the Venice Charter (article 16). This documentation was, of course, part of a wider range of technical studies of the interdisciplinary team of NTUA engineering experts.

In the past, several efforts for the geometric documentation of the Church of the Holy Sepulchre and the Holy Aedicule in it took place. Already since the 60's the Franciscan monk Corbo, documented, mainly as an archaeologist, a large part of the Church using of course the then available technological means [5]. Later [3] a team of British experts documented in high detail the Holy Aedicule. In the years 1993–1999, the Laboratories of General Geodesy and of Photogrammetry of NTUA undertook and executed (Fig. 16) the complete geometric documentation at a scale of 1:50 of the Church of the Holy Sepulchre for the Greek Orthodox Patriarchate [1, 8, 17]. Finally, in the years 2007–2009 a team of Italian experts embarked on terrestrial laser scanning for the complete 3D documentation of the Church [30].

For the current geometric documentation of the Holy Aedicule before the restoration works, several campaigns were necessary. The first one took place in May 2015 [21] and the second one in January 2016. Data acquisition included geodetic measurements, digital image acquisition and terrestrial laser scanning around and inside the Holy Aedicule.

Fig. 16. Sample of the geometric documentation 1993–1999 (© author)

This present geometric documentation aims at the production of the necessary base material on which the structural and material prospection studies will be based. For the needs of this documentation it was decided to produce a high resolution three-dimensional model and to perform specialized high accurate geodetic measurements for the production of conventional 2D base material on one hand and for the documentation of the deformations and deviations of the construction today on the other. Due to the peculiarities of the object of interest, the crowds of pilgrims always present inside and around the Aedicule, most of the works for the data acquisition took place after the closure of the Church. The methodology implemented for the production of the above described products applied the most contemporary geomatics techniques and specialized instrumentation. Briefly, an automated 3D imaging methodology based on high resolution digital images, terrestrial laser scanning and high accuracy geodetic measurements were implemented. These data were georeferenced to an already existing local plane projection reference system from previous work of NTUA [1].

Specifically, the geometric documentation produced an accurate three-dimensional (3D) model with the use of photogrammetric and geodetic methods, both for the interior and the exterior of the Holy Aedicule through images and scanned data collection for the reconstruction of the model in actual scale. This was realized via data processing (sorting of images, orientation, export 3D cloud points, dense point cloud processing, creation of surfaces and grouping them), for reconstructing 3D scenes of increased reliability and high accuracy. From this 3D model, the production of sections at specific positions was also possible, supported by suitable geodetic measurements.

For the image based approach, digital image sequences from varying distances were collected using a calibrated professional Canon EOS-1Ds Mark III full frame CMOS digital camera with 21MP resolution (5616 × 3744 pixels) and 6.4 µm pixel size, aiming to reconstruct the 3D scene of the Holy Aedicule through structure from motion (SfM) and Dense Image Matching (DIM) techniques. These techniques are the state of the art in reconstructing 3D scenes and offer high reliability and high accuracy as a cost and time effective alternative to the use of scanners. For this purpose, different lenses with a varying focal length (16 mm, 50 mm, 135 mm and 300 mm) were used. The image acquisition took place under low natural lighting conditions and during the night, exploiting the existing artificial lighting. No additional light sources were used (flash, studio flash, etc.). Therefore, the use of a photographic tripod was necessary since in some cases, the exposure time was up to 30 s. 3.757 images in total were captured requiring up to 59.3 GB of hard drive space. Image acquisition was carefully planned so that all details of the object were imaged on at least three consecutive images. Control points were not measured, but were extracted from the drawings of previous documentation effort [1] However, a selection process was applied in order to ensure a highly accurate result according to the requirements of the study and the significance of the object. Finally, distances were accurately measured on the Holy Aedicule in order to scale the final 3D model. Problems in the acquisition processes such as lighting conditions and camera-to-object relative positioning as well as difficulties in the alignment step and mesh optimization are also encountered without reducing the accuracy of the final results. These problems included, among others, the large distances between the object and the camera, the poor or inadequate lighting, the continuous population of the area by pilgrims, the smoke from the candles, which create faded areas on the images or unpredictable optical deformations due to the refraction effect caused by the temperature difference of the air.

In addition, laser scanning was also employed, in order to cover the areas where image acquisition was impossible, like e.g. the dark and smoked interiors of the two domes of the Holy Aedicule and the two staircases leading to the construction's roof. The two techniques act complementarily to each other. For this procedure, the terrestrial laser scanner FARO 3D X 330 was chosen as it is a lightweight third generation scanner, which uses the phase shift method for measuring the distance. It has the ability of collecting one million points per second with an accuracy of 2–3 mm in its space position. It can record points 360° around the vertical axis and 300° around the horizontal axis. For the complete coverage of the Holy Aedicule special scanning strategy was designed, in order to avoid gaps in the point clouds on one hand and to record all necessary details on the other. For that purpose, it was necessary to acquire overlapping scans from different scan positions. In total 58 scans were needed, of which 13 around the Holy Aedicule, 8 on top of its roof, 8 in the two staircases, 10 from the Rotunda Gallery and 19 in the inside. The total number of points collected was 65 million for the outside and 42 million for the inside. The density of the scans was selected to 1 point every 5 mm, in order to record all fine details, even those necessary at a later stage. The time required for each scan varied depending on the distance of the scanner to the object, a fact which differentiates the total number of points necessary. In any case the time for each scan was not more than a few minutes.

The creation of the final accurate three-dimensional model from the digital images is a complicated procedure requiring large computation cost and human effort. It includes the already mentioned collection of geometric data in limited space and time, the selection of the images, the 3D point cloud extraction, the creation of the surface, the noise filtering and the merging of individual surfaces. It is important to note that in such cases, the detail of the surface is very important, thus the noise filtering must be a carefully implemented procedure. The initial data were processed using various software packages in order to produce the final accurate 3D model of the Holy Aedicule. In the diagram of Fig. 17 the flowchart designed and adopted for the initial data processing procedure (images and measurements) is presented. After the careful selection of the necessary images and the creation of thematic folders, the radiometric correction of the imagery took place aiming at their quality improvement by minimizing the effects of the shadows and dark areas. Then, the images are imported into the software that implements SfM and DIM techniques. Subsequently, the dense point cloud is exported and imported to another software package in order to be subjected to a time-consuming process for removing outliers.

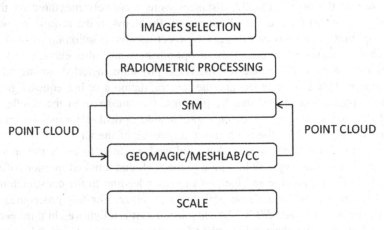

Fig. 17. Data processing workflow

Finally, the processed point clouds are merged and exported again in order to be scaled. The SfM technique for the orientation of the images and the 3D point cloud extraction procedure were realized through the use of Agisoft's PhotoScan® software, which has been extensively evaluated for increased accuracy in prior research internationally but also of the Laboratory of Photogrammetry. For the full coverage of the Holy Aedicule and the creation of a complete 3D model, images were captured from many different locations. It is important to note that for every part of the 3D model, the sparse point clouds consist of 10.000 to 60.000 points. After an inspection of the alignment results, the generation of the dense point cloud model took place. At this stage, the Agisoft PhotoScan® algorithms, based on the estimated camera positions calculate depth information for each camera to be combined into a single dense point cloud. It is noted that the dense point cloud of each part of the 3D model of the Holy

Aedicule consists of about 35.000.000 points and the entire model of about 280.000.000 points (Fig. 18). At this stage, colour is attributed to each point based on the images where it appears. In the outside coloured point cloud of the Holy Aedicule is presented.

Fig. 18. The coloured point cloud of the Holy Aedicule (© author). (Color figure online)

Fig. 19. The 3D model of the dome textured (left) and non-textured (right) (© author)

The processing of the Holy Aedicule point cloud was realized within the Geomagic Studio®, Meshlab® and Cloud Compare® software. Also, to sort out the outliers, several filtering algorithms are applied using the above mentioned software packages. In addition, algorithms were applied in order to make the point cloud uniform in terms of point spacing and reduce its density. Finally, the processed dense point clouds are wrapped into meshes. Figure 19 presents the part of the 3D model of the dome, which is one of the more complex parts of the Holy Aedicule. Through the created 3D model, it is possible to identify vulnerable and destroyed areas of the Holy Aedicule with not physical access on them.

The laser scanner data were thoroughly examined for their completeness in situ, i.e. before the departure of the team from Jerusalem. For that purpose, test registrations of the point clouds were performed in order to establish this possibility on one hand and their completeness on the other. After these tests, additional scans were required sometimes from very unconventional scan positions. The final point cloud registration was performed in the Laboratory of Photogrammetry of NTUA. As the volume of data was huge it was decided to perform the registration separately for the inside and outside parts of the Holy Aedicule. For the point cloud registration, at least three points are required. This role was undertaken by the special targets, whose coordinates in the common reference system were carefully determined, as ICP (Iterative Closest Point) algorithm does not provide reliable results in such cases. Hence after registration the point clouds were also referenced to the common system. The accuracy achieved for the registrations was of the order of 2–3 mm. In Fig. 20 a sample of the registered point clouds is shown.

For registering and georeferencing the three-dimensional models of the Holy Aedicule which were produced with the methods described to the common reference system, specially targeted points were put in suitable positions on inside and outside of the Holy Aedicule but also in the surrounding area. In total 38 control points were used.

Fig. 20. Part of the registered point clouds inside the Holy Aedicule (© author)

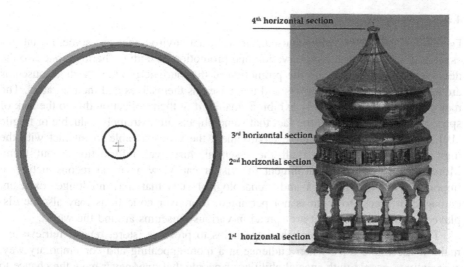

Fig. 21. The horizontal sections of the upper dome of the Holy Aedicule (© author)

Accurate geodetic measurements were performed in order to assess the verticality of structural elements, like the iron girder set up by the British in 1947 and some of the pillars of the monument. For that purpose, a local 3D network was established at the site around of the Holy Aedicule in order to support the creation of the 3D model of the Holy Aedicule and to determine probable deformations and displacements of the monument. The above mentioned geodetic network connected with the old geodetic network which had been established the period 1993–1999, in the framework of the Geometric an Architectural Documentation of the Church of the Holy Sepulchre in Jerusalem [1].

For checking the eventual deviations and deformations of the structural elements several measurements were performed. A longitudinal section of the upper dome of the structure, four horizontal sections of the same dome at 6.0 m, 8.0 m, 8.8 m and 12.0 m from the floor, two horizontal sections of the pillars and the marble supports of the Aedicule at 0.7 m and 4.4 m from the floor. In addition, special accurate measurements were conducted in order to establish the deviation from the vertical of the steel pillars of the cage built by the British.

Moreover, the change of the position of each the five basic columns at the north façade and the counterpart columns at the south façade of the Holy Aedicule, was determined from the corresponding position that the British as registered in 1947. These measurements led to the important conclusion that the upper dome of the structure does not present any significant deformations, as all sections were concentric circles within 7 mm (Fig. 21). This was also established by examining the longitudinal section of dome. The horizontal sections of the pillars revealed deviations between 40 and 90 mm. These results were also verified from the 3D model produced.

4.3   Developing Virtual Museums

Developing and displaying a museum in a virtual environment has some advantages especially concerning the preservation and promotion of cultural heritage but also the development of tourism and the promotion of the touristic product. Virtual museums are important to both the visitors and the museums themselves and their curators. The majority of the museums only exhibit a small part of their collection due to the lack of space and of course due to the fact that some objects are extremely valuable or fragile [19]. In a virtual and interactive environment the visitor is able to interact with the digitised exhibits and learn all the essential, historical information about them. Moreover, in a virtual environment the visitor can view a virtual reconstruction of important objects, buildings and archaeological sites that may no longer exist are damaged or access to them is not permitted. Moreover collections may also be displayed made of objects that are spread in various museums around the world.

The digitisation of cultural heritage helps to preserve, store, renew, retrieve and make it accessible for a wider audience in a more appealing and contemporary way, especially to people with special abilities or people that may never have the chance to visit the real museum [29]. The wide use of internet, social media and websites can make the digitised content of a museum more accessible and transport it to everyone all around the world. It is important to mention the result of the Colorado's University research according to which 70% of a total of 223 million people who visit a museum website would subsequently be more likely to go and also visit the real museum [11]. This means that the virtual museum functions in a complementary manner to the real museum. Finally, in virtual museum exhibitions the visitor is able to fully control the navigation as well as to freely explore, move around, manipulate the exhibits and create his/her own, unique virtual experience or collection of 3D digital exhibits even from different museums. It is obvious that every effort and innovation that concerns the digitisation of cultural heritage and the development of virtual museums and applications is a complicated, difficult, controversial task with many advantages and can only benefit and offer both the museums and the visitors. Especially in Greece, 65% of the tourists make an online search of their destination and 45% of them are interested in cultural heritage, monuments, museums and archaeological sites.

The Virtual Museum of the Stoa of Attalos is an application where the visitor is able to make a tour in the museum on his own, explore it, interact with the exhibits, rotate them and learn all the necessary information about them. The development of this application took into consideration various aspects such as the requirements' analysis, the architectural design, the planning of the exhibits' presentation, the user interaction, the programming process and the evaluation of the final product [19].

As far as the Virtual Museum of the Stoa of Attalos is concerned, the virtual environment hosts some of the exhibits which can be found on the ground floor of the Stoa of Attalos, in the Ancient Agora of Athens. For this project, 16 of the exhibits were chosen from the south part of the colonnade of the museum and the most important concern was to produce accurate, realistic and appealing 3D models that can be used in virtual applications, especially in a short period of time. That is why photogrammetric methods and 3D surveys were used for the mass production of the exhibits' 3D models and the development of the virtual museum. In order to process the data and build the accurate, textured 3D models of the exhibits PhotoScan Professional® v.1.1 software by Agisoft was used.

The application is available in Greek and English. In the beginning of the virtual tour the visitor has the chance to read the instructions that are available in order to freely navigate in the environment and understand the options and opportunities he/she has in the virtual museum (Fig. 22). The parameters that concern the movement, speed, rotation, height vision and behaviour of the visitor were extremely important in order to make the navigation friendly and easy for the visitor, as the majority of them may not have any previous experience with this kind of applications or even with the use of computers.

Moreover, the ambience and the depth of field were properly adjusted in order to have a more clear and realistic view of the exhibits, which is also important to the visitor and his/her virtual experience in the museum. The visitor has the chance to learn and find out more information about the exhibits that attract and interest him/her simply by clicking on them (Fig. 23). Moreover, the visitor is able to rotate the exhibits while the panel with the information appears on the right part of the screen. In that way the visitor is able to manipulate, closely examine and observe the details of every exhibit and at the same time learn not only the available information of the small panel that exists in the real museum, but also further information about it. The curator of the museum has the opportunity to choose the information that will be available to visitor and this is one of the advantages of this kind of applications. Finally, the last element that was added in the virtual environment was a mini-map to help the visitor move around and navigate in the environment without feeling disorientated, simply by offering him/her a view of the virtual museum from the top [9].

Fig. 22. The environment of the virtual museum (© author)

Fig. 23. The virtual museum with all included elements (© author)

5 Concluding Remarks

With the presentation of a few characteristic implementation examples, it has been shown that digital contemporary technologies can contribute decisively to the conservation of Cultural Heritage. The final products are 3D models and virtual restorations or reconstructions of monuments that either do not exist today or are at risk. Consequently, digital technologies and interdisciplinary synergies are of utmost importance. Equally important are the discussions and suggestions of scientists who have studied the monuments from an historical and archaeological point of view, proving once again that such interventions are a multi-disciplinary process.

Virtual reconstructions, virtual restorations, monitoring and 3D models on the other hand support many other disciplines involved in cultural heritage. They help architects and structural engineers in their work for monuments especially in cases of restoration, anastylosis etc. Archaeologists and Conservationists have a very good tool at their disposal for their studies. Many applications can be generated from a virtual reconstruction like virtual video tours of the monument for educational and other purposes for use by schools, museums and other organizations, for incorporation into a geographical information system (GIS) for archaeological sites, for the design of virtual museums and the creation of numerous applications for mobile devices (e.g. mobile phones, tablets etc.).

References

1. Balodimos, D., Lavvas G., Georgopoulos, A.: Wholly documenting holy monuments. In: CIPA XIX International Symposium, Antalya (2003)
2. Barsanti, S.G., Guidi, G.: 3D digitization of museum content within the 3D-ICONS project. ISPRS Ann. Photogramm. Remote Sens. Spatial Inf. Sci. **II-5/W1**, 151–156 (2013)

3. Biddle, M.: The Tomb of Christ. Sutton Publishing Ltd., Stroud (1999). 173 p. ISBN 0-7509-1926-4
4. Bochler, W., Heinz, G.: Documentation, surveying, photogrammetry. Paper presented at the XVII CIPA International Symposium, Olinda, Brazil (1999)
5. Corbo, V.C.: Il Santo Sepolchro di Gerusalemme. 3 vols. Publication of the Studium Biblicum Franciscanum, Jerusalem (1981)
6. Furukawa, Y., Ponce, J.: Accurate, dense, and robust multiview stereopsis. IEEE Trans. Pattern Anal. Mach. Intell. 32(8), 1362–1376 (2010)
7. Furukawa, Y., Curless, B., Seitz, S.M., Szeliski, R.: Towards internet-scale multi-view stereo. In: 2010 IEEE Conference on Computer Vision and Pattern Recognition (CVPR), pp. 1434–1441. IEEE (2010)
8. Georgopoulos, A., Modatsos, M.: Non-metric bird's eye view. Int. Arch. Photogramm. Remote Sens. 34(5), 359–362 (2002)
9. Georgopoulos, A., Kontogianni, G., Koutsaftis, C., Skamantzari, M.: Serious games at the service of cultural heritage and tourism. In: Katsoni, V., Upadhya, A., Stratigea, A. (eds.) Tourism, Culture and Heritage in a Smart Economy. SPBE, pp. 3–17. Springer, Cham (2017). https://doi.org/10.1007/978-3-319-47732-9_1
10. Georgopoulos, A., Lambrou, E., Pantazis, G., Agrafiotis, P., Papadaki, A., Kotoula, L., Lampropoulos, K., Delegou, E., Apostolopoulou, M., Alexakis, M., Moropoulou, A.: Merging geometric documentation with materials characterization and analysis of the history of the Holy Aedicule in the church of the Holy Sepulchre in Jerusalem. Int. Arch. Photogramm. Remote Sens. Spatial Inf. Sci. XLII-5-W1, 487–494 (2017). https://doi.org/10.5194/isprs-archives-XLII-5-W1-487-2017
11. Griffiths, J.-M., King, D.W.: Physical spaces and virtual visitors: the methodologies of comprehensive study of users and uses of museums. In: Trant, J., Bearman, D. (eds.) Proceedings of International Cultural Heritage Informatics Meeting (ICHIM 2007), Archives & Museum Informatics, Toronto, 24 October 2007. http://www.archimuse.com/ichim07/papers/griffiths/griffiths.html
12. Guidi, G., Russo, M.: Diachronic 3D reconstruction for lost Cultural Heritage. ISPRS-Int. Arch. Photogramm. Remote Sens. Spatial Inf. Sci. 3816, 371–376 (2011)
13. Kaliampakos, D., Benardos, A., Mavrikos, A., Panagiotopoulos, G.: The underground atlas project. Tunn. Undergr. Space Technol. 55, 229–235 (2015)
14. Karakosta, E., Papanagiotou, B., Tragaris, N., Chatzigeorgiou, Th., Arampatzi, O., Doggouris, S., Mpalodimos, D.-D.: Plaka Bridge: Survey-Check for vertical deformations, Diploma thesis, National Technical University of Athens (1984)
15. Kersten, T.P., Lindstaedt, M.: Image-based low-cost systems for automatic 3D recording and modelling of archaeological finds and objects. In: Ioannides, M., Fritsch, D., Leissner, J., Davies, R., Remondino, F., Caffo, R. (eds.) EuroMed 2012. LNCS, vol. 7616, pp. 1–10. Springer, Heidelberg (2012). https://doi.org/10.1007/978-3-642-34234-9_1
16. Kyriakaki, G., Doulamis, A., Doulamis, N., Ioannides, M., Makantasis, K., Protopapadakis, E., Hadjiprocopis, A., Wenzel, K., Fritsch, D., Klein, M., Weinlinger, G.: 4D reconstruction of tangible cultural heritage objects from web-retrieved images. Int. J. Heritage Digit. Era 3(2), 431–452 (2014)
17. Lavvas, G.: The Church of the Holy Sepulchre in Jerusalem, Academy of Athens (2009). 192 p. (in Greek). ISBN 978-960-404-139-8
18. Leftheris, B.P., Stavroulaki, M.E., Sapounaki, A.C., Stavroulakis, G.E.: Computational Mechanics for Heritage Structures. WIT Press, Southampton (2006)
19. Lepouras, G., Katifori, A., Vassilakis, C., Haritos, D.: Real exhibitions in a virtual museum. Arch. J. Virtual Reality 7(2), 120–128 (2004)

20. Makantasis, K., Doulamis, A., Doulamis, N., Ioannides, M., Matsatsinis, N.: Content-based filtering for fast 3D reconstruction from unstructured web-based image data. In: Ioannides, M., Magnenat-Thalmann, N., Fink, E., Žarnić, R., Yen, A.-Y., Quak, E. (eds.) EuroMed 2014. LNCS, vol. 8740, pp. 91–101. Springer, Cham (2014). https://doi.org/10.1007/978-3-319-13695-0_9

21. Moropoulou, A.I., Labropoulos, K.C.: Non-destructive testing for assessing structural damage and interventions effectiveness for built cultural heritage protection. In: Asteris, P. G., Plevris, V. (eds.) Handbook of Research on Seismic Assessment and Rehabilitation of Historic Structures, pp. 448–499. IGI-Global, Hershey (2015)

22. Munoz-Torres, M.C., Reese, J.T., Childers, C.P., Bennett, A.K., Sundaram, J.P., Childs, K. L., Anzola, J.M., Milshina, N., Elsik, C.G.: Hymenoptera genome database: integrated community resources for insect species of the order hymenoptera. Nucleic Acids Res. 39, D658–D662 (2011)

23. Oomen, J., Aroyo, L.: Crowdsourcing in the cultural heritage domain: opportunities and challenges. In: Proceedings of the 5th International Conference on Communities and Technologies, 19 June–2 July, Brisbane, Australia (2011)

24. Remondino, F., Del Pizzo, S., Kersten, T.P., Troisi, S.: Low-cost and open-source solutions for automated image orientation – a critical overview. In: Ioannides, M., Fritsch, D., Leissner, J., Davies, R., Remondino, F., Caffo, R. (eds.) EuroMed 2012. LNCS, vol. 7616, pp. 40–54. Springer, Heidelberg (2012). https://doi.org/10.1007/978-3-642-34234-9_5

25. Santagati, C., Inzerillo, L., Di Paola, F.: Image-based modeling techniques for architectural heritage 3D digitalization: limits and potentialities. Int. Arch. Photogramm. Remote Sens. Spatial Inf. Sci. 5(w2), 555–560 (2013)

26. Santos, P., Serna, S.P., Stork, A., Fellner, D.: The potential of 3D internet in the cultural heritage domain. In: Ioannides, M., Quak, E. (eds.) 3D Research Challenges in Cultural Heritage. LNCS, vol. 8355, pp. 1–17. Springer, Heidelberg (2014). https://doi.org/10.1007/978-3-662-44630-0_1

27. Stathopoulou, E.K., Georgopoulos, A., Panagiotopoulos, G., Kaliampakos, D.: 3D visualisation of lost cultural heritage objects using crowdsourcing. Int. Arch. Photogramm. Remote Sens. Spatial Inf. Sci. XL-5/W7 (2015). 2015 25th International CIPA Symposium 2015, 31 August–04 September 2015, Taipei, Taiwan (2015)

28. Stylianidis, E., Georgopoulos, A.: Digital surveying in cultural heritage: the image-based recording and documentation approaches. In: Ippolito, A., Cigola, M. (eds.) Handbook of Research on Emerging Technologies for Digital Preservation and Information Modeling. IGI Global Publishing, Hershey (2016)

29. Sylaiou, S., Liarokapis, F., Kotsakis, K., Patias, P.: Virtual museums, a survey and some issues for consideration. Arch. J. Cult. Heritage 10, 520–528 (2009). ISSN 1296-2074

30. Tucci, G., Bonora, V.: Geomatic techniques and 3D modeling for the survey of the Church of the Holy Sepulchre in Jerusalem. In: Proceedings XXIII CIPA Symposium, Prague, Czech Republic, 12–16 September 2011

31. UNESCO: Guidelines for the Preservation of Digital Heritage, CI-2003/WS/3 (2003)

32. Waldhäusl, P., Ogleby, C.L.: 3 × 3 rules for simple photogrammetric documentation of architecture. Int. Arch. Photogramm. Remote Sens. 30, 426–429 (1994)

33. Wu, C.: SiftGPU: A GPU Implementation of Scale Invariant Feature Transform (SIFT) (2007). http://cs.unc.edu/~ccwu/siftgpu

34. Wu, C., Agarwal, S., Curless, B., Seitz, S.M.: Multicore bundle adjustment. In: 2011 IEEE Conference on Computer Vision and Pattern Recognition (CVPR), pp. 3057–3064. IEEE, June 2011
35. Wu, C.: Towards linear-time incremental structure from motion. In: 2013 International Conference on 3D Vision-3DV 2013, pp. 127–134. IEEE, June 2013

Author Index

Printed in the United States
By Bookmasters